Foundations for Attachment
Training Resource

by the same author

Everyday Parenting with Security and Love
Using PACE to Provide Foundations for Attachment
Kim S. Golding
ISBN 978 1 78592 115 5
eISBN 978 1 78450 384 0

Creating Loving Attachments
Parenting with PACE to Nurture Confidence and Security in the Troubled Child
Kim S. Golding and Daniel A. Hughes
ISBN 978 1 84905 227 6
eISBN 978 0 85700 470 3

Nurturing Attachments
Supporting Children who are Fostered or Adopted
Kim S. Golding
ISBN 978 1 84310 614 2
eISBN 978 1 84642 750 3

Nurturing Attachments Training Resource
Running Parenting Groups for Adoptive Parents and Foster or Kinship Carers
Kim S. Golding
ISBN 978 1 84905 328 0

Observing Children with Attachment Difficulties in School
A Tool for Identifying and Supporting Emotional and Social Difficulties in Children Aged 5–11
Kim S. Golding, Jane Fain, Ann Frost, Cathy Mills, Helen Worrall, Netty Roberts, Eleanor Durrant and Sian Templeton
ISBN 978 1 84905 336 5
eISBN 978 0 85700 675 2

Observing Children with Attachment Difficulties in Preschool Settings
A Tool for Identifying and Supporting Emotional and Social Difficulties
Kim S. Golding, Jane Fain, Ann Frost, Sian Templeton and Eleanor Durrant
ISBN 978 1 84905 337 2
eISBN 978 0 85700 676 9

Observing Adolescents with Attachment Difficulties in Educational Settings
A Tool for Identifying and Supporting Emotional and Social Difficulties in Young People Aged 11–16
Kim S. Golding, Mary T. Turner, Helen Worrall, Jennifer Roberts and Ann E. Cadman
ISBN 978 1 84905 617 5
eISBN 978 1 78450 174 7

Using Stories to Build Bridges with Traumatized Children
Creative Ideas for Therapy, Life Story Work, Direct Work and Parenting
Kim S. Golding
ISBN 978 1 84905 540 6
ISBN 978 0 85700 961 6

Foundations for Attachment Training Resource

The Six-Session Programme for
Parents of Traumatized Children

Kim S. Golding

Foreword by Dan Hughes

Jessica Kingsley *Publishers*
London and Philadelphia

First published in 2017
by Jessica Kingsley Publishers
73 Collier Street
London N1 9BE, UK
and
400 Market Street, Suite 400
Philadelphia, PA 19106, USA

www.jkp.com

Library of Congress Cataloging in Publication Data
Names: Golding, Kim S., author.
Title: Foundations for attachment training resource : the six-session
   programme for parents of traumatized children / Kim S. Golding.
Description: London ; Philadelphia : Jessica Kingsley Publishers, [2017] |
   Includes bibliographical references.
Identifiers: LCCN 2016054736 | ISBN 9781785921186
Subjects: LCSH: Attachment behavior in children. | Psychic trauma in
   children. | Parenting.
Classification: LCC BF723.A75 .G6537 2017 | DDC 649/.154--dc23 LC record available at
https://lccn.loc.gov/2016054736

British Library Cataloguing in Publication Data
A CIP catalogue record for this book is available from the British Library

ISBN 978 1 78592 118 6
eISBN 978 1 78450 600 1

Printed and bound in Great Britain

The accompanying resources can be accessed at
www.jkp.com/voucher using the code
GOLDINGFOUNDATIONS

For my mum whose connection has been ever present and in memory of my dad whose connection made his correction safe. They offered me safety that I took for granted.

Contents

The following materials can be accessed at
www.jkp.com/voucher using the code
GOLDINGFOUNDATIONS

4. ACCOMPANYING RESOURCES

Foreword

Dan Hughes, PhD

What does it take to raise a child well? We are likely to know the answer to this question intuitively – if we were raised well – but it might be more difficult to describe it in words. But we know that it involves many factors and that these factors need to evolve based on our special knowledge of our unique child, our child's age and the immediate circumstances. Most likely we would include the following when we speak about what parenting well entails:

- discovering what is unique about our child and responding to their needs in various ways that are guided by our sense as to what is best for them

- providing safety through staying close and being responsive to their various needs

- demonstrating love through our expressions and our actions

- helping them to manage big emotions by being with them in the experience

- noticing their inner lives of thoughts, feelings and wishes that lie under their behaviours

- reflecting with them about stressful events, confusing thoughts, and significant doubts so that they develop the ability to make sense of themselves and the events of their world

- modelling for them the values and habits that we want them to have as they mature

- repairing our relationship with them whenever conflicts cause stress to it

- helping them to learn that their behaviour has natural consequences that will help to guide their future behaviours.

- ensuring that they can trust that our care for them will be comprehensive, unconditional and lasting.

Whilst this list might be incomplete, it gives some sense of how difficult it is to reduce the very complex activities of caring for our child into a few concepts.

Too often efforts to describe what type of parenting is needed for children who have experienced family trauma and attachment losses are limited in their recommendations. These efforts tend to stress the child's needs for a safe and predictable environment that includes clear expectations for desired behaviours which are reinforced with positive consequences when the child attains – or is making progress towards – these expectations. These recommendations tend to be based on social learning theory, which emphasizes the importance of influencing children through providing them with clear goals with instructions, modelling, coaching and reinforcing the child's efforts to engage in behaviours that we want them to achieve. These efforts might be effective when the child is habitually safe – physically and psychologically – within their relationships with their parents. (Most of us would say that our parents' efforts to teach us and reinforce our correct behaviours were reasonably effective.) What we need to consider is that efforts based on social learning theory might not be nearly so effective when the child does not trust the motives of their parents, nor that the care that they are receiving will continue to be present. Children who habitually mistrust their caregivers develop strategies of self-reliance (control, manipulation, concealment, intimidation, suppressing vulnerable emotions as well as the wish for close relationships). This state of mistrust is known as 'blocked trust' (Baylin and Hughes 2016). In cases of blocked trust, the foundation for facilitating change for these children is to first develop their trust that the care that they are receiving from their parents will meet their many needs more fully than will their efforts to meet all of their needs through going it alone.

Attachment theory summarizes well the child's need for safety within his relationships with his parents, along with the factors in the attachment relationship that are crucial for establishing and maintaining the sense of safety. The various factors mentioned above that are thought to characterize good caregiving all have their foundation in attachment theory. A strong attachment is crucial for many areas of our children's development, including the following:

- the ability to regulate complex affective states

- the ability to manage stress, first through turning to their parents for comfort and support and gradually being able to manage stress with self-reliance as well

- the ability to reflect on their inner lives and be aware of what they think, feel and want, enabling this awareness to lead to acting in a way that is in their best interest

- the ability to develop mind-mindedness, which refers to the child's ability to understand the intentions, thoughts and feelings of his parents and others

- the ability to be engaged in relationship repair when conflicts create stress on the attachment

- the ability to be safe, to experience positive emotions including reciprocal joy and delight, as well as to become interested in the world and how to be successfully engaged in it

- having empathy and compassion for others

- being able to inhibit behaviour leading towards immediate gratification and to be motivated by long-term goals.

Parenting is often difficult but what keeps parents going through the hard times is the sense of satisfaction and pride that comes from their child's positive response to their caregiving. When parents received good care when young, the challenges of parenting are likely to be managed fairly well without any consistent disruptions to the quality of care being given. When children often respond to their parents' initiatives to provide care by accepting their guidance with signs of development, contentment and satisfaction over being their child, the caregiving becomes reciprocal. It means a lot to both the parent and child. When the child consistently rejects their parents' care, little reciprocity is experienced and the parent is at risk for 'blocked care'. When this occurs continuing to provide consistently good care becomes neurologically harder and harder to do (Hughes and Baylin 2012). Over time the parents may be able to do the job of caregiving, but their heart is no longer in the efforts. When this occurs, the child who is experiencing blocked trust is not likely to risk learning how to trust.

Kim Golding's Foundations for Attachment Programme is remarkable in its ability to provide practical assistance within six group sessions to parents of children with difficulties in their attachment relationships, whilst at the same time covering the core components of the challenges facing both child and parent. The organizing principle of her programme is attachment theory and she is able to present clearly to parents and carers how developmental trauma and attachment challenges make it very difficult for these children to trust the relationships which they need in order to resolve the traumas and develop secure attachments. She enables parents to understand the shame that these children consistently experience and how it impairs their ability both to express what they need and also to accept the care that they desperately need.

After describing why children who have experienced trauma and attachment difficulties do not trust relationships with their parents, Dr Golding presents the attitude that parents are wise to adopt if they are to begin to build connections with their children. She shows how the manner in which a parent approaches a child – from an open and engaged stance rather than a defensive one – is at least as important as what the child is being told. This attitude, along with the closely related manner of engaging with PACE (being playful, accepting, curious and empathic), is crucial if the child is to remain safe, not become defensive, and allow himself to be influenced by the parents' guidance. Efforts to enable the child to begin to trust his parents are best made through first establishing a connection with the child within which the child is likely to be more receptive to any correction. With such a connection, the child is more likely to understand and accept the positive motives of the parents that lead to the limits placed on their child's behaviours.

A full third of Dr. Golding's Foundations for Attachment Programme is devoted to assisting the parent in managing the distress of providing care for children who are frequently rejecting their care in a variety of ways. She focuses on how the parents are at risk of having stressful issues from their own childhood being activated by their child's opposition to their caregiving. She is able to help parents to be aware of the tendency to experience blocked care when their caregiving is rejected. Dr. Golding also provides a variety of ideas and activities to assist parents in being able to manage the difficulties secondary to the activation of their own attachment histories and/or blocked care.

Kim Golding's success in assisting adults to better care for their children rests on her ability to help parents and caregivers to truly understand the inner lives of these children who no longer trust that caring adults will keep them safe. With that understanding in hand, Dr. Golding shows parents how to become engaged with them and also guide them into a world where good care is able to be safely received.

Kim Golding has once again provided us with an excellent resource for understanding, being engaged with, and facilitating development for children and youth who have experienced familial trauma and attachment difficulties. Her guidance over the years for parents and carers, teachers and residential workers has been consistently sensitive and practical in meeting the complex needs of these children. Dr. Golding invariably uses attachment theory and research as her guide in designing her very effective programmes. Her prior programmes repeatedly demonstrate success in assisting the adults who are providing care for these children. I am confident that this programme will as well.

Dan Hughes

Acknowledgements

This programme would not have been possible without the wisdom and mentoring of so many people. The parents and children have taught me more than they can possibly know and will be properly acknowledged in the accompanying book. In addition, I have developed this programme over a number of years and whilst being in touch with a lot of people. Apologies if I don't name you all.

With thanks to Joe Tucci who invited me to participate in the Australian Childhood Foundation Trauma conference in Melbourne, 2014. This gave me an opportunity to develop my ideas for this programme whilst planning my presentation. Whilst there it was a pleasure to meet a number of researchers and clinicians whose work has been inspirational: Allan and Judy Schore; Stephen Porges and Susan Carter; Dan Siegel; Ed Tronick. Their work has made mine infinitely stronger. Similarly, thanks to Ben Monaghan and Craig McKenzie who invited me to tour Australia and New Zealand; presenting the ideas many times around these beautiful countries continued to help me develop them. It is fitting that I am finishing writing this manual as I embark on another training tour with them.

Back home in Britain I have always had huge support from friends and colleagues within the Dyadic Developmental Psychology (DDP) community. Thanks to Julie, Geraldine, Edwina, Alison and many others who work to ensure we in the UK do justice to the DDP model. Thanks also to Anne-Marie who has supported and protected my work. Discussion and sharing with friends and colleagues in my peer study group has further enhanced my ideas; Jane, Sue, Cas, Emily, Ruth, Liz, Eleanor and Gill.

The DDP Institute (DDPI) has brought Britain, America and Canada together and given me more friends. Thanks to all board members past and present. Of course none of this would have been possible without the most important influence of all: thank you, Dan Hughes for your inspiration and for the generous sharing and support that you always provide. It goes without saying that your DDP model is at the heart of this work.

I would like also to give thanks to the many people who have been involved in the piloting of this programme, and whose ideas have helped me to strengthen my own. Emily Barnbrook, Louise Hankon, Debbie Rainscourt and all in Worcester who have supported me with the group work for many years and willingly took on another programme to pilot – sorry about all the questionnaires! Additionally, Lucy Wheen and her team at Bryn Melyn Care, Joanne Peterkin, Helen O'Shea, Marie Kershaw, Pam Wilkinson, Sarah Mundy, Bonita and those at Children Always First, and Sue Knowles have all helped by offering pilot sites. Thanks also to Vicki Roberts who analyzed all the data. Without her, the evaluation would not have been done. I also want to give a shout out to all the great people at Clover Childcare who helped me work up my ideas into the coherent 'parenting in the moment model'.

As ever, thanks to my ever-patient family who put up with my distractions and keep things going around me: Chris, Alex and Lily, and to my mum who I do not see enough. My dogs too have always provided regulation although they don't know it; most recently, Bilbo, who I still miss, and Hera and Jess, my current cocker spaniels, whose energy just keeps me going.

Thanks to Steve and all at Jessica Kingsley Publishers for continuing to support my work.

Introduction to the Foundations for Attachment Programme

The Foundations for Attachment Programme is a six-session programme for those parenting children who have relationship difficulties, especially children who have experienced attachment problems, trauma, loss and/or separation early in their life. Parents can come to parenting in many ways: children born to them, fostering, adoption, kinship or residential care. My hope is that this programme will be helpful for any parents who are having parenting challenges and enable them to increase their emotional connection with their children.

This is a Dyadic Developmental Psychotherapy (DDP)-informed programme based upon the Dyadic Developmental Psychotherapy and Practice model developed by Dan Hughes (2009, 2011). It introduces parents to four significant challenges of parenting children whose capacity to emotionally connect with them has been compromised. These are:

- the child experiencing blocked trust

- the child fearing intersubjective connection within reciprocal relationships

- the child experiencing high levels of shame

- the child miscuing their attachment needs through a pattern of expressed and hidden needs.

This programme has been written with the aim of helping parents to:

- Gain an understanding of these challenges and explore ways of building emotional connections with the children. This can increase trust in reciprocal and attachment relationships leading to increased attachment security and reduced levels of shame.

- Understand how to provide support for behaviour alongside building these connections. This has been termed 'connection with correction' by Dan Hughes (2009).

- Explore the dangers of blocked care when caring for children with blocked trust and understand the importance of looking after themselves.

- Understand the significance of exploring one's own attachment history when caring for children with attachment difficulties.

The programme has been developed around the Foundations for Attachment model.

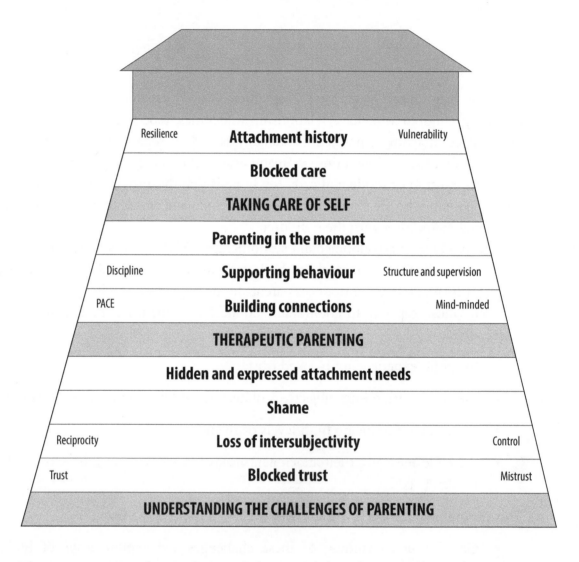

The programme is designed around three modules of two sessions per module. This can be delivered in six half days (three hours, including a break) or three full days.

MODULE ONE: UNDERSTANDING CHALLENGES OF PARENTING

This module introduces group members to the challenges often associated with parenting children with attachment difficulties. These are linked to attachment theory, an understanding of the theory of intersubjectivity, and the impact of trauma upon development. Throughout these two sessions thought will be given to the implications of parenting children who experience these difficulties.

SESSION ONE: BLOCKED RELATIONSHIPS

Understanding challenges of parenting

Parenting challenge one: blocked trust

- Fear of abandonment

- Impact of blocked trust on the nervous system

- Parenting children experiencing blocked trust: comfort, curiosity and joy

Parenting challenge two: fear of intersubjectivity

- Parenting children who fear intersubjective connection

SESSION TWO: HIDING AND MISCUING

Parenting challenge three: shame

- Parenting children living in shame

Parenting challenge four: miscuing through hidden needs

- Parenting children to meet hidden and expressed needs

Introducing a DDP-informed therapeutic parenting approach

MODULE TWO: THERAPEUTIC PARENTING

Module Two explores DDP-informed therapeutic parenting. This is based upon the Dyadic Developmental Psychotherapy and Practice model developed by Dan Hughes (2009, 2011). This pays special attention to the parenting attitude of PACE (playfulness, acceptance, curiosity and empathy). Parenting with PACE requires the capacity to mentalize, especially to be mind-minded. The parent strives to understand, without judging, the internal experience of the child. Group members are encouraged to explore how to be less defensive and to stay open & engaged with the children so that they can connect emotionally with them. They additionally explore how to maintain this connection whilst also providing structure, supervision and discipline in order to support behaviour.

SESSION ONE: BUILDING CONNECTIONS

Therapeutic parenting

The ability to be mind-minded

Open and engaged or defensive

The ability to maintain an attitude of PACE

SESSION TWO: SUPPORTING BEHAVIOUR

Difficulties for developmentally traumatized children when parents use traditional parenting strategies

Exploring behaviour support instead of behaviour management

Regulation-based parenting with PACE

Some parenting principles: 'connection with correction'

Putting it all together, parenting the insecure child: 'parenting in the moment'

PACE: Frequently asked questions

MODULE THREE: LOOKING AFTER SELF

Module Three moves the focus away from the child towards the parents having good self-care as they look after themselves. Whilst in some ways it would make sense to begin with this module it is felt that the first two modules will provide a sense of safety for the group members, allowing them to feel comfortable doing the self-reflection required in the final module. Additionally, group members will understand the importance of this as they realize the complexity of caring for children with attachment difficulties. This module explores the impact of one's own attachment history when parenting the children and helps group members to consider their own histories and identify their own strengths and vulnerabilities. The idea of blocked care (Hughes and Baylin 2012) is then introduced and group members explore how to recognize when they are experiencing blocked care and ways to unblock their care.

SESSION ONE: UNDERSTANDING ATTACHMENT HISTORY	SESSION TWO: SELF CARE AND BLOCKED CARE
Exploring past relationships and attachment history	Self-care
	Blocked care
	Conclusion: Revisiting the Foundation Model of Parenting and previewing the House Model of Parenting

WHO IS THE GROUP PROGRAMME SUITABLE FOR?

The Foundations for Attachment Programme has been used successfully with a range of parents, parenting in different circumstances. Its success has been dependent on the skill and knowledge of the facilitators. Understanding the challenges and sensitivities of the group members, and being able to adapt the delivery of the programme in line with these, is an essential part of its success.

This programme is likely to be helpful for all parents who are caring for children who have had experience of developmental traumas and are struggling to experience attachment security. These are children who have experienced trauma from within their family in their early years, and this trauma has impacted upon their development. Because of the early experiences of children in care or adopted from care it is especially suitable for parents of this population.

Potential parents can participate in this programme before children are placed, as well as parents who are currently parenting.

This programme has been successful with biological parents, but additional sensitivity is needed from the facilitators. It can be difficult exploring the impact of early experience on children when the parent was parenting during this time, and thus potentially contributed to the difficulties. This can raise complex feelings for the parents. A non-judgemental stance, and sensitivity and support for feelings raised, are especially important. Facilitators will need to ensure that there is sufficient time for parents to discuss the feelings that the group work is evoking.

Similar sensitivity is needed with kin carers who will be confronted with exploring difficulties the children are having which stem from a time when the parenting was provided by relatives.

This programme has been successful with residential carers. It is important that facilitators understand the particular challenges that living in residential care can pose. Children and young people often arrive in residential care with a lot of failed relationships behind them. They are likely to be more resistant to the possibility of trusting the residential support worker. They are also often acutely aware that this is a job for their carers and they have separate lives when off shift. This can make it harder for them to believe that the worker does care about them and wants a relationship with them. Coupled with this, young people struggling with adolescence and the pull towards independence can present an extra challenge to those trying to provide an experience of safe dependence. On the other side, residential workers can find the idea of being a parent to the children uncomfortable, and may struggle with the idea that they are providing unconditional love to a child who they are caring for but have not brought into their own homes. Shift patterns and a range of parenting ideas held by different team members can pose significant challenges. The material in this programme does not fully address the challenges of residential care, and therefore the experience of the facilitators to ensure relevance in delivery will be essential. Feedback from a facilitator who took part in the pilot study for this programme highlighted some of the difficulties:

> These units felt they were fire-fighting and overwhelmed with the limitations of what they could provide in the timescale, anxiety re Ofsted inspection, reduced level of staffing, use of casual staff and lack of funding leads to a sense of failure and lack of hope.

This facilitator suggested having an extra module to focus on translating ideas for the residential setting. Following the pilot I have included more case examples relevant for residential workers. A further module could be included as suggested to explore these examples in more depth.

THE FOUNDATIONS FOR ATTACHMENT PROGRAMME AND THE NURTURING ATTACHMENTS PROGRAMME

The Foundations for Attachment Programme is a prequel to the Nurturing Attachments Programme which I have previously published (Golding 2014). These programmes are therefore fully compatible. The Nurturing Attachments Programme is based around the House Model of Parenting. This is a model of parenting ideas which aims to help parents to develop their parenting skills matched to the emotional and behavioural needs of the children. In the Foundations for Attachment Programme I have developed the Foundation model. Again these models can be combined to provide a more intensive overview of the parenting approach. These programmes can therefore fit together or be used as stand-alone programmes. Parents who want to explore DDP-informed parenting in greater depth can progress from Foundations for Attachment to Nurturing Attachments.

WHAT EXPERIENCE DO GROUP FACILITATORS NEED?

This programme is based on a DDP-informed approach to parenting as conceived by Dan Hughes (Hughes 2009, 2011). Therefore, it is essential that facilitators have had some DDP training provided by a trainer certified by the DDP Institute (DDPI). I would recommend that facilitators have done both the level one and two DDP training, each of which is four days long. A good understanding of, and comfort in using, PACE is essential. Facilitators will also need to feel confident in explaining theory, including attachment, intersubjectivity and trauma, and relating this to the parenting of the children. Experience of working with parents and children where children have experienced developmental trauma is also an essential experience for delivering this programme.

Facilitators will also need to feel confident in supporting parents when emotionally distressed. This programme can evoke powerful feelings for group members. The session on exploring attachment history can be especially evocative and facilitators need to be prepared to provide individual support to some group members.

Facilitators have an important affective-reflective role within the group. The affective-reflective dialogue is an important principle of DDP. Communication between facilitator and group member will be both cognitive (reflective) and emotional (affective). This will be verbal and also non-verbal as emotional states aroused within the group are regulated and new meanings and understanding are co-created.

- *Reflective.* A groupwork programme inevitably has a lot of content. This is the cognitive or reflective part of the groupwork experience which is detailed within this manual. The facilitator will need to understand the content and be able to explain this to group members so that they can develop new knowledge and understanding. This is a collaborative process as, alongside the knowledge of the facilitators, the group members bring their parenting experience to the discussion; meaning is co-constructed from the experience of both group members and facilitators.

- *Affective.* The affective component that complements this reflection will be led by the facilitators in response to group members. A PACE attitude aided by being mind-minded towards group members and the experiences they bring is an essential part of facilitating the delivery of this programme.

Stories will also give affective and reflective meaning to discussions. This programme is not just about delivering the content; it is also about discovering the stories within the content, and within the experience of group members and facilitators alike. The telling of stories is an important way of learning about, sharing and experiencing the parenting of the children, and the changes that can be made to this. If we want parents to have an attitude of PACE, bringing the affective and the reflective to their parenting, then it is important that facilitators have this attitude also.

DELIVERING THE FOUNDATIONS FOR ATTACHMENT GROUP

The Foundations and Nurturing Attachment groups are delivered in a similar way, with the groupwork experience being interactive and participative. A combination of psychoeducation, small and large-group discussion, role play and activities provides group members with a varied learning experience.

Group size

There is no ideal size of group, as this will depend on the skill of the facilitator. Having said this, a smaller rather than a larger group will allow more interaction and participation. Group size of 10 to 12 is reasonable. Such a group would require a minimum of two facilitators.

Facilitators

One facilitator will lead the session, or part of the session if they are swopping this role. When leading the facilitator has responsibility for delivering the content, helping group members to engage with the material and activities associated with this. This facilitator is also mindful of timing. A second facilitator will support the lead facilitator and will have a bigger role in helping group members to participate in the session. This facilitator can monitor group members, noticing any difficulties that they might be having, such as struggling to be heard amongst the louder members. The second facilitator is most likely to notice if a group member is becoming upset or emotionally overwhelmed. If one of the group needs to leave the room and needs support it would typically be the second facilitator who would do this.

Both facilitators are likely to plan the sessions together, and to reflect on it following each session. In this way adaptations can be made in line with the needs of the unique group attending at the time. If group members are absent, facilitators can plan how they can help them to catch up in time for the next session.

It is also helpful if the facilitators can be available during breaks and at the end of the group, as some group members will want to seek advice or get support in their parenting with things that they are not comfortable sharing within the whole group.

Style of delivery

This programme works best when group members are actively engaged, with lots of discussion. There will inevitably be quieter group members, but facilitators will make sure that all those who want to join in will do so. It is hoped that quieter group members will make more use of small-group activities to make their own unique contributions. Participation works best when facilitators are part of the group, sitting within the circle rather than standing at the front. This is a collaborative approach within which the facilitators are not seen as the experts. All have expertise to bring to the group; the facilitators have responsibility for holding expertise to do with the content of the programme, but group members bring their own personal expertise related to their experience of parenting. It is the combining of this expertise that makes the group powerful. Group facilitators will be learning alongside the group members as well as facilitating the group.

I do not recommend PowerPoint, as this tends to signal the facilitator as expert and can reduce discussion. Some limited use of slides, for example to show a visual image, can be helpful as long as this does not detract from the engaging and interactive style of the facilitator. Less experienced facilitators will sometimes want to use slides to help them remember key points and ideas. As they get more experienced they might find it liberating to move away from this and to be led by the group more. Key points and ideas for each session are still given, but these can be interwoven with group discussion more easily when not structured by PowerPoint slides. However it is done, it will be the facilitators' responsibility to ensure that discussion and participation are encouraged, and anecdotal information that facilitators and group members share can be used to enhance the richness of the material being presented.

Within the process, notes and suggestions for using a variety of styles of delivering the programme are provided. This includes whole-group discussion which can flow naturally from facilitator-presented material, and discussion structured around an activity. All group members will then benefit from the experience found within the group as a whole. Facilitators will make sure that the group stays on track, allowing some diversion but then gently guiding back to the current topic. Working with the group as a whole will be combined with small-group activities. These latter tend to use up more time, including setting them up and collecting feedback afterwards. They can be useful to give quieter group members an opportunity to engage, and also to provide some exploration of ideas at greater depth.

There is less use of role play within this programme, compared to the Nurturing Attachments Programme. Role play can be very helpful but also creates a lot of anxiety. The longer groups lend themselves to this as there is more time to help group members to feel safe with each other. However, if there are confident members of the group it can be helpful for facilitators to dip into some role play to explore experience with a child in relation to the topic being discussed. Facilitators might also want to demonstrate ideas using role play. I would certainly expect that some demonstration of PACE will be provided, alongside modelling of this throughout facilitators' interactions with group members.

Video material can be helpful, particularly in the first module when exploring early parent–child interactions. There are excellent resources commercially available, or freely given via the internet, which can enhance a session. Bringing children 'into the room' can be enlivening for the group.

Balance of education and practical ideas

There are a large amount of psychology concepts and theory in the facilitators' notes, especially in Module One. Facilitators will need to make a judgement about how much depth to go into. In general, some understanding of why the children struggle and present such challenges can be helpful, and actually very reassuring for parents who perhaps are wondering if they are failing and getting things wrong with the child. However, some parents can be put off by the extent of psychology. Modules Two and Three have a more practical focus, with lots of activities to engage with the ideas. Facilitators need to find a balance for the group they are working with, giving sufficient theory to help group members understand why the parenting ideas are being suggested, but reducing some of the theory if this is not being appreciated. More time can be spent on exercises and ensuring that understanding is embedded into practical experience. Stories, metaphors, personal anecdotes and relating ideas to group members' experience can all help to reduce the intellectual nature of sharing theory and to make it accessible to all. A glossary is included to help group members understand the terms.

Embedding into practice

One of the challenges of any training experience is how to help group members take this forward, so that it doesn't become yet another training that is forgotten within six months. We want parents to take the ideas that they have found helpful and embed them into their day-to-day parenting. Some parents might go on to attend a Nurturing Attachments group. As this is based on a longer programme they have more opportunities to explore their experience of using the ideas at home and to settle into using these in a way that starts to feel natural. Other parents might benefit from some ongoing support, and maybe the possibility of top-up sessions to help them take the ideas forward. Exercises that have not been used within the programme could be used within such top-up sessions. Parents might keep in touch after the group, perhaps meeting up at intervals to share experiences and provide support to each other. Some parents will have regular support already; for example, foster carers will have a fostering social worker supporting them. It might be helpful if this social worker has knowledge of the programme, or even works through it with his foster carers. A practitioner supporting the parent might be able to review how things are going, for example, looking at the self-care plans created at the end of the group and reviewing progress in meeting this plan. If time has been short within the group session the parent could be supported to create or expand this plan after the group work has ended. Imaginative ways of reviewing and revisiting parenting ideas built into follow-up support can be really helpful in embedding learning into practice.

USING THE MANUAL

This manual contains everything that you will need to run the programme. I have provided session-by-session notes which include:

- *Session aims and overview:*
  This provides a quick overview of the session, helping facilitators to ensure that session aims are met.

- *Example session plan:*
  The session plan is a guide, including timings. This is for guidance only, but gives facilitators a starting point.

- *Trainer notes:*
  This provides a summary of the key theoretical material for each session. It provides background information that facilitators need to understand, although they do not need to cover all the detail. Key points need to be covered, but the depth and breadth of cover will be at the facilitators' judgement.

- *Description of activities:*
  The activities are provided to help facilitators engage the group with the material. A selection of activities is suggested but they do not all have to be used. Some of the activities can be used for reflection between sessions if there is insufficient time within the sessions. These suggestions provide some choices for the sessions. Many of the activities draw on case scenarios. These are all fictional but are consistent with my experience of children, young people and parents. I have tried to give a breadth of these in terms of age of child, living situation, etc. I am aware that these will not all be relevant to the group members. I would encourage facilitators to adapt these or write their own scenarios tailored to the group they are delivering to, where this would be helpful. I am also aware that I am influenced by my own culture when writing these, with only a few examples of children from different cultures. Again, where facilitators are running groups which include group members from different cultures I would encourage them to adapt or write new scenarios to take account of this different context.

  I have included reflections on some of the activities as part of the handouts. These can guide the facilitators when feeding back from these activities, as well as being available to group members for reflection between sessions. These are not definitive answers, just reflections for thought and discussion.

- *Process notes:*
  This provides guidance for structuring the sessions. Again this is only a starting point, but will help facilitators to plan how to deliver the content whilst incorporating the activities.

- *PACE: frequently asked questions*
  At the end of Module Two, I include a list of questions that are often asked about using PACE, together with answers to these.

- *Glossary of psychological terms and theory used in the programme.*

- *References and reading list.*

The manual is supplemented by photocopiable online materials which include:

- activity sheets

- handouts

- glossary of psychological terms and theory used in the programme

- references and reading list.

NOTES

1. Throughout the manual the generic term 'parent' is used to describe the range of caregivers who parent children with attachment and trauma difficulties. This is in recognition that they all take on a parenting role for the children they are caring for.

2. To avoid clumsiness, I have alternated gender for both parent and child throughout the manual.

3. There is a range of photocopiable handouts and activity sheets available as an online resource to accompany this manual. These can be photocopied for all group members. Also included are the glossary and references/reading list so that group members can also have copies of these. These materials can be accessed at www.jkp.com/voucher using the code GOLDINGFOUNDATIONS.

Evidence for the effectiveness of the Foundations for Attachment Programme

A pilot study was carried out during the development of the programme. This occurred across seven sites geographically spread through England. Facilitators delivered the programme to a total of 112 group members.

The breakdown of the groups studied was as follows:[1]

- Two sites delivered the programme to staff working in residential settings. A total of 88 residential carers participated in the programme and 80 completed the programme. Group size was between eight and 18. Just under half of the carers participating were male (43%) with 57% being female. Eighty-five per cent of the children and young people they were caring for were between 12 years and 16 years; 13% were between 17 and 19 years and 2% were under 11 years old. Seventy-one per cent of the young people had been living in the home for under a year, with the other 29% having lived there between one and five years.

- Five sites delivered the programme to a range of parents including adoptive, foster and kinship parents. A total of 36 parents participated in the programme and 32 participants completed the programme. Sixty-eight per cent were adoptive parents with the remaining being foster or kinship carers. Group size was between four and seven. Nineteen per cent of these parents were male whilst 81% were female. The children being cared for ranged in age from one to 19 years. The looked after children were all under 14 with an average age of ten years; 87% were over five years of age. The adopted children ranged in age from one to 19 years of age but with a younger average age of seven years. All the looked after children had been in placement for less than a year.

---

1   A minority of participants did not provide information about themselves and their families so numbers are extrapolated from the information that was collected.

This compares to the adopted children, where only 13% had lived with their families for under a year. Fifty-nine per cent of the adopted children had lived within their families for between one and five years, 6% between five and ten years and 22% over ten years.

- A further site piloted the programme with four biological parents caring for children with acute mental illness. Three parents completed the programme. The group size was not sufficient for pre- and post-group questionnaires to be used, and therefore this site is not included in the whole-group analysis.

Across the seven sites, group members were asked to complete a range of pre- and post-group questionnaires immediately prior to and upon completion of the programme. Not all questionnaires were completed by the participants therefore the total numbers for each measure varied.

- Knowledge quiz (n=101)

- The Warwick-Edinburgh Mental Wellbeing Scale (n=112)

- Brief parental self-efficacy scale (n=98)

- Parental reflective functioning questionnaire (with permission from Patrick Luyten, University College London) (n=78)

- Carer questionnaire. A self-report questionnaire which explores parent knowledge, skills and understanding in relation to parenting their child(ren) (n=81)

- A satisfaction questionnaire post group (n=102).

The data collected was input into IBM SPSS Statistics 21. It was established that the data was suitable for parametric testing and paired t-tests were carried out. Analysis for the whole group was carried out. Further analysis was carried out to see if any significant difference existed between residential carers and adoptive/foster carers. This was achieved by using independent t-testing of the difference in pre- and post-programme scores.

Summary of results for whole group of parents and residential workers across seven sites

Group members reported gains in knowledge through attending the group, and this was confirmed by statistically significant changes as measured by the knowledge quiz. In addition, small but statistically significant positive changes were recorded for wellbeing. Prior to the group programme 15 per cent of participants reported low wellbeing whilst 11 per cent reported high wellbeing. After attendance at the group low wellbeing had dropped to 9 per cent whilst high wellbeing had increased to 23 per cent. Small but statistically significant differences were also reported for feelings of efficacy and reflective functioning. The carer questionnaire revealed statistically significant positive changes. Details of these results can be seen below.

KNOWLEDGE QUIZ

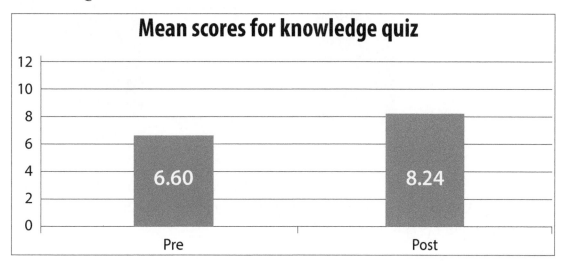

There was a significant difference in the scores for pre-programme (M=6.6040, SD=1.83346) and post-programme (M=8.2376, SD=1.70967) conditions; t (100) = 7.109, p<0.05.

THE WARWICK-EDINBURGH MENTAL WELLBEING SCALE

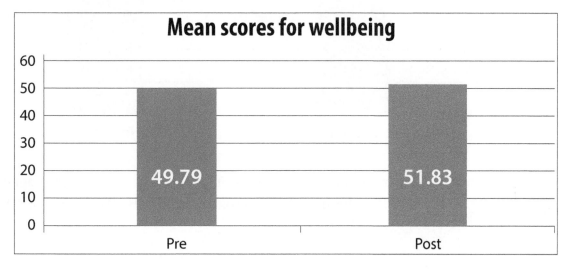

There was a significant difference in the scores for pre-programme (M=49.7946, SD=8.15076) and post-programme (M=51.8304, SD=7.92065) conditions; t (111) = 2.444, p<0.05

BRIEF PARENTAL SELF-EFFICACY SCALE

There was a small but significant difference in the scores for pre-programme (M=20.3163, SD=3.43000) and post-programme (M=20.9592, SD=2.40668) conditions; t (97) = 1.984, p<0.05.

PARENTAL REFLECTIVE FUNCTIONING QUESTIONNAIRE

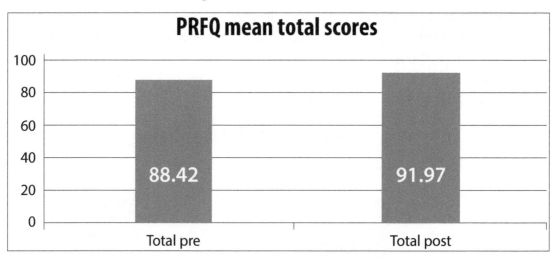

There was a small but significant difference in the total scores for pre-programme (M=88.4231, SD=10.79985) and post-programme (M=91.9744, SD=8.30580) conditions; t (77) = 2.910, p<0.05.

CARER QUESTIONNAIRE

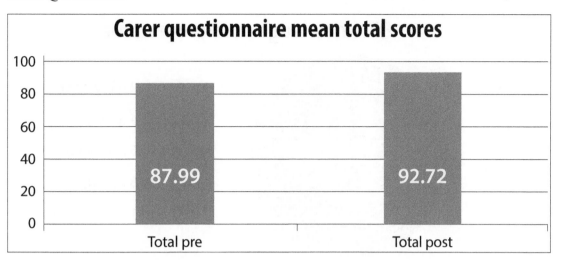

There was a significant difference in the total scores for pre-programme (M=87.9877, SD=17.02681) and post-programme (M=92.7160, SD=14.62125) conditions; t (80) =2.782, p<0.05.

Satisfaction questionnaire

Group members reported high levels of satisfaction with the groupwork programme, with 83% of participants rating overall satisfaction between 7 and 10. Group members were satisfied with all aspects of the group, with group discussion being especially appreciated. Group members rated their estimate of their knowledge before and after attending the group. Knowledge was rated as increased following the group (see below).

SATISFACTION QUESTIONNAIRE Q1

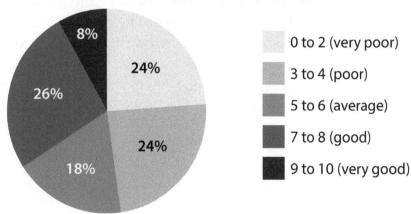

SATISFACTION QUESTIONNAIRE Q7

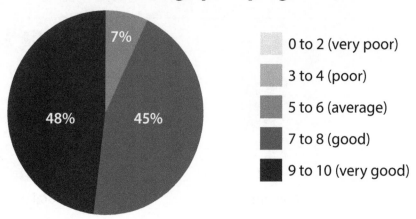

Summary of results for residential workers compared to parents

When results for parents were compared to residential workers, differences were revealed. They all appeared to benefit from attending the group, but they differed in how they benefited.

Wellbeing and efficacy was higher for residential workers compared to parents prior to attending the group with wellbeing increasing slightly (not statistically significantly) whilst efficacy stayed the same. The parents but not the residential workers reported statistically significant increases in wellbeing and self-efficacy. Therefore, parents appear to gain more benefit from the group in improving wellbeing and efficacy, possibly because these were initially lower compared to residential workers. This suggests that more attention needs to be given to providing emotional support to the parents.

Both parents and residential workers had the same reflective functioning scores prior to attending the group. This only changed for parents with statistically significant increased reflective functioning upon completion of the group. More attention to reflective functioning might therefore be needed by group facilitators when delivering to residential workers. This could be achieved with ongoing support to help them to reflect on the children in their care.

Parents had high scores pre- and post-group attendance on the knowledge quiz (mean score of 8) whilst residential workers had lower pre-group scores (mean score of 6) which increased to 8 post group. The residential workers but not the parents showed a statistically significant increase in knowledge on the knowledge quiz, possibly a reflection of their lower knowledge prior to attending the group.

Both parents and residential workers reported positive and statistically significant change on the carer questionnaire.

Feedback from birth parents in one site

A group was run for parents who had a child struggling with mental illness, requiring admission to an adolescent inpatient unit. The group was attended by four birth parents with three of these completing the programme. Three of the parents had a child who was currently an inpatient, with one parent whose child had recently been discharged from the day service. The average age of the child was 16 (range 15–17).

Group members reported high levels of satisfaction with the groupwork programme, with the three parents who completed the programme rating overall satisfaction between 7 and 10. Group members were satisfied with all aspects of the group, although satisfaction with handouts was lower (average 5 out of 10). The group size is too small to draw conclusion from this. It might suggest that handouts need some adapting for use with birth parents. Group members rated their estimate of their knowledge before and after attending the group. Knowledge was rated as increased following the group with average rating changing from 1 to 7 out of 10.

MODULE ONE

UNDERSTANDING CHALLENGES OF PARENTING

SESSION TITLE: BLOCKED RELATIONSHIPS

AIMS OF SESSION

- To provide group members and facilitators with an opportunity to introduce themselves and to get to know each other.

- To establish a non-judgemental and safe environment for group exploration of issues relevant to parenting that is challenging because of relationship insecurities.

- To explore the idea of 'blocked trust' and to increase understanding of how children can develop this difficulty.

- To explore the concept of 'intersubjectivity' and to discover what happens when children don't get the early intersubjective experiences that they need.

- To consider how to parent children who experience blocked trust and fear of intersubjectivity.

SUMMARY OF SESSION

This session provides group members with an opportunity to get to know each other whilst reflecting on their own child, or the parenting task that is lying ahead of them. It also provides the facilitators with an opportunity to set a non-judgemental tone, thus building safety and increasing the confidence of those attending. Group members are helped to reflect on the many reasons why children and young people might present challenges to being parented and to notice that characteristics in the child or parent or between them might contribute to this. There is also an opportunity to reflect on any special challenge which might be presented that is common to the group of parents who are participating in the programme (e.g. foster carers, adopters, birth parents, residential support workers).

The remainder of the session introduces the first two challenges that children or young people might experience when they have attachment insecurities. The idea of blocked trust is introduced, and related to experiences that can occur in the first year of life. This is then closely linked with the fear of reciprocal relationships that can develop. Group members are introduced to the idea of 'intersubjectivity'. Some thought is then given to ways of parenting children who experience blocked trust and fear of intersubjectivity.

SESSION PLAN

Example session plan	
Introductions	15 minutes
Discussion: Understanding the challenges of parents	10 minutes
Discussion: Understanding complexity	10 minutes
Reflection on child/young person	15 minutes
Discussion: Parenting challenge one: blocked trust	30 minutes
Break	20 minutes
Parenting challenge two: Fear of intersubjectivity	40 minutes
Reflection on child/young person	40 minutes

TRAINER NOTES[1]

UNDERSTANDING CHALLENGES OF PARENTING

KEY POINTS

* Developmental trauma can have a devastating impact on a child's development and sense of security.

* There is a range of reasons why children have difficulties related to their attachment experience.

* This is about understanding the context and not blaming the parents.

This groupwork programme is for parents of children or young people who have difficulties related to their attachment experience, leading to relationship difficulties. The focus is on parenting children who have experienced developmental trauma. This is traumatizing experience which occurs from within the family, caused by the nature of the parent–child relationship. This trauma impacts on the development of the child, hence the name. Developmental trauma is devastating because the trauma comes from the relationship which would usually be supporting a child through trauma. The child experiences trauma without parents who can provide the safety needed to recover and heal.

This can be difficult for birth parents to reflect upon, as an important role for a parent is to be an attachment figure for her child. Parents need help to understand that attachment difficulties can arise for many reasons, even though parents' motivations are good and they are committed to being a good parent for their children. Even if parents provided an environment which was developmentally traumatizing for their children they are showing a commitment to reducing the impact of this by engaging with this programme.

Parenting children through kinship care can also have a resonance when exploring the early experience of the child provided by a relative, whether this is son, daughter, niece, nephew or some other relationship.

---

1 The accompanying online materials can be accessed at www.jkp.com/voucher using the code GOLDINGFOUNDATIONS.

Parents who are parenting a child later in life through adoption, fostering or residential care may experience less personal impact in exploring the early experience of their children, but are still likely to be affected by an exploration of early experience and how it can impact on attachment experience and later relationship experience. Understanding their child's experience more deeply can be very painful.

There are a range of reasons why early attachment experience can be poor. For example:

- Difficulties can arise during pregnancy (e.g. exposure to drugs), at birth (e.g. prematurity) or following birth (e.g. infection). The infant might need to spend time in a special care unit, impacting on the early bonding experience between parent and child. The mother might be ill following the birth, further adding to this.

- Childhood illness. Illness in early childhood can lead to difficulties in developing security. Hospitalization can add to this, making it even more challenging. Alternatively, illness or hospitalization of a sibling can mean that the parents become less emotionally available to their other children. Death of a sibling can have an even bigger impact.

- Parental illness. Physical or mental illness can both reduce the parents' capacity to be available, attuned and sensitively responsive to their child. A mother may have struggled with post-natal depression or longstanding mental or physical illness or have episodes of acute mental or physical illness. Hospitalization will be an added stressor further compromising the child's security, and of course death of a parent can be unavoidable but extremely traumatic.

- Family stress. Any chronic or acute stress upon the family can lead to less emotional availability from the parents and thus insecurity for the child. Employment, poverty, relationship troubles between parents or with extended family members or illness/death within extended family or with close friends can all be reasons why parents may struggle with parenting their children.

- Child characteristics. Children born with a learning, or other genetic, difficulty may have difficulty signalling clearly to their parents. This can make it harder for the parent to emotionally attune, understand what her child needs and meet these needs. This can be further complicated when parents are struggling with feelings of grief and loss for the child they expected to have. Similarly, children born with fussy, hard to soothe temperaments can place additional demands on the parents, which can make parenting stressful.

- Parents who have their own early history of trauma or experience of poor parenting will not have had the experience to know how to be available and responsive to their child. Parenting styles can end up being repeated between generations or parents can over-compensate, trying so hard not to be the parent they experienced that they become insensitive in other ways.

• Sadly, for some children the experience of the parent goes beyond insensitive to being frightening (abuse) or absent (neglect). Both can have a profound impact on the child's ability to feel safe and secure within the family. This includes experience of parents who are frightening because of domestic violence, alcohol or drug abuse.

• Experience of separation and loss, often compounded by abuse and neglect and multiple placements within the care system can leave a child emotionally distressed and with defensive patterns of relating to caregivers that can make it challenging for later parents. Children looked after and adopted are a highly vulnerable group of children who can be developmentally traumatized by their early experience and who struggle to trust and feel secure in their current families.

PARENTING CHALLENGE ONE: BLOCKED TRUST (BAYLIN AND HUGHES 2016)

KEY POINTS

* Early experience can help children develop trust or mistrust in their caregivers, depending upon the parenting provided.

* This in turn can lead to a sense of being unconditionally or conditionally loved.

* This can lead to changes in brain functioning as defensive and socially engaged systems adapt to experience, leading to blocked trust.

* Children will learn to behave in ways that adapt to blocked trust, most notably through a range of controlling behaviours.

* Expectations and adaptations move with them into new homes.

Parents have the challenge of building connection and trust alongside providing boundaries and discipline, rather than sequentially, so that the child can feel unconditionally loved whilst managing restrictions in his environment.

Blocked Trust is when young children block the pain of rejection and the capacity to delight in order to survive in a world without comfort and joy. (Hughes and Baylin 2014)

Trust

Secure parent–infant interactions rely on parenting that is attuned, sensitively responsive and empathic. This experience is necessary for the development of a healthy nervous system. Consistent, predictable, reliable and stable nurturing care will lead to a sense of trust in caregivers.

This can be related to Erikson's stages of development (Erikson 1963). The first stage he labelled the crisis of trust versus mistrust and he linked this to the experience of safety or danger in the first stage of the infant's life. Erickson suggested that trust relates to the development of hope.

Mistrust

When infants experience a frightening early environment without parental protection, their development will organize around a nervous system that is prepared for danger. Erickson suggested that mistrust relates to the development of fear; an idea that resonates with children's experience of developmental trauma.

It is this sense of hope/trust or fear/mistrust that is taken forward to later relationships. This will determine whether a child can feel secure and appropriately trusting of others even when threatened or insecure or mistrusting even when the relationship is benign and loving. This in turn leads to a sense of being unconditionally or conditionally loved.

Trust leads to experience of being unconditionally loved

Infant behaviour is relatively simple and focused on eliciting care and learning about the world. The infant is not considered to be responsible for his behaviour and therefore does not need discipline. Parenting therefore communicates to the infant that he is loved unconditionally as there are no conditions on the relationship or on the behaviour. The parent communicates that I will love you 'no matter what'.

The focus of parenting efforts is on providing the infant with nurturing and responsive care. This experience of trust leads to the development of secure attachment and the experience of unconditional love.

Toddlers move further away from parents to explore the world around them. The children are becoming mobile and can start to get into mischief! There are now conditions on behaviour – 'If you do this…then…'; 'When you do this…then…'. However, the secure child will experience this within the context of a relationship that remains unconditional. The parent communicates that I will still love you no matter what, and I will make things okay when I put limits on your behaviour.

The parents ensure that their children are kept safe and are taught how to behave, matched to the values of the community they are living within. The children experience safety in this new aspect to their relationship with their parents because they continue to have the experience of being unconditionally loved. The children trust in the good intentions of their parents.

Mistrust leads to experience of being conditionally loved

In the case of mistrust, the infant is perceived as responsible for his behaviour. Parenting therefore communicates to the infant that he is loved conditionally. The parent communicates that I will love you 'only if'.

Even at infancy, children experience love as conditional. For the growing child, the provisions of boundaries, restrictions, irritation, frustration or anger from the parents, especially in the absence of empathy or warmth, only serve to reinforce this conditionality. The children experience unregulated shame and learn to associate boundaries with their developing sense of self as bad.

The brain-based development of blocked trust

Growing in an atmosphere of mistrust and fear impacts on early brain development; in particular, the brain organizes around the need for self-defence and at the same time suppresses the need for social engagement. This allows survival in a world which is harsh and non-nurturing; reliance is on self rather than trust in the caregiver.

Jon Baylin and Dan Hughes (2016) use the term 'blocked trust' to describe this process of suppressing the need for comfort and companionship to survive neglect and abuse. The children learn not to trust that comfort and companionship will be safely given to them by their caregiver, because their initial cues to elicit these were met with pain, fear or silence. The children learn to suppress these innate, instinctive needs which are common to all human children when born. This means that they suppress feeling the social emotions. These are emotions which relate to care and companionship from within relationships, such as pain of separation and joy of connection. When relational experiences have been frightening and painful the child feels safer being asocial. The child develops into a state of chronic defensiveness, defending against the real and anticipated pain were the child to be open to social engagement. The much-needed and enduring emotional bonds with caregivers are sacrificed along the way. The child learns to suppress his relational needs and to keep the parent at a safe distance by becoming self-sufficient.

When children experience blocked trust they:

- learn to resist authority and to oppose parental influence

- avoid the parent as a potential source of comfort

- can't relax and enjoy playful moments

- can't be open, able to share thoughts and feelings

- remain vigilant to danger, with reduced curiosity and learning

- don't trust in their parents' good intentions

- don't trust in the unconditional support and love that's on offer to them

- trust in themselves rather than others

- develop controlling behaviours as they try to take charge of their own safety; it feels safer to be in charge than to be influenced by another.

As will be explored in Module Three, blocked trust in a child can trigger blocked care in the parent. Neither can engage healthily in the relationship. There is mutual mistrust and defensiveness within the parent–child relationship. Jon Baylin describes how this can block the potential for change. Thus, child blocked trust and parental blocked care results in blocked change (Baylin 2016).

Change of parenting environment

When the parenting environment changes, children with blocked trust will move into the home anticipating the same difficulties as they experienced previously. The new parent wants to demonstrate their unconditional love, but as the children are older they cannot be shown unconditional love and care without the parents also attending to their behaviour. This makes it harder for the children to trust in the parents' good intentions, or to experience love as unconditional. Instead of behaviour support as being part of an unconditional relationship ('I will love you no matter what and even when I don't approve of your behaviour'), it is perceived as an indicator that love is conditional ('I will only love you if…'; 'If you can't behave in this way I will not love you'). The child's early experience has predisposed him to make these assumptions when he is being nurtured and supported; including with behaviour. Even though this is not what the parent is trying to communicate, the child hears that love is conditional, and it is likely that he will come up wanting. 'I love you but don't like your behaviour' is not a message that developmentally traumatized children can make sense of.

This is also true when children are living with parents who were previously insensitive but have made some changes in the parenting that they now offer. Perhaps they have recovered from illness or have made changes in their life that now means they are more available and accepting of their children. The children continue to anticipate what they have previously experienced.

Therefore:

- Children need discipline and boundaries but they still need to experience unconditional relationships. When the unconditional relationship is provided first, and discipline and boundaries sit on top, the children can manage this later experience whilst continuing to experience love as unconditional.

- When children have not experienced unconditional love early in life, and when they are now being parented by a different parent, the development of trust and the provision of socialization experience through discipline and boundaries must develop together rather than sequentially.

- Parents try to get around this by telling the children that they love them, but they don't like the behaviour. The children however experience such strong feelings of shame, experienced as a sense of being bad, that they cannot make this distinction; if their behaviour is bad it is because they are bad. This leads to blocked trust.

- To help a child recover from blocked trust the parent must help him to develop a different, less shame-based sense of self.

- The parent offers the child connection and understanding through which unconditional love is communicated whilst also empathically providing structure and boundaries.

FEAR OF ABANDONMENT

> **KEY POINTS**
>
> * Blocked trust leads to core anxieties about not being good enough.
> * This leads to fears of rejection and loss of parents, described as fear of abandonment.
> * Baby abandonment is part of our cultural history, still apparent in some parts of the world. Thus ancestral memories of strong babies being cared for and others being abandoned might contribute to modern fears of abandonment.

The experience of blocked trust and conditional love is closely associated with fears of abandonment.

- The children who cannot trust have core anxieties about not being good enough.

- They anticipate that they will lose their parents one day.

- This is a fear that resonates with children who have experienced separation and loss of parents already, sometimes multiple times.

The fear of abandonment may also resonate from ancestral memories. For example, anthropologists and evolutionary biologists have explored the practice of baby abandonment. This is a practice that is relatively common both in Western history and in some modern tribal communities where resources are scarce (see Sarah Blaffer Hrdy in Daniela Sieff 2015). Therefore, there may be an evolutionary and anthropological perspective on why the experience of conditional love can so easily trigger fears of loss and abandonment.

This perspective suggests that:

- modern mother–infant relationships have been shaped by our ancient history

- in resource-rich modern societies mothers no longer must make decisions about whether to rear or abandon a baby

- in less affluent communities these decisions are still being made.

For example, mothers of the !kung of the Kalahari desert, Botswana, will abandon an infant in the bush if still nursing a child when the infant is born.

This can also be seen in parenting practices in Western cultures through the ages:

- Foundling hospitals of previous centuries led to thousands of infants being left, with two thirds dying before their first birthdays.

- In the 1800s in London, many infant deaths were reported to be due to accidental smothering, a condition described as overlaying, in numbers much larger than this relatively rare accident should suggest.

- Folk legends of changeling children provided a culturally sanctioned way of abandoning babies in the forests.

- The ancient need to invest in healthy children may be why mothers of pre-term twins were found to unconsciously direct more attention to the healthier twin when observed eight months after the twins' birth (Mann 1980, in Blaffer Hrdy and Sieff 2015).

Blaffer Hrdy and Sieff speculate that children have evolved to be hypersensitive to signs of a lack of commitment, especially from the mother. Deep-rooted fears of abandonment are triggered when the child senses any signs that he is not worth being cared for. For children who have experienced a lack of love and conditionality early in life, even ordinary boundaries and discipline might provide such indicators.

IMPACT OF BLOCKED TRUST ON THE DEVELOPMENT OF THE NERVOUS SYSTEM

KEY POINTS

* We are born with immature brains. Development is influenced by experience.

* Sensitivity of the alarm system, especially the amygdala, is set by this experience. Frightening early experience leads to brains that are sensitized to danger.

* This can bias children towards feeling unsafe even in safe situations, and responding defensively rather than being open and engaged to others.

* Blocked trust develops as core brain systems respond to danger and lack of social support.

* Parents are likely to feel less safe themselves and also move into defensive responding.

* If parents can stay open and engaged to their children it can help children move from defensive to social engagement. This increases safety and security, effectively resetting the sensitivity level in the brain.

Overview of nervous system

The nervous system consists of:

* central nervous system (CNS) = brain and spinal cord

* peripheral nervous system (PNS) = connects CNS to limbs and organs

* autonomic nervous system (ANS) = division of PNS consisting of a sympathetic (accelerator) and parasympathetic (brake) branch

* somatic nervous system (SNS) = takes sensory information or sensations from the peripheral organs (those away from the brain e.g., limbs) to the CNS

* vagal nerve = carries messages within the nervous system (NS).

The nervous system controls the body by transmitting signals to and from different parts of the body, co-ordinating the individual's voluntary and involuntary actions. Importantly for helping developmentally traumatized children, this is also dependent upon information that the nervous system gets from the environment. This information is processed in the central nervous system, determining how to respond and sending signals to muscles and glands to make this response. When a child experiences a frightening environment, this will influence how the nervous system develops, including the brain's level of sensitivity to danger.

Experience and the brain

The brain is immature at birth; therefore, there is a lot of scope for its development to be influenced by experience. For example, the amygdala is sensitized by early experience which feels dangerous. It gives messages to the ANS based on this sensitivity. Thus, the sympathetic NS moves into fight/flight rather than play. Similarly, in dangerous circumstances the parasympathetic NS will shut down rather than relax.

Stephen Porges suggests we have an ancient nervous system which evolved to deal with dangerous environments. A modern nervous system developed on top of this as we evolved into a social species needing the ability to socially engage with each other (Porges 2011). We therefore ended up with a complex mix of ancient and modern. We move between these depending on whether we are experiencing safety or danger, as detected by the monitoring system in our brain, especially the amygdala, supported by the hippocampus.

The defence and social engagement systems therefore work in a complementary fashion. If a person is in one system they cannot at the same time be in the other system (see Figure M1.S1.1).

In early experience of danger:

- the social monitoring system becomes sensitized by this early experience and the children become hyper-alert to danger within the social world

- this deactivates the social engagement system, and activates the social defence system within the brain

- the children are left socially defensive and not open and engaged to the influence of others.

The nervous system becomes sensitized to perceptions of danger leading to mobilization (fight, flight and freeze mediated by the sympathetic nervous system) and immobilization (faint mediated by the parasympathetic nervous system) in response to this perceived danger. These behaviours which are not considered to be socially acceptable only serve to increase the children's sense of badness and to reinforce the mistrust of others.

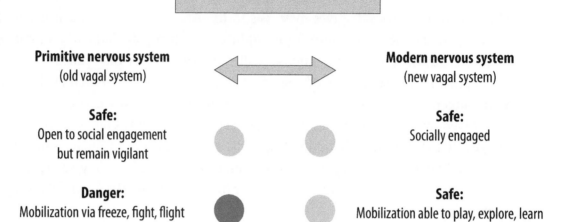

Figure M1.S1.1 Summary of the defence and social engagement systems (adapted from Porges 2014)

The defensive responding that children develop when exposed to poor and frightening caregiving has been described by Baylin and Hughes (2016) as blocked trust. These authors suggest that five brain systems are affected in the development of blocked trust. These are core brain systems which are responsive to the quality of care that a child receives.

- *Self-defence.* At times, everyone needs to defend themselves, whether against physical or emotional threat.

- *Social engagement system.* This is the system that is strengthened by good care. It helps us to stay socially engaged with others, even when those interactions are a bit tense. This facilitates social bonding and taking care of each other.

- *Social switching system.* This allows movement between social engagement and self-defence depending upon circumstances and as the current state of safety and threat are appraised during interactions.

- *Social pain.* From early in life children will experience the pain of social separation. This is a necessary part of the development of a call and response dyadic relationship between an infant and his parent. The infant signals distress (the call) and the parent responds to reduce the distress. A neuroscientist called

Nim Tottenham has described this as social buffering. The parent has an important role in providing regulatory support whilst the child matures and develops his own capacity for emotion regulation (Tottenham 2014, cited in Baylin and Hughes 2016).

- *The stress system.* How a child will respond to stress is determined early in life dependent upon the quality of care received. This system supports the ability to respond to challenge, by mobilizing physical, cognitive and emotional resources to deal with the challenge. We all need some activation of our stress system, with its associated release of cortisol, to deal with both good and bad challenges. It is this response to stress and moderate levels of cortisol that help us to learn and remember new things. Problems arise when the stress system is activated at more extreme levels.

In infancy, these systems develop in a subcortical, bottom-up fashion, with top-down support coming from the parent. The parent's brain supports the more immaturely developed infant brain. This social buffering provides the child with the experience of safety in closeness to the parent. This releases oxytocin which is taken up by receptors on the amygdala, leading to a reduction in sensitivity to danger. The social buffering provided tames the child's defensive systems, reducing the child's sensitivity to stress (Gee *et al.* 2014, cited in Baylin and Hughes 2016).

As the infant matures these early brain systems connect to the developing higher brain regions. By 18 months of age, with good care, the toddler has his own executive system for the social brain, reducing the need to respond defensively. The child is comfortable with social engagement. He has capacity to engage with others, and to sustain this engagement even when interactions are tense. These interactions support the development of self-awareness and empathy as the ability to think about self and others increases. Introspection and reflection arise in safety.

Thus, good-quality care of an infant will support the shift from bottom-up to top-down functioning and the development of the social engagement system. The child is learning to regulate and to reflect; this supports learning from new experiences. As social engagement occurs, instead of defensive reactions, trust is developed and the child can attune to inner experiences through the development of empathy.

Poor care, on the other hand, will leave the child's brain in an under-developed, less connected state adapted for more dangerous environments (see Figure M1.S1.2). As Jon Baylin and Dan Hughes put it:

> Maltreated children are forced, in a way, to shift into a trajectory of brain development more suited for life in the wild than for living in very safe environments. Knowing this can help therapists and caregivers better understand the seemingly wild, over-the-top emotional reactions and behaviour exhibited at times by maltreated children living in tame environments. (Baylin and Hughes 2016, p.49)

The self-defence system is favoured over the social engagement system as the child experiences the world as dangerous and himself as bad. This defence system, which shuts down the higher brain systems, allows the child to become vigilant to the external world rather than reflecting on his inner life. In effect this protects the child from the dual dangers of a dangerous world and an inner life of terror and shame. The stress system becomes chronically activated, easily triggered and hard to turn off. This allows social pain to be blocked but also, tragically, it blocks new learning.

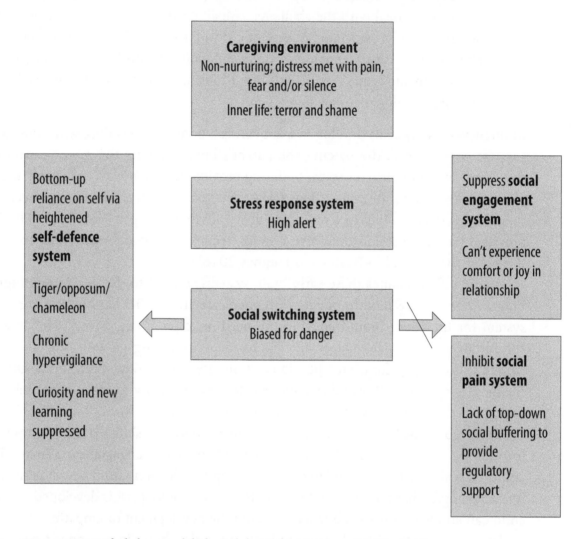

Figure M1.S1.2 Blocked trust and the brain (adapted from Hughes and Baylin 2016)

From this description of blocked trust, we can see how children can develop styles of relating that are angry, controlling and highly intrusive towards the safe care that the parent is offering: the fight/flight of the sympathetic nervous system. The child is oppositional, ready to fight and defend himself. Baylin and Hughes (2016) describe such a child as a 'tiger'. Parents always know when they are trying to nurture a tiger. They must resist being drawn into cycles of negative, aggressive reactions which leave both experiencing mistrust.

This, however, is not the only way that children express blocked trust. These authors also point to 'opossums' and 'chameleons'.

The opossum will keep a very low profile; more the feigning death of the parasympathetic nervous system than the fight/flight responses described in the tiger. Opossum-like children will try to appear small and silent as they attempt to stay out of sight and out of mind. They do not want to draw attention to themselves. The parent reaches out but finds the child not there. The parent feels rejected and a sense of failure as they try to reach these shut-away children. They find it hard to stay engaged with the children and end up caring out of necessity as they are receiving so little back. This too can end in a cycle of mutual mistrust.

The third animal Baylin and Hughes (2016) use to represent blocked trust is a chameleon. Chameleons are expert at blending in and these children have this ability also. They will constantly assess the mood of those around them and try to adapt their behaviour to this mood. These children suppress their own needs as they attempt to accommodate to the needs and moods of the adults. This is a way of staying connected with them, superficially social, but without any substance to the connection they are forming. Parents of chameleons will describe a 'fakeness' about these children which makes any connections they have with them feel manipulative and unreal.

When environments change, the child is likely to remain defensive and not open to social engagement. New learning does not happen easily. If a child anticipates that he is going to be hurt, rejected or not responded to he will behave defensively. However, if the parent can help him to feel safe, over time he will move across to the open and engaged state. When we are in a relationship we tend to move into the same state as the other person. If a child is defensive, it can pull the parent into matching this and becoming defensive in turn. If, however, the parent can remain open and engaged at these times, a level of safety will build up; mistrust becomes trust, and the child will be able to match the parent and become open and engaged in turn. Over time, this can reset the sensitivity of the stress system so that children are less likely to react to innocuous events as if they are dangerous. This, however, is not an easy or quick process. The children are hyper-focused on threat or potential threat, and much less able to attend to signs of safety.

Facial recognition provides a good example of this. Studies have shown that a child who has experienced abuse will detect anger in face and voice faster than children who have not experienced abuse. They also cannot withdraw this attention to notice other things (Pollak 2003, cited in Baylin and Hughes 2016). Thus, children will miss signs of safety in their environment because of this hyper-focus to signs of threat, a phenomenon that Baylin and Hughes (2016) have called 'safety blindness'. The task of the parents is to hang on in there, calming the children's defensive reactions through their open and engaged state and thus providing the regulatory support needed. As they are doing this they will be cracking the door open on the children's blocked attachment system as the children learn to anticipate safety and care from their current parents.

PARENTING CHILDREN EXPERIENCING BLOCKED TRUST: COMFORT, CURIOSITY AND JOY

KEY POINTS

* Blocked trust impacts on children's capacity to seek comfort, engage in curiosity and experience joy.

* Open and engaged parenting which increases trust for the child can awaken comfort-seeking, curiosity and joy.

When children have blocked trust, they lose the capacity to seek comfort, to experience curiosity and to experience joy in relationship. In building trust for the child, the parent is also helping the child to discover the comfort of nurture, the wonder of curiosity and the fun of joy (Hughes and Baylin 2014).

Parenting needs to help children to recover from blocked trust so that they can feel unconditionally loved. The parent continually demonstrates and makes explicit that the child is unconditionally loved through her attuned, empathic, responsive care and her use of relationship repair at times when attunement is lost. This might be because of the need for discipline in the form of a boundary or consequence, because the parent says no to the child or because the parent has responded defensively. The child learns that none of these are because he is a bad child, and that parents always make things right again. He really is loved 'no matter what'.

In this way, the children start to build trust in the parent and can use this trust to let the parent help them to have new experiences of comfort, curiosity and joy.

Children need their parents to help them to recover the capacity for sadness

Children traumatized within relationships will adapt by blocking the experience of pain because comfort isn't available. The release of opioids helps this social pain management. If social pain is blocked, then the children won't need comfort. This, therefore, is an adaptation to a lack of available comfort.

- If the child is going to experience that comfort is now available, the parent will need to awaken the pain of disconnection. This then awakens the need for comfort which the parent can respond to.

- Sadness is the hardest emotion to experience for traumatized children. They are afraid to feel sad, anticipating no comfort.

- They experience resistance to empathy, fearing the emotional experience that receiving empathy awakens.

- The parent helps the child to experience empathy, and to trust and anticipate that the parent will be available to comfort him with her emotional experience.

- Thus, the parents help the child to feel sad and become open to comfort again. That is, they help the child to feel safe to be sad and need comfort; to be able to cry in his parent's presence. Displaying emotional distress can be a sign of recovery in developmentally traumatized children.

Children need their parents to help them to recover the capacity for curiosity

Children are born to be curious. They may not yet have words, or understanding, but infants still express a sense of wonder about the world around them. Even the smallest thing can be a thing of intense wonder to the immature infant. Anything novel or unexpected is a special source of interest. The child is learning about the world around him as he experiences it. Later, this innate curiosity will be the precursor to the development of reflection. The child will be able to step back and think about what he is experiencing; so sad, then, for curiosity to be stamped out of a child. Living in danger leaves the child so alert for external threats that wonderment is obliterated. The novel increases concern or fear and threat needs be defended against. Curiosity is not the friend of those in danger; it needs be replaced with vigilance.

- Parents remain open and engaged to the children, using their own curiosity to awaken the curiosity of the children.

- The children experience it as safe to be curious and to share in a state of wonder about the world, themselves and others.

- Children will start to ask, 'Why...?'

Children need their parents to help them to recover the capacity for relational joy

When children are mistrusting and predominantly defensive, they will have few experiences of shared playfulness; pleasure, laughter and delight are luxuries when the child's focus is upon anticipated danger. The child learns to mistrust these experiences, which then create anxiety and a need to withdraw from them and the relationship. Opportunities to experience moments of joy or fun are important to help the child to relax within these aspects of the relationship. The child can then learn to regulate positive emotional states through the co-regulating sharing of these moments.

- When children resist relationship, they cannot experience joy within the relationship.

- The parents need to help the children to shine in the delight of the other and to mirror their joy in being with them.

- Some children will display a kind of 'manic happiness'. This is a defence against sadness but it is not relational. Parents will help the children to experience relational happiness.

PARENTING CHALLENGE TWO: FEAR OF INTERSUBJECTIVITY

KEY POINTS

* Children need and will instinctively seek primary intersubjective experiences in their early relationships.

* These relationships give them safe experience of influencing and being open to influence within the relationship.

* This provides a foundation for later experiences of secondary intersubjectivity. Children can enjoy exploring the world from within connected relationships.

* Being open to influence but receiving fear, pain and loss is frightening.

* Children will learn to fear and avoid intersubjective relationships. They disconnect, learning to influence without being open to influence, i.e. controlling behaviours.

Attachment and intersubjectivity

Safety and intersubjectivity are interwoven. The attachment relationship is a hierarchical relationship: 'I look to you to keep me safe and well; I do not need to keep you safe and well.' This is complemented by the intersubjective relationship which is non-hierarchical: 'I influence you; I'm open to influence from you.' Children need both relationship experiences to thrive.

Theory of intersubjectivity

Trevarthen (2001) observed infants and children interacting with caregivers. He observed the relationship dance between them and noticed how fundamental this is to the relationship experience that children need.

An intersubjective relationship is a contingent and responsive relationship which allows each partner to discover what is unique and special about the other, and they share this understanding together. That is, it is a relationship within which each impacts upon the other. The relationship is immediate, present, and with each response being contingent on the action of the other.

This relationship begins with an absorbed relationship between child and parent within which the focus is on each other and not the outside world. Trevarthen called this *primary intersubjectivity*. This is an attuned relationship within which the infant and parent discover each other and, in the process, discover more about themselves.

- The infant discovers he can influence the parent – this is the beginning of autonomy.

- The infant is open to influence from the parent – this is the beginning of the capacity for reciprocal relationships.

These interactions mean that children experience emotional regulation within the relationship: a precursor for the development of self-regulation.

Children develop a sense of self, reflected in the responses to them from the parents. Later in the relationship parent and child remain intersubjectively connected whilst discovering the world beyond the relationship. This is *secondary intersubjectivity*. The child learns about the world of people, events and objects. The child and parent together focus their attention outwards. This shared attention helps them both to explore the world and learn about the impact of this world on each other. The child learns about the world through the meaning the parent gives it. As the parent helps him to make sense of the world the capacity to think develops. In this way children learn that the world, themselves, and other people make sense. This in turn allows children to reflect upon, process and learn from experience.

These primary and secondary intersubjective experiences become a part of the relationships that the children go on to develop.

A relationship is intersubjective when there is:

- *Joint attention.* Both partners in the relationship are attending to the same thing at the same time. They each bring their own unique perspective to this, leading to a different experience of the event. Children need these experiences to learn to regulate attention.

- *Matched affect.* Within contingent relationships both partners share the emotional experience. For example, the parent and child may share a sense of joy and fun. The positive emotional state of each is magnified as each shares the same affective experience. On the other hand, the child might be experiencing some distress. When the parent matches the affective experience associated with the distress but stays regulated by not getting distressed herself, the child will be soothed. Children need these experiences to learn to regulate their emotional states.

- *Complementary intention.* Both partners have an intention which is complementary to the other's intention. Children need these experiences to learn to engage in co-operative behaviour.

Intersubjective experience = reciprocity. Children are open to influence and enjoy influencing. These experiences provide an experience of safety.

Autonomy without reciprocity = controlling; lack of intersubjectivity leads to a sense of shame and social defensiveness. The child needs to take control of relationships rather than engage in mutual influence.

- Children who experience neglect lack early intersubjective experience. They feel not special and not loveable.

- Children who experience anger, fear or rejection experience terror and shame when they seek connection. They avoid these connections.

- These children learn to avoid intersubjective experience. They disconnect from relationships and become controlling instead.

PARENTING CHILDREN WHO FEAR INTERSUBJECTIVE CONNECTIONS

KEY POINTS

* Parenting a child who rejects can lead to parents experiencing a sense of failure.

* The parents also withdraw from the relationship.

* Parents need support to remain connected to their children.

* They can then lead the child back into connection.

Impact on parents

Parenting children who are not open to connection within the relationship can have a negative impact upon the parents. The parents offer relationship and the children respond with rejection and hostility or with a clinginess that suggests the parents cannot soothe and comfort the children. This can trigger worries, fears and beliefs within the parent. 'Am I a bad parent?'; 'Maybe I can't do this'; 'Maybe this is the wrong placement?'

The lack of intersubjectivity impacts on the parents' beliefs about themselves; they start to feel a sense of failure as parents; they feel unsafe with the children. The parents now withdraw from the intersubjective relationship. They try to manage the children without connecting with them.

Staying connected

At this stage the parents need support more than they need behavioural advice; that is, they need their own connections to stay connected to their children despite their rejection. Support leads to resilience to continue caregiving despite their fears and doubts.

If the parents can find ways to stay connected to the children, then they can help the children to become more open to relationship. As intersubjectivity becomes possible the children experience a relationship within which they can heal.

SUGGESTIONS FOR ACTIVITIES

Activities to support the exploration of 'understanding the challenges of parenting'	
As a whole group	Using the question 'Why parenting might be a challenge?' 1. Flipchart responses in four sections: child characteristics; developmental experiences (as any child); parent characteristics; life experiences (specific to a child). Focus the group members to think about early as well as current experiences. 2. Extend the discussion to reflect on challenges for the population attending the group. Add this layer of complexity to the flipchart.
In small groups	Use Activity Sheet 1 to reflect on the above, but specific to an individual child or children. Activity Sheet 3 or 4 can be used if the group member does not have a child to reflect on.
Activities to support the exploration of challenge one: blocked trust	
As a whole group	Ask how group members currently support behaviour whilst encouraging prosocial behaviour. The responses are tabulated into two columns; one will later be labelled as 'connection', and one as 'correction'. This chart is then used to introduce 'blocked trust'.
Activities to support the exploration of challenge two: fear of intersubjectivity	
As a whole group	Use photos and video clips to introduce the concept of intersubjectivity.
In pairs	A speaking and listening exercise with the listener staying in control and then switching to listening empathically. Notice the difference.
As individuals or small groups	Reflect on the questions in Activity Sheet 2, relating to a specific child or young person.

PROCESS NOTES

INTRODUCTIONS

Begin the session with introductions. The facilitators introduce themselves and outline the aims and objectives for the session, alongside general housekeeping and setting of ground rules.

Ask participants to introduce themselves, including their current and past parenting experience, and what they would like to achieve from the programme.

Next, the facilitators will introduce the Foundations for Attachment Model and explain how the programme will be organized around this model.

UNDERSTANDING CHALLENGES OF PARENTING

Activity: This provides an opportunity to reflect on why group members are attending this group, and to think about why parenting might be a challenge. Ask them to consider as a whole group what things can make parenting challenging. It is important to focus group members on early as well as current experience for the child.

This exercise also provides the facilitators with an opportunity to establish this group as non-judgemental and to help group members reflect on the range of things that can influence a child or young person which can then impact upon their experience of parenting the child.

The facilitators will flipchart the responses as in the example that follows.

Child characteristics	Developmental experiences (for any child)
Temperament (e.g. hard to soothe, slow to warm up, fussy)	Going to nursery
	Coping with a new sibling
Neurodevelopmental difficulties (e.g. rigid thinking, poor regulation, poor impulse control, struggles to switch attention or to change activities, doesn't cope with the unexpected)	Moving house
	Starting school
	Changing school
	Joining clubs and activities
Genetic difficulties (e.g. autism, learning difficulties, dyspraxia)	Looking after a pet
	Loss of pet
Physical difficulties	Loss of family, e.g. grandparents
	Starting a job – paper-round, Saturday job
Parent characteristics	**Life experiences (specific to a child)**
Temperament	Unexpected loss
Neurodevelopmental difficulties	Trauma within family
Genetic difficulties	Trauma external to family
Physical difficulties	Bullying and other peer difficulties
	Illness in child or family member
	Hospitalization in child or family member

Understanding the complexity of the children

This could mean by developmental stage, for example, adolescence, or by population, for example, adopted.

Activity: Extend this discussion to focus on issues that are relevant for the population attending the group: for example, foster carers, adopters, birth parents, parents of a child with mental illness, learning difficulties or challenging behaviour, etc.

Some of these factors might have been captured on the flipchart but now help group members to see how this adds an additional layer of complexity which adds to the challenge of parenting the children. Add this layer of complexity to the flipchart as in the example below.

Child characteristics	Developmental experiences (for any
Parent characteristics	Life experiences (specific to a child)
Additional complexity for being adopted	**Additional complexity for child with mental illness**
Experience of multiple families	Time out of school
Poor early experience of being parented	Time in hospital
More complicated to figure out who they are (sense of identity)	Difference from peers
	Impact of illness itself
Desire to search for birth family	Moving between poor health and improved health
Sense of not being good enough, being kidnapped, etc.	Having to take medication
Feeling of difference from other children	Sense of identity as a young person with mental illness

Reflecting on a child or young person

Activity: Now give group members time to reflect on their own children or young people. Using Activity Sheet 1, they can map out the factors in each of these areas that apply to them, providing them with a sense of why they may be finding it hard to parent their child. It is important to encourage parents to reflect back to the earliest years to explore challenges throughout the child's life.

Thought needs to be given to group members who do not yet have children placed with them. These group members might:

- Work with group members who have children placed, maybe adopters or foster carers who are caring for young children.

- Foster carers might reflect on a child who has previously been in their care.

- Alternatively, these group members might work through one of the alternative activity sheets which provide them with case studies of a child and an adolescent.

PARENTING CHALLENGE ONE: BLOCKED TRUST

Explore current parenting practices. This provides a good introduction to thinking about trust and mistrust, firmly rooting it in parenting.

Activity: How do you manage challenging behaviour and help children to develop prosocial behaviours? Invite participants to talk about how they currently try to exert an influence on children and young people they are caring for or have cared for. If they do not have experience of parenting they could reflect on how they were parented.

Tabulate the responses on a flipchart; include a column for approaches that connect to the children and a column that focuses on correcting behaviour, but don't label these now. It is likely that the second column will be more extensive than the first, unless the group is already knowledgeable about DDP principles.

EXAMPLE: INITIAL CONNECTION AND CORRECTION TABLE

Connection	Correction (behavioural support)
Spending time with them	Time out; ignoring
Understanding reasons for behaviour	Consequences, e.g. grounding, removal of privileges or items
Building relationship	Praise and rewards
	Distraction; diversion
	Positive activities
	Guidance; suggestions
	Explaining; reasoning

Now label the columns. Explain that the first column is the 'connection' column. In this column, the focus is more on the children themselves rather than their behaviour. Secure children grow up knowing and believing in this connection. They know that they are loved unconditionally and that their parents are interested in their experience of the world. Thus, when parents use 'correction', the children already feel connected.

Explain that the second column is the 'correction' column. Be clear that this is not about punishment. In this context, correction refers to how parents can guide their children to behave in ways considered acceptable. The emphasis is to help the children to behave in a way which is acceptable within their culture. This will fit in with the parents' own values and beliefs as well as the norms of the culture they were brought up in. This is behaviour management, based on social learning theory; i.e. that the children's behaviours are influenced by the consequences that follow. Pleasant consequences tend to increase behaviours whilst unpleasant consequences tend to decrease behaviours. Secure children will modify their behaviour in line with the consequences provided by their parents without doubting the parents' love and security.

Insecure children, lacking this security, are less likely to modify their behaviour in line with the parent's wishes. Instead, they will behave in ways which help them to feel some increased sense of safety and security usually via more controlling behaviours. This may or may not involve the parents. When parenting insecure children more attention needs to be given to connection before we can 'correct' the children. The 'correction' then becomes more empathic and more collaborative; behavioural support rather than behavioural management. That is, the empathic connection helps the child move from shame and to experience remorse. The child wants to make amends and will think with the parent how to do this.

This will be explored more in Module Two, along with the important step of helping children to regulate before they will be able to experience the connection. In this session, the goal is to help the group members to understand the importance of connection and to be curious about how they might do this.

The chart now looks like the example below.

Connection	Correction (behavioural support)
Spending time with them Understanding reasons for behaviour Building relationship	Time-out; ignoring (reframed as need for time-in so child does not experience rejection and shame) Consequences, e.g. grounding, removal of privileges or items (connection allows this to be done collaboratively in a way which lets child make amends) Praise and rewards Distraction, diversion Positive activities Guidance, suggestions Explaining, reasoning
First year: development of trust and experience of unconditional love Mistrust – child does not know he is loved unconditionally and will move into shame and fear of abandonment	Discipline, boundaries, socialization build on top of trust. Can manage discipline if know loved unconditionally Blocked trust develops as brain adapts to mistrusting environment.

Having explored the development of trust and mistrust over the first couple of years and experienced what it is like to mistrust, the facilitators can now provide some deepening exploration of this parenting challenge and how mistrust becomes blocked trust, using the trainers' notes.

FEAR OF ABANDONMENT

The development of mistrust is closely linked with fears about abandonment, which can have ancestral roots in the practice of baby abandonment as well as resonating with current experience. Not only may children have experienced separation and loss in their early experience, ancestral memories of baby abandonment can also be triggered by the development of mistrust. This has been explored by anthropologists and evolutionary biologists. Some understanding of this can help parents understand why mistrust can be so deeply rooted, and can take such a long time to recover from. It also explains intense sibling rivalry which can occur when parenting sibling groups.

IMPACT OF BLOCKED TRUST ON THE DEVELOPMENT OF THE NERVOUS SYSTEM

There is a lot of material that can be covered here. What is covered and what depth to go into will be a judgement that the facilitators make. Some groups will benefit from more time spent on reflective exercises and less on psychoeducation, whilst other groups will enjoy exploring theory in more depth, giving a foundation for understanding the parenting ideas presented later in the programme. The main points that group members need to get from this session are that:

- Children who have early frightening experience can develop blocked trust, which affects how they experience normal parenting.

- Blocked trust leaves children with big fears of not being good enough and of being abandoned.

- This is a biological process; it is not only about behaviour. The development of the brain responds to early experience in a way that can sensitize it to danger and this impacts on the way children react defensively.

- When children are being defensive they are not open to social engagement.

I have found that even if parents find a lot of biology confusing, they get the simple traffic light model. This helps them to see the difference between being defensive and being open and engaged, and they understand that they are trying to help the child move from being defensive to social engagement. As one foster parent once said to me, and with reference to my putting the defensive responding on the left-hand side of the traffic lights: 'Ah, I need to help my child to move from left to right then!'

PARENTING CHILDREN EXPERIENCING BLOCKED TRUST: COMFORT, CURIOSITY AND JOY

The final part of the challenge of mistrust is to notice with group members how blocked trust impacts on the capacity to experience comfort, curiosity and joy. Explore how to parent the children so that they can recover from blocked trust and learn to trust in comfort, curiosity and joy.

The response to children who are behaving defensively and how it can pull parents into defensive responding can also be mentioned here. Similarly, the risk of blocked care can be referred to. These will not be covered in any depth until the last session. Understanding that there is a biological impact on parents' own capacity to care when parenting children with blocked trust can be helpful to parents who have had this experience or maybe are even in it at the current time. Knowing this is a normal experience and will be explored later might help to sustain them.

PARENTING CHALLENGE TWO: FEAR OF INTERSUBJECTIVITY

This links very closely with development of mistrust; it might be considered a consequence of the development of mistrust. The facilitator introduces the term 'intersubjectivity' and explains how this describes the reciprocal relationship; one in which both members of the relationship will influence the other but also be open to the influence from the other. This is described in the trainer's notes.

Activity: This can be difficult to grasp but can be powerfully demonstrated using photographs and video.

- Show human and animal photographs of intersubjective relationships.

- Show a video of an intersubjective connection.

The facilitators now demonstrate the impact of a relationship that is not intersubjective. This relates to the impact of trauma and loss upon the child.

- Illustrate with video clips, e.g. still face; depressed parent and child.

Ask group members to reflect on times they found themselves becoming more controlling in their behaviour towards someone else, usually at a time of increased stress. Help them to notice that controlling behaviour tries to influence others whilst trying not to be influenced back.

Activity: If there is time divide the group into pairs and ask them to talk together. Choose a speaker and a listener, but ask the listener to try to stay in control; this can be by trying to problem solve or to reassure by responding defensively, as if they are feeling criticized, for example. Notice how this shuts down the listener's openness to being influenced by the speaker. Listeners can then try listening empathically and notice the different impact this has on them.

The facilitators help the participants to explore the impact on a parent of parenting a child whose previous experience of loss of intersubjectivity means that he no longer trusts relationships and prefers control to reciprocity. It is important to emphasize how this is rooted in fear of emotional connection and therefore of experiencing an intersubjective relationship. Notice how challenging it is to continue caring for a child who resists reciprocity, leading parents to be vulnerable to staying in defensive modes of parenting. The risk of blocked care is high in these situations, as will be explored in the final session.

Facilitators now focus on helping participants to reflect on the parenting needed to help children reduce their fear of intersubjective connection. This helps the children to feel effective influencing and safe being influenced. This will mean not getting pulled into control battles, but gently increasing the children's trust in their influence so that their need to control can reduce. In the next module, we will explore the use of PACE in order to do this. Parents will need to understand that control will increase at times of stress and learn to focus on reducing the stress rather than trying to stop the controlling behaviours.

Activity: If there is time group members can reflect on Activity Sheet 2, helping them to reflect on a child or young person. This helps them to recognize mistrust, fear of intersubjective connection and need for control. If time is short, this can be completed between sessions or modules.

SESSION TITLE: HIDING AND MISCUING

AIMS OF SESSION

- To explore the emotion of shame and to increase understanding of how children can get stuck in toxic shame.

- To understand the impact that the experience of shame can have on a child's behaviour.

- To explore how to parent in order to reduce the experience of shame.

- To explore attachment theory and how difficult attachment experience can lead to miscuing in a pattern of hidden and expressed needs.

- To explore how to parent in ways that meet the hidden as well as the expressed needs.

- To introduce the principles of DDP-informed parenting in preparation for Module Two.

SUMMARY OF SESSION

This session continues to explore the challenges of parenting. This builds upon the challenges of blocked trust and the fear of the intersubjective relationship which were explored in the previous session. Now the group will explore the related difficulties that the child can have when parenting has led to the development of unregulated shame. The shield the child erects to defend against the pain of this can lead to some challenging behaviours which can only reduce when the parent provides regulation rather than behavioural management.

The final challenge is explored within the context of attachment theory. The group considers the pattern of hidden and expressed needs that can develop when the child has experienced insensitive and sometimes frightening parenting early in life. There is an opportunity to reflect on specific children in relation to these two challenges.

The session ends with a preview of Module Two through the introduction of the DDP-informed parenting principles.

SESSION PLAN

Example session plan	
Exploring shame, and the shield against shame	30 minutes
Activity: Andrew and Joseph	20 minutes
Hidden and expressed needs – miscuing through hidden needs	30 minutes
Break	20 minutes
Activity: Exploring through 'strange situation' scenarios	30 minutes
Reflection on a child or young person	20 minutes
Introducing DDP-informed therapeutic parenting	30 minutes

TRAINER NOTES[2]

PARENTING CHALLENGE THREE: SHAME

KEY POINTS

* Experiencing shame is part of normal development.

* Parents regulate shame in their young children through attuned experiences and relationship repair.

* As children mature experience of shame reduces and guilt increases; children can then experience remorse and seek to make amends.

* If shame isn't regulated it becomes bigger and more toxic.

* To defend against dysregulated shame, children develop a 'shield against the shame', most typically evident through lying, blaming others, minimizing and raging.

Shame is an emotion that develops in toddlers at the same time as parents are starting to provide boundaries and discipline. The experience of shame is part of the process of teaching children acceptable behaviour. This is done through attunement–break–repair sequences. Attunement represents the emotional connection. Breaks to this connection are experienced as shame and can happen for a range of reasons. The parent might be distracted by other things, or experience some irritation, frustration or other defensive response. At times, the parent breaks the attunement to provide some discipline. However the break occurs, it is important that the parent then attends to relationship repair. This communicates his continuing love for the child and demonstrates that even when things go wrong the relationship can remain strong. This regulates the shame and returns the child and parent to a state of attunement again.

---

2   The accompanying online materials can be accessed at www.jkp.com/voucher using the code GOLDINGFOUNDATIONS.

Attunement–break–relationship repair

- The attunement–break–repair experience is an important part of the parenting; the child needs to experience being loved unconditionally whilst having limits put on his behaviour.

- This allows the child to regulate the shame, and then to experience guilt. Guilt is a more positive emotion in that it can be other-focused. The child feels remorse and wants to make amends.

- When a child experiences poor attunement and the parent does not repair the relationship the child becomes trapped in feelings of shame without being able to regulate this emotion.

- The experience of shame then builds up into toxic unregulated shame which influences the child's developing sense of identity; the child develops a sense of being bad. Now the child is self-focused. She cannot experience guilt and remorse and therefore cannot make amends. She remains focused on her own sense of badness.

- The children have to develop a shield to defend against how horrible this feels (see Figure M1.S2.1). This shield against shame is demonstrated through a range of behaviours including lying, blaming others, minimizing and raging.

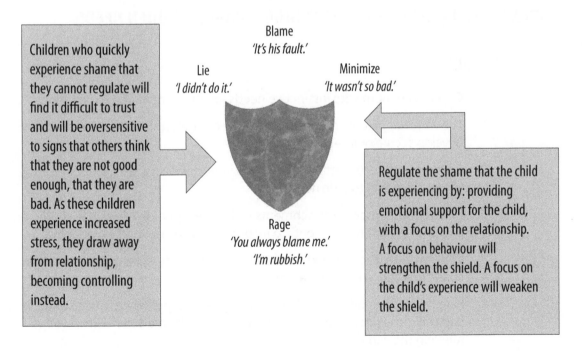

Children who quickly experience shame that they cannot regulate will find it difficult to trust and will be oversensitive to signs that others think that they are not good enough, that they are bad. As these children experience increased stress, they draw away from relationship, becoming controlling instead.

Blame
'It's his fault.'

Lie
'I didn't do it.'

Minimize
'It wasn't so bad.'

Rage
'You always blame me.'
'I'm rubbish.'

Regulate the shame that the child is experiencing by: providing emotional support for the child, with a focus on the relationship. A focus on behaviour will strengthen the shield. A focus on the child's experience will weaken the shield.

Figure M1.S2.1 Shield against shame

PARENTING CHILDREN LIVING IN SHAME

> ### KEY POINTS
>
> * Behavioural management can increase feelings of shame.
>
> * Children need parents to connect with them and regulate the shame.
>
> * The children will then be helped by behavioural support.

Behavioural management strategies are aimed at children reducing the shame-based behaviours, demonstrating remorse and making amends. This just serves to increase the sense of shame and the shield is reinforced. The children need parents to help them to regulate the shame first. This is done through connection with the children's internal experiences. As the children experience the parent understanding their anxieties, worries and fears, the behaviours will start to reduce. Now the children can experience remorse and want to make amends. Correction becomes a collaborative process as the parents support the children in figuring out what to do. Connection with correction allows children to experience an attuned relationship. They learn that relationships can always be repaired, and that they are loved unconditionally.

PARENTING CHALLENGE FOUR: MISCUING THROUGH HIDDEN NEEDS

> ### KEY POINTS
>
> * Children are born with instinctive needs for attachment and exploration.
>
> * The way that parents respond to these needs determines whether children develop secure or insecure attachments.
>
> * Children with secure attachments can signal needs in a straightforward way without needing to hide needs.
>
> * Children with insecure attachments will express or hide needs depending on how they expect their parents to respond. This is described as miscuing.
>
> * Children with disorganized-controlling attachments will express a need for control, hiding a need for parents.
>
> * Parents trying to offer sensitive parenting can get pulled into these attachment patterns if they don't gently challenge to meet the hidden need as well as meeting the expressed need.

Attachment theory was originally conceived by John Bowlby (1988/1998), a child psychiatrist who bucked the trend of his day and became especially interested in the interpersonal world between child and caregivers. He suggested that a child develops an attachment bond with the caregiver. This relationship is used to gain security and comfort when experiencing distress and to gain support to explore the world when feeling secure and settled.

This attachment experience leads to the development of an internal working model. This is a template of how relationships work which can guide the child with future relationships. This experience leads to expectations of others, as well as providing the child with an understanding about herself, for example, 'Others are kind and I am loveable.'

Mary Ainsworth (Ainsworth *et al.* 1978), Mary Main (Main and Solomon 1986) and others explored the way that patterns of attachment develop depending upon the experience of parenting. Sensitive parenting leads to secure patterns; insensitive parenting leads to insecure but organized patterns; and frightening or frightened parenting leads to disorganized patterns. As the child matures these disorganized patterns develop into extreme patterns of controlling behaviours. Notice how the development of the controlling patterns represents the loss of the ability to feel soothed and comforted by the parent. It also affects the ongoing development of the intersubjective relationship. The children, in learning to avoid these connections, become controlling and are therefore less open to intersubjective experiences. They try to influence the other without being influenced by the other.

Secure attachment patterns of relating

Much like the connection between the two ends of a seesaw, attachment and exploration inter-relate. When the child needs comfort and protection, attachment needs are activated, and the child seeks comfort and protection. As these needs are met, the attachment needs can deactivate and exploration needs increase with the associated drive to learn about the world.

The secure child moves smoothly between seeking comfort and seeking exploration, supported by the attuned, sensitive caregiver. Notice how the child does not need to hide any of her needs from the caregiver. She is confident expressing how she feels, secure that these expressed needs will be met and satisfied.

This in turn leads to the development of an internal working model of self and others. The child develops a sense of self as effective, worthwhile and loveable and others as loving, supportive and protective. This model builds resilience, helping the child to be successful in later relationships, and to manage adversity when it arises.

Insecure attachment

Children who do not have the experience of a secure attachment will develop patterns of relating adapted to the anticipated unavailability of the parent. They miscue the parents as to their attachment needs by displaying attention-needing behaviours (ambivalent-resistant attachment pattern) or self-reliant behaviours (avoidant attachment pattern). The children behave in ways that maximize the chance that parents will be available when needed.

The disorganized controlling pattern emerges as children take these patterns to extremes in the face of frightening caregiving. These children anticipate that parents will be frightening and therefore make strenuous efforts to take control to reduce their sense of fear. When this fails, their behaviour disorganizes into highly stressed, dysregulated or dissociated behaviours.

Impact on new caregivers

Mary Dozier (2003) studied what happened to attachment patterns of relating when toddlers moved into their foster/adoptive homes. These children would lead the attachment dance and the parents responded in kind. Therefore, parents would behave as if the children did not need them when the children demonstrated avoidant attachment patterns or would behave angrily when the children demonstrated ambivalent-resistant attachment patterns and would not be comforted by them. It appears that the parents would respond to the miscuing of the children and try to meet the needs that were being expressed but overlook the pattern of hidden needs that the children were not displaying.

Ambivalent attachment patterns of relating

These children express their continuing need for comfort and protection. They express, 'You are unpredictable, I can't trust in your availability. I need you to attend to me all the time.' In order to keep expressing this need they have to hide their exploration needs. 'I will not show my need to separate and explore. I will pull you in and push you away to keep you noticing me.' The parents are miscued about what the children are experiencing because the children are expressing their needs based on their expectations of the parents rather than upon how they feel internally. They express, 'Stay with me, notice me, attend to me'; they hide 'Okay, I can do this. I'm comfortable enough to be apart from you now.' The parents try to meet the expressed need: 'I will reassure you that I am available. I will be here when you really need me.' This does not soothe the child, and the parents express frustration that they can't meet the need. The child's expectation that parents will be inconsistent and unpredictable is confirmed.

Avoidant attachment patterns of relating

These children display a lack of need. They miscue the parent by acting like they want to explore at times when they need comfort. The children anticipate that any displays of need will lead the parents to withdraw and become unavailable when they are most needed. They express, 'I will do it by myself. I fear my need of you. I will push you away'; they hide 'I will not show my need for comfort and soothing.' The parents try to meet the expressed need by letting the children manage on their own. The children's expectation that parents will not be there when needed is confirmed.

Disorganized attachment patterns of relating

Children with disorganized, controlling patterns of relating are more complex. The secure base is frightening; the world is scary and so the children try to take charge. They express, 'I will not rely on you. Relying on you is dangerous. I must be in control.' They control through highly self-reliant, rejecting behaviours that keep parents at a distance and/or through highly coercive behaviours that keep parents attending to them. They hide away their need to explore the world and their need for comfort and nurture, except on their terms. It is a challenge for the parents to meet the hidden needs whilst trying to deal with the impact of the expressed needs.

PARENTING CHILDREN TO MEET HIDDEN AND EXPRESSED NEEDS

KEY POINTS

* Sensitive parenting is likely to meet the expressed needs, leaving hidden needs unmet.
* Parents need to recognize all the child's needs despite the miscuing.
* Parents need to meet expressed needs whilst gently challenging to meet the hidden needs as well.

Miscuing occurs through patterns of hidden and expressed needs. Parents need to be available, responsive and gently challenging. The parents are challenging hard-won beliefs. 'Parents can't keep you safe'; 'Parents are dangerous'; 'I am so bad, nothing you can do or say will change this'; or, 'I should take care of you, and not expect you to take care of me.' Children need parents who can accurately interpret their need for nurturance despite the miscues the child is giving. They connect with the hidden experience of the child whilst at the same time providing the boundaries needed to keep the child safe: 'connection with correction'.

Ambivalent attachment patterns

Parents need to provide a high level of structure and consistent routines so that the child can begin to trust in the predictability of the parenting. They need to co-regulate the emotion that the child is expressing but not managing. They also need to be mindful of the hidden needs. Mary Dozier (2003) suggests that they gently challenge the hidden needs. The child needs help to be apart and to feel secure that the parent will be there when needed.

Avoidant attachment patterns

Parents need to gently challenge the hidden needs by providing comfort and safety at times when they predict that the children will need this. The children can begin to trust that their emotional needs will not overwhelm the parents. Parents also need to co-regulate the emotion that the children are hiding but not managing. In this way parents can help the children to feel comfortable needing and being helped by them.

Disorganized-controlling attachment patterns

These children need safety and low-stress environments but behave in ways that reduce safety and increase stress. As stress reduces and safety increases the amount of controlling behaviours will reduce.

INTRODUCING A DDP-INFORMED THERAPEUTIC PARENTING APPROACH

KEY POINTS

* The DDP model developed by Dan Hughes provides an approach for parenting children which helps parents to connect with the children's internal experience.

* Connection builds safety and security leading to developing trust in the parents.

* The attitude of PACE will help parents to emotionally connect with their children.

* 'Correction' in the form of behaviour support can then be provided with high levels of warmth and nurture.

* The DDP model provides a set of principles that can be applied in parenting.

The therapeutic parenting approach provided within this programme is based on the Dyadic Developmental Psychotherapy and Practice model (DDP) developed by Dan

Hughes (Hughes 2009, 2011). This is a model that is based on observations and understanding of early child development, alongside understanding the experiences that children have missed out on when their early development has occurred with parents who were not able to meet their developmental needs.

Within the DDP model family members are helped to develop healthy patterns of relating and communicating so that they can all feel safe and emotionally connected. As connection starts to become more comfortable for the developmentally traumatized child, her trust in her parents will start to develop. Trust and connection then provides a foundation for the children's safe experience of discipline and boundaries. Behavioural support is matched to developmental age, ensuring that the children are getting the level of structure and supervision that they need. This will reduce the need for consequences.

DDP-informed parenting is therefore connection with behavioural support. The parent takes on the dual task of building trust and providing boundaries and discipline because the opportunity to do this sequentially earlier in the child's life has not been possible. Dan Hughes has described this parenting as 'connection with correction'. This is a phrase that is used in this programme. It is important to note that 'correction' equates with behaviour support. It refers to parenting which helps children develop prosocial behaviours by providing appropriate boundaries, limits and consequences within the context of highly warm and nurturing environments.

Central to helping children develop safety in connection within DDP is the parenting attitude of PACE (Golding and Hughes 2012). This allows the parent to become attuned to the child through a stance of playful parenting, acceptance of the child's inner world, curiosity about the meaning underneath the behaviour and empathy for the child's emotional state. In this way the parents stay emotionally engaged and available to the child, demonstrating their unconditional love whilst also providing the safety that comes from appropriate boundaries and discipline.

DDP principles and parenting developmentally traumatized children

Qualities of the relationship offered by the parent:

- *Intersubjective.* Past experience has led the children to fear the intersubjective relationships they need in order to feel safe and to trust, and for healthy emotional and social development. Children use controlling behaviours as a way of avoiding reciprocal interactions. They influence but are not open to influence. The parent connects with the child to help her to feel safe in relationships within which she is open to influence.

- *Attitude of PACE.* The parent holds an attitude of PACE, offering an unconditional relationship which is expressed through playfulness, acceptance, curiosity and empathy. The parent maintains a curiosity about the inner life of the child and accepts this without judgement or evaluation. This acceptance is communicated with empathy for the struggles this experience can bring. PACE also offers the child fun and joy within the relationship: moments of healthy relationship and respite from the day-to-day struggles.

- *Open and engaged.* An open and engaged parent uses PACE to connect intersubjectively. Often the children respond by being closed and defensive. The parents try to avoid joining them in this closed, non-engaged defensive state. Such responses would close down the relationship. Of course, the parent will at times lose the attitude of PACE and will become defensive, evaluative and/or judgemental. At these times the parent can avoid the relationship being damaged through relationship repair as described below.

The relationship helps the child to:

- *Feel safe and secure.* The parents notice the child's verbal and non-verbal communications and whether these signal that the child is feeling safe or not. Safety can be increased by accepting and acknowledging the child's experience with PACE, and providing co-regulation as needed.

- *Co-regulate affect.* The child feels emotion which is expressed bodily through her affect. The parents match the vitality, intensity and rhythm of the affect. They can then respond with empathy, verbally and non-verbally. This helps the child to feel understood and aids regulation.

- *Co-construct meaning of experience.* The parents help the child to make sense of both present and past experience. When the child responds to PACE and her attention is held by the parents' attentive stance there is an opportunity to put words to experience. This increased understanding can provide the child with flexibility to respond to events verbally and not just through behaviour. The world is explored in new ways, creating new meanings from within the relationship.

The parent can help the child by:

- *Discovering the narrative or story.* Instead of trying to change the children through reasoning, lecturing or reassuring, the parents engage them in understanding what is happening. In other words, they discover and tell the story of the moment as it is occurring in the present and influenced by the past. The immediate aim is not to change the child but to be genuinely interested in understanding her experience.

- *Affective-reflective dialogue.* As in any good story the parent talks with the child in a way that is affective (expressing emotion) and reflective (providing the content through the narrative). This will involve both verbal and non-verbal communication. It is the interweaving of curiosity and empathy that carries the narrative forward.

- *Follow–lead–follow.* To connect with a child, the parent needs to start where she is. The child experiences being understood. Now the parent can lead her into deeper understanding. The child will respond to this; the parent follows again. In this way, the parent sets a rhythm to the telling which allows the story to emerge.

- *Talking with and about.* This way of communicating is emotionally intense, especially for children who have found ways to exist without connection in their past. The parent helps the child to tolerate this without becoming overwhelmed by it. This can be helped by not always talking directly to the child. At times, it can be helpful to talk about her. This can be a wondering out loud or perhaps sharing a thought with another person. The child may quietly listen, but if she joins the conversation again the parent can resume talking with her.

- *Attending to verbal and non-verbal communication.* Every communication is non-verbal; some are also verbal. Noticing discrepancies between verbal and non-verbal can help the parent understand the experience of the child. When verbal and non-verbal again match the communication becomes deeper and more open.

- *Relationship repair.* The parent will notice ruptures in his relationship with the child. The parent may have become defensive, or the child may have misunderstood. It is important that the parent takes responsibility for repair at these times. With mistrusting children, relationship repair will need to occur much more frequently as the child seeks signs of rejection and abandonment. As the child experiences repair and connection she may experience remorse herself and want to make amends. At these times the parent can support the child, helping her to repair the relationship with anyone hurt by what has happened.

SUGGESTIONS FOR ACTIVITIES

Activities to support the exploration of shame and the shield against shame	
In a small group or as a whole group	Use Activity Sheet 5 to reflect on the difference between shame and guilt.
Activities to support the exploration of hidden and expressed needs	
As a whole group	Explore patterns of attachment through viewing video clips of the 'strange situation'. Notice needs that are being expressed and those that are being hidden.
As individuals or in small groups	Reflect on the questions in Activity Sheet 6.
Activities to support the exploration of the DDP-informed approach to parenting	
In a small group or as a whole group	Explore the scenarios described in Activity Sheet 7 and match these to the DDP principles.

PROCESS NOTES

The facilitators will begin the session by checking in with group members, and exploring any reflections that they have had since the first session.

PARENTING CHALLENGE THREE: SHAME

In the previous session, the group members explored the intersubjective relationship and watched how children tried to avoid contact with caregivers when this relationship experience was absent or painful for the child. In this session, the group will go on to explore the emotional experience when intersubjective connection goes wrong and the avoidance of connection that develops. This is most obviously evident in reluctance to look at the caregiver's face, and can be linked to the emotional experience of shame.

Facilitators explain the development of shame and the subsequent development of the experience of guilt, exploring this as a normal developmental process.

What happens when a child does not have sufficient experience of attunement and repair of relationship ruptures by the caregiver? The group now considers the process by which unregulated shame leads to a defensive shield.

These defences can be explored as a shield against shame (Golding and Hughes 2012). Help group members to understand this shield.

PARENTING CHILDREN LIVING IN SHAME

The facilitators explore with the group ways of parenting the children to regulate the shame and to understand why behavioural approaches aimed at trying to reduce lying and get the child to accept responsibility will tend to reinforce the shield.

Activity: Activity Sheet 5, with the case study of Andrew and Joseph, can be used to explore this in more depth.

PARENTING CHALLENGE FOUR: MISCUING THROUGH HIDDEN NEEDS

This is the fourth and final challenge that the facilitator will explore with the group. This challenge is informed by our understanding of attachment theory: the way that the innate need to attach and to explore are connected and work in a complementary fashion. The facilitator will start by telling the story of attachment as conceived by John Bowlby and developed by Mary Ainsworth, Mary Main and others. The idea of sensitive parenting will be explored, but linked to the idea of good-enough parenting, i.e. sensitive parenting enough of the time for the child to feel secure. Parents cannot be sensitive all the time. However, when parenting is too inconsistent, rejecting of the child's emotional needs or frightening to the child, then security of attachment will not develop. The internal working model develops and this impacts on the way the child approaches future relationships.

The facilitator will then outline the different attachment patterns. It can be helpful to use the analogy of a seesaw to show how the attachment needs and exploratory needs are expressed or hidden in the different attachment styles. For example, in secure attachment the seesaw is freely moving as the two ends of the seesaw, representing the attachment needs and the exploratory needs respectively, move up and down. In the ambivalent attachment pattern, the seesaw is stuck with the attachment needs up and the exploratory needs down whilst in the avoidant attachment pattern the seesaw is stuck the other way around.

Now explain that the disorganized controlling pattern recognizes the lack of an organized strategy for the young child to protect herself against the fear. As the child matures, however, she develops a strategy organized around control. These children develop the coercive ambivalent patterns and the self-reliant avoidant patterns into controlling patterns to provide rigid and inflexible behaviours that provide some feeling of safety in what is experienced as an unsafe world.

Activity: Group members can explore the patterns of hidden and expressed needs through video examples of children in the Strange Situation. Consider first a secure child and notice how easily the child can express what she is feeling. Now, notice what is being expressed and wonder about what is being hidden in the insecure examples. Reflect on how these patterns could be gently challenged.

Parenting children to meet hidden and expressed needs

As these patterns are outlined, the parenting needs are highlighted through Mary Dozier's work. This identified the pattern of hidden and expressed needs represented by the different attachment styles. The parent needs to meet the expressed needs, but also provide a gentle challenge to the child by meeting the hidden needs. This will move the child towards a more secure pattern of responding within which she can express needs without the compulsion to hide some of them.

Activity: The facilitators will now return to the exercise begun at the start of Session One, using Activity Sheet 6. Revisit the reflection of a child. Is there anything they would like to add having worked through these four challenges? If time is short this activity sheet can be used for reflection between modules.

The last part of this session introduces the DDP-informed approach to parenting which will be used in Module Two. Facilitators introduce this model and provide an overview of the principles:

- the intersubjective relationship

- attitude of PACE

- open and engaged

- safety and security

- co-regulating affect

- co-constructing meaning of experience

- discovering the narrative or story

- affective-reflective dialogue

- follow–lead–follow

- talking with and about

- attending to verbal and non-verbal

- relationship repair.

As these principles are explored they can be linked to the challenges of parenting that have been explored during Module One so that group members can see how the principles will be helpful in meeting these challenges. It will also be helpful to find a way to display these principles so that they can be referred to when working through Module Two, which will focus primarily on the use of PACE.

Activity: Working in small groups or as a whole group, explore the scenarios described in Activity Sheet 7 and match these to the DDP principles. As a whole-group exercise, this could be done using the scenarios on small cards, and matching these to the principles which will be displayed around the room. Let group members know that there are no right or wrong answers, and the scenarios illustrate multiple principles as described in Handout 8. The point is not to get this right but to have discussion that helps group members to become familiar with the principles and how they relate to day-to-day parenting; in doing so they will also be getting a deeper understanding.

MODULE **TWO**

DDP-INFORMED THERAPEUTIC PARENTING

SESSION TITLE: BUILDING CONNECTIONS

AIMS OF SESSION

- To explore the importance of emotional connection within DDP-informed therapeutic parenting.

- To explore the parenting skills of being mind-minded and using PACE.

- To notice and practise being mind-minded when talking to children.

- To notice and practise using PACE within parenting.

SUMMARY OF SESSION

This is a key session within the programme for developing parenting skills. It explores DDP-informed parenting and the importance of emotional connection with children. Specifically, facilitators will help group members to understand and explore the ideas of being mind-minded in parenting and using the attitude of PACE (playfulness, acceptance, curiosity and empathy). Group members are also helped to recognize the difference between defensive and open and engaged responding. A large focus of this session is upon skills practice using narratives, discussion, written conversations and role play.

SESSION PLAN

Example session plan	
Catch-up and reflections	10 minutes
Activity: Write a description	5 minutes
Exploring DDP-informed therapeutic parenting and the importance of emotional connection	20 minutes
Parenting skills for therapeutic parenting – mind-mindedness	10 minutes
Activity: Dialogues	10 minutes
Activity: Writing mind-minded conversations	10 minutes
Activity: Reflect on own descriptions	5 minutes
Break	20 minutes
Role play: Open and engaged and defensive responding	20 minutes
Parenting skills for therapeutic parenting – PACE	20 minutes
Activity: Exploring PACE through day in the life role play	30 minutes
Activity: PACE before discipline, choose from the different activities	20 minutes

TRAINER NOTES[1]

THERAPEUTIC PARENTING

KEY POINTS

* Therapeutic parenting helps parents to be trauma informed rather than trauma organized.

* Parents need to meet the therapeutic, developmental and behavioural needs of the children.

* DDP-informed parenting focuses on 'connection with correction' which helps parents to meet the developmental and therapeutic needs alongside behavioural support.

Therapeutic parenting is a general term given to ways of parenting children that offer a healing environment alongside the parenting that all children need. Children are helped to feel safe so that they can recover from past trauma or distress alongside helping them to fulfil their developmental potential. The DDP model lends itself to helping parents to become therapeutic within their parenting.

Sandra Bloom has created the Sanctuary Model to provide hospital environments within which traumatized patients can heal. She persuasively argues that these environments need to be informed by the traumas that the patients have endured, often in childhood. If this does not happen then these environments will instead become organized by the trauma. This leads to unhealthy environments, and a lack of healing (Bloom 2013). This is an interesting distinction which I think can also be provided to parenting. Ordinary parenting of traumatized children can lead to the parent becoming organized by the trauma, as parents start to respond to the impact on them of blocked trust, fear of relationships, shame and miscuing of attachment needs in their children. This can lead to defensiveness in parenting. Therapeutic parenting can be a way of becoming trauma informed rather than trauma organized. This can allow the parent to be more open and engaged to the child, and more able

---

1   The accompanying online materials can be accessed at www.jkp.com/voucher using the code GOLDINGFOUNDATIONS.

to return to this when he does become defensive. As Jon Baylin and Dan Hughes (2016, p.73) describe:

> Parents who can resist the natural tendency to respond defensively to a child's defensiveness and can recover effectively from inevitable moments of losing empathy with a mistrusting child are the trust builders these children need to have.

Therapeutic parenting provides this open and engaged experience for children, which helps them to trust in the parent and to become comfortable with reciprocal intersubjective relationships, being open to influence as well as influencing. Parents need to regulate powerful feelings of shame in the child and meet hidden as well as expressed attachment needs. All of this occurs alongside parenting that provides consistent and developmentally appropriate boundaries and discipline.

The parenting task is therefore to parent in a way which meets the behavioural, developmental and therapeutic needs of the children. DDP-informed parenting and its emphasis on 'connection with correction' is a useful parenting approach to achieve these goals.

Behavioural parenting

All children thrive with *authoritative parenting* that provides a high level of warmth, clear and consistent boundaries and an appropriate level of autonomy. The child experiences warmth and nurture in an unconditional relationship alongside the structure and supervision that he needs at his stage of development. This will allow him to find out ways to be appropriately independent whilst also learning it is safe to be dependent upon parents.

Developmental parenting

Children will be at their own developmental stage depending on prior experience as well as their genetic constitution. Parenting needs to be adjusted to take account of:

- *Emotional age.* This includes the ability to make sense of and regulate emotional experience.

- *Developmental age.* This includes the stage of development the child is at, as illustrated by success with cognitive tasks.

- *Social age.* A combination of the above two will lead to the child's ability to make and retain friendships.

These may differ from each other and vary day to day. For example, emotional age can become younger when stress increases.

Therapeutic parenting

Therapeutic parenting helps a child recover from trauma and loss. It is relationship focused, building connections through attuned, responsive parenting. This helps the child to emotionally regulate and to make sense of experience.

In order to be able to provide therapeutic parenting, there are some key capacities that the parent will need to draw upon. These will be explored next.

THE ABILITY TO BE MIND-MINDED

> **KEY POINTS**
>
> * Connection relies on understanding the internal experience of the child.
>
> * The ability to be mind-minded helps parents to understand the child's emotional world.
>
> * This is different from traditional parenting which focuses on external behaviour but less on internal emotional experience.

In order to connect with the child, parents need to be able to understand the child's internal experience: what the child feels, thinks, believes, desires and wishes for. This relies on the ability to be mind-minded, to know what is in the child's mind.

Mind-mindedness is a part of our ability to mentalize: being able to make sense of the internal worlds of ourselves and others (see Figure M2.S1.1). We understand that our own internal experience, what we think and feel, impacts on the other's thoughts and feelings. Similarly, we are aware that the internal experience of others impacts on our thoughts and feelings. We can reflect on this (psychologists call this reflective function) and this allows us to connect with other people.

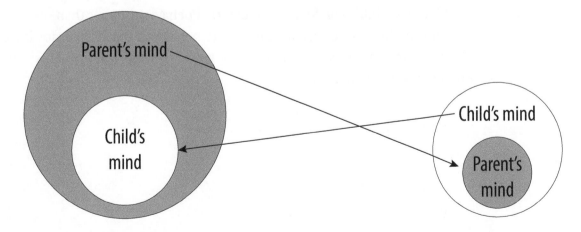

Figure M2.S1.1 Mentalization

Mentalization is an ability that we develop as we mature (Fonagy *et al.* 2002). It relies on having good theory of mind: the ability to understand that you and others have minds, with their internal world of thoughts, feelings, beliefs and desires. In order to connect with children, the parent first has to be able to make sense of the internal experience of the child. In turn the parent can help the child to discover his own mind, to organize his experience, and eventually to put into words what he is experiencing. This increases the child's capacity for regulation that has begun to develop within the relationship with an attuned, sensitive parent.

Being mind-minded towards the child, as part of our mentalization ability, is an important part of connecting; it also slows us down. Defensive, reactive parenting is not mind-minded and happens very quickly. This is great for dealing with immediate dangers, pulling a child back from a road as the bus approaches, for example. It is less helpful when there is no immediate danger because it cuts off understanding the internal experience of the child. We react without fully understanding. By maintaining some curiosity and wondering what is going on for the child, we can hold off on our reactive responses, reflect, and then respond in ways that increase the connection with the child, whilst also dealing with any behaviour that needs support.

It is also important that parents notice their own minds, especially understanding and managing the emotional impact that the child is having upon them. This might be, for example, berating themselves, feeling a failure, reacting with frustration. Reflecting on this reduces these defensive responses. Parents can remain connected with themselves and this strengthens the connection with the child.

This is different from more traditional parenting based on social learning theory. Traditional parenting relies on problem solving based on understanding the environmental contingencies that make behaviours more or less likely to happen. Parenting techniques are suggested with the goal of managing these contingencies in order to increase the frequency of behaviours the parent wants the child to display. Put simply, the parent is advised to reward good behaviour and ignore or provide a negative consequence for bad behaviour. This does not require understanding the internal world for the child. The focus is on external behaviour rather than on internal experience. This might help to manage immediate behaviour but it does not increase emotional connection, a connection that helps recovery from trauma. This will be explored more in the next session.

OPEN AND ENGAGED OR DEFENSIVE

KEY POINTS

* Connection with a child relies on a parent being open and engaged.

* It is hard to stay open and engaged when the child is being defensive.

* The parenting attitude of PACE relies on the parent staying open and engaged.

* PACE and open and engaged parenting increase a child's trust whilst defensive parenting increases mistrust.

The idea of open and engaged has been referred to already; noticing when we are defensive or open and engaged is an important part of DDP-informed parenting. As parents, indeed as human beings, we are all going to become defensive at times. We get caught up in our own internal experience, our own thoughts and feelings. We are not reflecting on these, but are being driven by them. Hence we might become frustrated or hopeless, have a sense of failure, or experience any of a range of difficult thoughts and feelings. These drive our behaviour: we might get angry, we might move to reassure or solve the problem, we might become withdrawn. All of these responses are unconscious ways of coping with the difficult experience we are having. In becoming defensive we lose sight of the other person.

Parents' capacity to stay open and engaged to their children rests on the strength of their ability to emotionally regulate. Remaining emotionally regulated, even when the child is behaving in a way that increases stress, will lead parents to be less defensive in their parenting. This in turn allows them to stay open and engaged to their children so that they can connect emotionally with them.

Connecting intersubjectively to the child's internal experience is only possible if the adult can stay open and engaged. We might still have the difficult experience, but we are aware of this and have compassion for ourselves. We don't move into defensive behaviours but instead can focus on the other person. We are open to thinking about what their experience might be. Instead of being driven by our internal experience we respond in relation to our understanding of the child.

Dan Siegel uses the analogy of a river which can be helpful to understand this (Siegel 2010). I have illustrated this in Figure M2.S1.2. Siegel talks about the river as representing us in an integrated state, able to link parts of our internal world and our relationships; energy and information within ourselves and coming from within our relationships are regulated. The flow of the river represents a sense of harmony: we are flexible and adaptive. This is coherent, and provides us with both energy and stability. If, however, we lose this integration we move from the river to the banks. One bank is rigidity and the other is chaos.

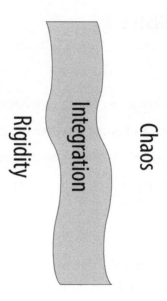

Figure M2.S1.2 River of integration (adapted from Siegel 2010)

The open and engaged state puts us into the flow of the river. We are able to be adaptive to the child and flexible in our responses. We can attend to what the child is experiencing, and gain a deeper understanding of him and why he is doing what he is doing. We take the time to understand what the child is experiencing rather than trying to change this experience. If we do move to reassure the child, we only do this once we have endeavoured to understand him. Reassurance is then about letting the child know we get it and that we have hope that we can get through it, i.e. we accept the child's experience rather than wanting to change it. Similarly, problem solving comes from a position of understanding and being with the child. Parent and child can jointly find a way forward, when this is appropriate to the situation.

When we become defensive we have moved onto one of the banks.

If we move to rigidity we might become very task focused, and rational. We might try to sort out the problem, or reassure or talk the child into feeling or being differently. We are keen to make the difficulty go away and this is driving us. Alternatively, we might become very critical, judging the child rather than understanding him. We are rigid in our responses to the child.

If we move to chaos we are likely to become more emotional. We react to our feelings and express this in an unprocessed way. We might become very angry, or move into feelings of hopelessness. These are acted out in the way we behave towards the child.

You might notice that these two banks fit with the two attachment styles of avoidance (dismissing state of mind), which tends to be more rigid, controlled and self-reliant, and ambivalence (preoccupied state of mind), which tends to be more emotionally reactive. Thus, our attachment experience can influence which bank we move towards.

When young people become closed, defensive and/or hopeless, and move to their own banks of rigidity or chaos, it can be easy for the adult to join them in this closed, non-engaged state. The adults also become defensive through their experience of feeling irritated, frustrated, hopeless, etc. All of these responses will close down the intersubjective relationship.

This difference between open and engaged and defensive becomes very important as we go on to explore the parenting attitude of PACE. When the parent is defensive, she loses the attitude of PACE and instead becomes punitive, evaluative or judgemental. The relationship is less connected and the child's mistrust increases. When the parent stays open and engaged by maintaining the attitude of PACE, or by repairing the relationship when this attitude is temporarily lost, the connection is strengthened and the child's trust increases.

THE ABILITY TO MAINTAIN AN ATTITUDE OF PACE

KEY POINTS

* Dan Hughes coined PACE to describe a parenting attitude that facilitates the parent's connection to the child.

* PACE is a way of being that helps a child feel more secure, not a strategy to change a child.

* Playfulness, joy in relationship; Acceptance of internal experience; Curiosity to discover the child's world; Empathy communicates understanding and compassion for the child.

* Explore PACE as a way of being to help parents stay open and engaged to self and child.

* Understand and be with the child without immediate motive to change the child.

* Parents need to figure out how to helpfully be with PACE with their child. This can be modelled on how parents are naturally with infants, toddlers and older children.

* Parents connect with PACE before discipline; this helps the child to feel understood and the child is more likely to respond to the discipline as a result.

When parents are mind-minded they are better able to understand their own and their children's internal experience. They now need a way to use this understanding in a way that helps them to connect to the child.

PACE is at the core of therapeutic parenting. This parenting attitude facilitates a connection between child and parent which is not possible with a narrower focus on managing the behaviour. This connection builds the trust and security in relationship that has previously been missing from the child's experience of being parented. With this connection, the child will cope better with the normal boundaries and discipline that parents need to provide for their children.

PACE was suggested by Dan Hughes as a way of helping parents remain emotionally engaged and available to the child (see, e.g., Golding and Hughes 2012). PACE helps parents to demonstrate to the child that they are available and sensitive to his needs. The parent becomes attuned to the child through a stance of acceptance, curiosity and empathy. Playfulness at appropriate times provides an opportunity to increase the fun and joy in the relationship. PACE combined with unconditional love for the child means that the parent is meeting the emotional needs of the child to be loved, nurtured, protected and understood.

Parents will need to adopt an attitude of PACE; to maintain this attitude even when they are beginning to feel challenged by the child and thus defensive towards them; and to return to the attitude at those inevitable times when it is lost under stress. The ability to do this is strengthened when parents have good ability to stay emotionally regulated themselves. Emotional regulation strengthens PACE whereas dysregulation weakens it. In the final section of this book I explore self-care, social support and self-understanding. These all help to strengthen parents' capacity to stay emotionally regulated when under stress.

PACE rests on the ability of parents to become attuned to the children's inner experience. An attuned response to children helps them to feel connected to the adults. This does not have to be conveyed as a conversation with the child. If the parents are generally curious and understanding about the child's inner world, acceptance and empathy will come through in the way they are with that child. In this way, PACE is not a strategy to get children to talk, to open up, or to behave differently. It is a way of being to help children feel more secure. At its best, PACE is a habitual way of engaging with the child, not a technique to turn on and off as needed.

If the child is verbal and at a developmental stage where he can also join in the curiosity about his inner world, then it may be that the child will listen to what the parents are saying and join in some exploration of his experience with them. The parent needs to match the child's mood so that the child can feel understood. Thus, if the child is sad the parent will talk quietly and slowly. If the child is angry the parent will talk without anger but with more vitality and intensity. With this understanding the child might feel ready and able to think with the parent about what has been going on for him.

There are four parts to PACE:

P = Playfulness

The first part of the PACE attitude is playfulness. Parents will help children to develop security in part by helping them to be playful. This is not about providing appropriate toys and activities, important though these are. For playfulness to build security, it needs to develop the relationship. The parent helps the child to experience joy in the relationship. Experience is amplified when it is shared in a playful way. It dramatizes that the child is special and loveable. Fun and play is protective; a child can't experience shame when being happy and joyful. Play provides optimism that things can be different. The child discovers his strengths and uniqueness; he experiences having a positive impact on another within a reciprocal relationship. This builds trust as the child enjoys feeling connected to another. Relationship-building playfulness is an important part of the parenting that the children need.

A = Acceptance

Perhaps the hardest part of using PACE is being able to accept without evaluating the child's inner experience of thoughts, feelings, beliefs, wishes and desires. Parents need to be aware of the inner life of their child, understanding it without trying to change it. When this inner experience is distressing or difficult for us, it is understandable that we move into evaluation, trying to reassure or talk the child into feeling something different. The child will experience this as being not good enough for the parent; shame increases. Instead the parent needs to embrace mistrust as well as trust from the child, accepting that the child will move backwards and forwards between these. The child experiences the parent as interested in him, rather than as wanting to change him. In this way shame will reduce and the child will experience unconditional love: you love me in all my parts. We want this experience to be different so that it is more comfortable for the child and the parent; however, security comes from having a parent who accepts the child's internal experience without evaluation. Sitting with the uncomfortable is part of providing a secure base.

C = Curiosity

Parenting that builds relationships is parenting that is also curious and reflective. Through an attitude of not knowing, and a desire for discovering who the child truly is, the parent can understand the child more fully. If the parent is not curious, she is more likely to make rapid judgements about the child and this is more likely to lead to non-reflective action. This in turn can shut down the relationship. Curiosity is an act of discovery that can lead to responsive, non-judgemental care.

E = Empathy

Curiosity leads to a different understanding and thus a deeper acceptance of the child and his experience. The child experiences this increased understanding and acceptance through empathy. Empathy builds secure attachment. The child feels more secure when inner experience is understood, accepted and empathized with.

PACE as a way of being

PACE can be an emotional compass for the parents, helping them to remain open and engaged to themselves as well as to their children. When parents are feeling frustrated, despairing or a sense of failure, it is important that they are PACE-ful towards themselves. In this way, they can find a sense of equilibrium again, with support from others if helpful, and then calmly return to PACE for the child.

In this way PACE becomes a way of being. The parent wants to be with and to understand the child without an immediate motive to change him. Trust that change will come out of the process as the connection between parent and child becomes stronger. PACE to try and change the child will weaken this connection. In PACE the parent has no immediate agenda beyond empathically connecting with her child through understanding and acceptance.

This is especially difficult when a child is demonstrating mistrust towards the parent. Embracing the mistrusting child so that the child feels accepted is difficult when the parent so wants the child to trust her. It is also difficult when a child starts to develop some tentative trust. This will be cautious and temporary as the child moves between mistrust and trust. The parent will be delighted to accept the trust, and the progress that this represents. This can make it challenging to also accept mistrust when it inevitably pops up again. If a child experiences his trust but not his mistrust as being accepted, he will experience love and acceptance as conditional. This can only strengthen the mistrust. Accepting and embracing the child in all his parts, with a consistent attitude of PACE, can be difficult but is important if the trust is to strengthen.

PACE is both verbal and non-verbal. When these don't match, it is likely that the parent is struggling with acceptance and is trying to use playfulness, curiosity and empathy without feeling it. It is becoming a technique, not a way of being. The lack of acceptance will be felt by the child non-verbally and he is likely to become angry or withdrawn as a consequence. The parent needs time and compassion as she deepens her understanding of her child. Acceptance for her struggles will help her to find acceptance for her child. As the parent discovers acceptance, PACE will be conveyed both verbally and non-verbally. The non-verbal components reflect a way of self-expression that is unique, deepens and makes the communication more trusted, and most importantly is received authentically by the child. PACE expressed non-verbally will not be a technique.

It might be helpful to think about how the elements of PACE link together, so that it is appreciated as a whole, rather than a series of elements. Notice that there is not one place to start; it is a circular process of combining the elements into a whole.

Notice how ACE will always be present; starting with any of these elements and P will come in and out as appropriate (see Figure M2.S1.3).

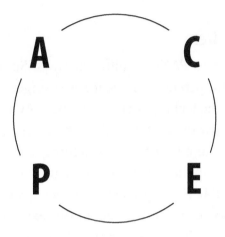

Figure M2.S1.3 PACE as circle

It can also be helpful to think about how curiosity can deepen acceptance and empathy (see Figure M2.S1.4). The parent responds to the child's mental state with acceptance and empathy: 'You are having a hard day today' or 'You are enjoying yourself today.' The parent's curiosity about the child's experience can then increase her understanding, leading to a deeper A and E response. 'It is so hard when it feels like I don't love you enough to give you the sweets' or 'You are loving the way that sand feels as it trickles through your fingers.'

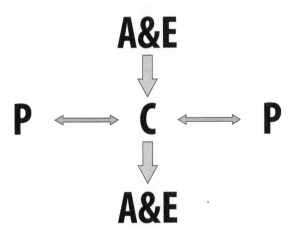

Figure M2.S1.4 Deepening PACE

It is worth emphasizing that PACE is not about doing; it is not a technique to coerce the child to behave in a different way. It is instead a way to get to know the child. PACE is a way of being, allowing the parent to get alongside the child and to support and share the experience the child is having. When a child experiences the parent as trying to change him, he is more likely to be oppositional and non-compliant. When, instead, the child perceives the parent as wanting to know him, he is more likely to be engaged in the relationship.

Introducing PACE to children

Children will respond to PACE in different ways. Some children respond positively straight away and the parents experience a stronger connection with them. Other children might resist the feeling of closeness that PACE brings. It may feel too strange to them, not fitting their sense of who they are. Empathy, in particular, can expose the child to being known in a way that is unsettling. Older children might comment on how the parent is reading their mind. The parents will need to approach these children more slowly; lighter PACE can gradually deepen over time, allowing the children to get used to being known and to feel safe in this experience.

Jon Baylin describes PACE as surprising the brain. The child has adapted to a world where negative reactions and rejection are anticipated. When the parent does not respond in this way, the child experiences something which is surprising and unexpected. Novelty allows new learning and adaptation to occur (Baylin 2016).

It is helpful to think about how parents naturally have a PACE-like attitude to their infants and young children. They accept the child and what the child experiences and try to make sense of this experience so that they can nurture and soothe, or stimulate and play with their child. They have no expectation of the child; they just strive to be with him in a way that supports and connects. As the child matures the parent begins to make this more explicit, telling the toddler what he is experiencing so that the toddler can come to understand himself more deeply. It is no good asking the toddler to describe what he is experiencing; he has not yet got the reflective capacity to do this. A toddler needs others to make sense for him, and over time this will develop his capacity to do this for himself. Only with the older child does the parent ask the child how he is feeling. Now the child can join the parent in wondering about his mental states; it becomes natural to be curious and to express what is being felt.

When introducing PACE to a developmentally traumatized child it can be helpful to keep this developmental sequence in mind. Notice how the children make sense of their internal experience. Do they need the parent to be with them in the external experience, as with an infant; to help them to know what they are experiencing, as with a toddler; or can they wonder about this experience with the parent, as with an older child? As the parents match the developmental stage of the children they will be able to connect with them in a way that the children are ready for. Over time the children will learn to reflect on their experience and will be comfortable with this. At times of stress, this fledgling ability to connect will reduce again, and the parent can return to sitting with acceptance without any pressure on the children to talk about what they are experiencing.

PACE with discipline

If PACE is used as a technique in the hope that the child will change his behaviour, then the parent is not experiencing acceptance. The parent might, for example, decide to use empathy, rather than have a genuine curiosity from which empathy naturally arises. 'I know this is hard for you but...' The parent is trying to use PACE to bring about change. PACE as a technique is likely to lead to resistance. Children will react to this with shame, as they experience not being good enough for the parents. This only strengthens the behaviour that the parent hoped would change. When the parent sits alongside the child, understanding and accepting his experience, empathy will naturally emerge. The child experiences a sense of being good enough for the parent. If he has hurt someone, this acceptance can enable the child to experience guilt and genuine remorse. The child wants to make amends and does not need to be coerced into doing this by the adults, through the sanctions they might apply.

Change, therefore, is not something that is coerced by the parent. Rather than: 'This is so hard...but' to try to make the child behave differently, PACE, with true acceptance of the child's experience, can lead to increased security from which behaviour change can arise. The essence of PACE is being able to be with the other without expectations of change; in this way, the use of PACE sits in the background with the relationship in the foreground.

Of course, PACE does not mean that parents will tolerate behaviour that is unacceptable to them. However, by connecting with PACE before discipline, the parent has a greater understanding of the child's experience; the child feels more understood and the child is more likely to respond to the discipline as a result.

PACE continues to be held as an attitude alongside the discipline, so that it becomes a way of supporting the child's behaviour, helping the child to behave in a way that is more comfortable for him as well as everyone else. This in turn helps the child to experience unconditional love even though discipline is present. Through the connection that PACE brings the child will experience shame being regulated. Now the child can experience guilt and want to make amends. The connection with the parent provides the continuing support needed to help the child to do this. Consequences become collaborative rather than imposed by the parents, and the ongoing PACE before, during and after discipline allows the child to continue to feel understood, accepted and unconditionally loved. It also allows any relationship ruptures caused by the discipline to be repaired.

PACE and discipline will be explored further in the next session.

SUGGESTIONS FOR ACTIVITIES

It is not anticipated that all these activities will be used in the delivery of this session. These are suggestions for facilitators to select from. An example of how these activities can be incorporated into the session is provided within the process notes. In this session, in particular, I have included a lot of different activities around the use of PACE. Selection of these will depend upon how the group members are understanding the content. If top-up sessions are planned for group members, some of these exercises could potentially be reserved for these.

Activities to support the exploration of therapeutic parenting	
As individuals	Group members write a couple of paragraphs describing a recent time with their child or young person.
In small groups	Reflect on children who have experienced developmental trauma and loss. Consider: *What has happened? What do they feel?* and *What do they do?*
Activities to support the exploration of mind-mindedness	
As a whole group	Explore mind-mindedness using the dialogues in Activity Sheet 8.
As a whole group or in small groups	Explore the conversations in Activity Sheet 9 to explore parental mind-mindedness.
As individuals	Return to the descriptions written at the beginning of the session. Reflect on mentalizing words that were used or could have been used.
Activities to support the exploration of 'open and engaged' and defensive responding	
Facilitators demonstrate through role play	Explore the difference between open and engaged and defensive responding through role plays of parents being defensive and using PACE.

Activities to support the exploration of PACE	
As a whole group	Volunteers will read through one of the scripts in Activity Sheet 10 or 11, whilst the rest of the group reflects on this. Go through the non-PACE and then the PACE version and notice differences.
As a whole group or in small groups	Consider the different interactions described in Activity Sheet 12. Spot the motive of the parents. Are they trying to be with the child in PACE, using curiosity to understand, accept and empathize, or are they using PACE coercively, in the hope of getting some behaviour change?
Between sessions	Facilitators might suggest that parents are PACE-ful with their partners between sessions.
As a whole group or in small groups	Consider the examples on Activity Sheet 13. Ask group members to consider how they might hold an attitude of PACE with these different children.
As a whole group	Explore PACE using transcripts chosen from Activity Sheets 14–17.

PROCESS NOTES

Begin the session with a general catch-up and opportunities for reflections following the first module.

Activity: At the beginning of this session the facilitators ask the group members to spend a few minutes writing a couple of paragraphs describing a recent time with a child or young person. Ask them to describe a time which has been a bit challenging, but not to choose anything that was very upsetting, and to describe the child at this time. If a participant is not currently having much experience with children, they can choose a time with another adult instead. This narrative will be referred back to later in the session.

THERAPEUTIC PARENTING

Traditional parenting

Now the facilitators introduce the idea of therapeutic parenting, with a focus on the importance of building connections with the child to enhance feelings of security. Group members will have their own experience of being parented, have probably used these ideas with varying levels of success with their own children, and may have received advice and previous training based on traditional ideas. It is helpful therefore to spend a short time providing an overview of why these parenting strategies tend to be less helpful for developmentally traumatized children.

This can facilitate discussion about the difficulties of receiving different advice from different people. Facilitators will acknowledge that they are going to be offering another set of parenting ideas. They can encourage group members to explore what makes sense to them and what appears to be helpful for their children.

The facilitators will move on to help the group members reflect on the idea of DDP-informed therapeutic parenting, with its additional focus on connection with emotional experience.

Start by asking participants to reflect on the connection between experience, feelings and behaviour.

Activity: In small groups ask participants to reflect on children who have experienced relational trauma and loss. Complete the following table, considering the children's experience, behaviour and feelings. Guide the participants to reflect on the content as described in the example. It can be helpful for participants to complete this exercise with a specific child in mind, for example, the child they wrote about in their narrative.

What has happened? (past and recent context)	What do they feel? (emotional experience)	What do they do? (behaviour)

As groups feed back, the facilitators explore with participants the connections between early experience, internal life and behaviour, relating this to ideas of connection and discipline, as in the example on the following page.

What has happened? (past and recent context)	What do they feel? (emotional experience)	What do they do? (behaviour)
Separation and loss of birth family Abuse and neglect Exposure to frightening events Moves Loss of safety and stability No security of attachment All this impacts on development of child	Feel helpless and abandoned Emotionally overwhelmed with poor emotional regulation Dissociation as coping mechanism Feel ineffective, helpless, unlovable, blaming of self, attacking of others Excessive and unregulated shame	Poor behavioural regulation: Under-controlled = aggression, oppositional Over-controlled = compulsive compliance, resistance to change Cognitive difficulties = poor problem solving, inflexible and attentional difficulties Adapt patterns of relating to others through excessive dependency or excessive self-reliance.
⬇	⬇	⬇
Need for understanding	Need for connection	Need for behavioural support ('correction')
= therapeutic parenting		

THE ABILITY TO BE MIND-MINDED

The facilitators will now move on to explore with the group members what parenting skills will be helpful to them if they are going to successfully build more connection into their parenting.

This focuses on the importance of the ability to mentalize, allowing parents to be mind-minded in their parenting. This ability is essential to maintain the attitude of PACE in parenting.

Activity: Understanding experience from dialogue (see Activity Sheet 8)

The facilitator will help the group members to understand mind-mindedness through exploration of parent–infant; parent–child and parent–teenager dialogues.

This can be done as a whole group or in small groups. There are a lot of activities in this session to help exploration of mind-mindedness and PACE; decisions will need to be made about which to do, and how much to do in small groups, which does take up more time. This particular activity works well as a whole group. The facilitators read through each of the dialogues parents might have with their children. Ask the group members to identify what they have learnt about the inner experience of the children and young people from what the parent is saying.

Begin with the non-mind-minded example of a parent talking to an infant. Group members will quickly notice that they are learning more about the experience of the parent than the infant. Reflect on what the infant might be learning about self.

Now repeat this for the mind-minded example and notice how much more we understand about the infant's inner experience, and therefore how much more the infant is being helped to understand his inner experience.

This is then repeated for the other dialogues with toddlers, older children and adolescents.

As children grow up and become more verbal, experiencing parents as mind-minded can lead to an increasing capacity to understand their own internal experience.

Activity: Writing mind-minded conversations (see Activity Sheet 9)

The conversations of parents and children of different ages can now be explored to help the group members reflect on non-mind-minded conversations, and how these could be re-written to be mind-minded. Again, this can be done as a whole group or in small groups depending on how many of the activities the facilitators decide to use. Ideas for reflecting on these conversations are given in Handout 13.

Activity: Return to the descriptions written at beginning of the session. Now ask group members to return to the paragraphs they wrote at the beginning of the session. Reflect on the description they wrote and notice if they were mentalizing or not. Advise group members that neither is right; they weren't specifically asked to write about the child's internal experience. Just notice and reflect on the descriptions:

- How many mentalizing words were used?

- Can they now add more mentalizing words to their narratives?

OPEN AND ENGAGED AND DEFENSIVE

One of the important things we need to do when parenting children is to try to stay open and engaged with them even when they are becoming defensive. This can be very hard, however, when the parent finds all their buttons being pushed. (This will be explored more in Module Three). If the parent can stay open and engaged, then it is more likely that the child will also be able to move to this more open stance.

Activity: The differences between open and engaged and defensiveness can be explored through role play.

1. The facilitators role play a child becoming defensive, angry and hostile and the parent becoming equally defensive in turn.

2. The facilitators enact the same role play but this time the parent stays open and engaged, using the PACE attitude.

Notice the difference in the children and the parents in these two role plays. Consider what makes it difficult for the parents to move from defensiveness. What might be helpful for them so that they can do this? How can the parents look after themselves when they do not avoid the pull to defensiveness? It is important to help parents to be compassionate for themselves.

Notice too how relationship repair is always available for the parents to restore their connections with the children. Acknowledging that they did not do very well, apologizing and helping the child to feel that the parent wants a continuing relationship with him is an important part of parenting. It also demonstrates to the child that things can go wrong in a relationship but this can be put right.

It can be helpful for parents to acknowledge that sometimes it is difficult to remain open or to repair the relationship following a time of defensiveness. Parents need to look after themselves, so that they can stay open to their children. In particular, the experience of blocked care, when caring for a child becomes a chore with little or no joy, can lead to difficulties in staying open and engaged. This will be explored further in the final session.

THE ABILITY TO MAINTAIN AN ATTITUDE OF PACE

PACE is chosen as the focus of this session, as it is a central parenting skill within the DDP principles introduced at the end of the last module. As facilitators discuss and explore PACE, make sure to relate this to the range of principles introduced. It can be helpful to have these principles displayed in the room for easy reference.

The previous activity and discussion about open and engaged begins to introduce an exploration of PACE as an attitude. There are a range of activities to explore this. The choice of which to use will best be made in response to how the parents are understanding the ideas.

The facilitators will need to work hard to convey the essence of PACE, both by talking about it and describing the different components, but more importantly by modelling it within the sessions.

Describe PACE: the elements and the role each of these plays in the whole. Notice examples of PACE that have cropped up earlier in the session or in previous sessions.

Activity: This activity does take a bit of time to set up but can be used to help people understand the experience of PACE and non-PACE from others. The day in the life role play provides a way of demonstrating PACE (see Activity Sheets 10 and 11). There are two versions of this script. Choose the one most appropriate to the group. Assign roles to group members volunteering to read through the scripts, and bring them into the centre of the room. Others will watch from the outside and reflect on what they notice. First ask the volunteers to read through using the non-PACE responses, next use PACE responses. Ask the 'child' or 'young person' how the two felt and what differences they noticed. Now ask observers to comment on what they observed. (My thanks to Julie Hudson for suggesting this exercise.)

It is important to acknowledge that PACE isn't easy. Group members are unlikely to be able to stay with PACE all the time; this is okay. They will however get good at noticing when they have moved away from PACE; when they are nagging, lecturing, scolding or generally moving too quickly into problem solving or reassurance. In noticing this, they will be able to gently return to PACE.

A challenge when introducing PACE to parents is to convey it in a way that isn't seen as a technique to change the child. Conveying PACE as a way of being is difficult. When parents talk about PACE not working, or relate an anecdote and ask if this is a time they could use PACE, you know they are not quite getting it. They are likely to be looking for some immediate answers, with PACE being used to change the way the child feels. Of course, parents want children to change but when this becomes the immediate goal it is likely that the child's internal experience is not fully accepted. Children can feel not good enough when they experience the parent trying to change or talk them out of how they feel. Ironically, the child's internal experience is more likely to change when the parents are not focused on this. With acceptance, the child's security increases.

Acknowledge how difficult this is when a child is demonstrating mistrust towards the parent. Embracing the mistrusting child so that the child feels accepted is difficult when the parent so wants the child to trust her. It is also difficult when a child starts to develop some tentative trust. The movement back and forwards between trust and mistrust can be unsettling and discouraging for parents. Times of trust feel unreal and times of mistrust feel like being back at the beginning. Maintaining a consistent PACE attitude when the child is transitioning between these states is especially hard. Accepting and embracing the child in all his parts, with a consistent attitude of PACE, can be difficult but is important if the trust is to strengthen.

It can be helpful to explore how parents can be PACE-like towards themselves so that PACE becomes an emotional compass. Help group members to notice that when they are feeling frustrated, despairing or a sense of failure, PACE can help them to find a sense of equilibrium again, with support from others if helpful. As they accept and understand their internal experience they naturally feel less frustrated and despairing. They have not tried to change how they are feeling, but feelings change nevertheless.

Now, focus group members on how they can do the same for their children. By holding the attitude, PACE becomes a way of being with them too. Facilitators will help group members to consider whether they are trying to use PACE to bring about change. PACE as technique is likely to lead to resistance. Explore how children are likely to react to this with shame, as they experience not being good enough for the parents. Rather than a technique to coerce the child to behave in a different way, the parent gets alongside the child and supports and shares the experiences that the child is having.

Notice the verbal components of PACE and also reflect on the non-verbal elements. Reflect on what happens if these don't match. This is a sign that the parent is not fully accepting the experience of the child.

The next activity can be used in session, or maybe as homework, to help group members understand the difference between way of being and technique. This may be helpful when parents are struggling to make sense of how PACE can be a way of being with a child rather than doing to the child.

Activity: Consider the different interactions described in Activity Sheet 12. Ask the group members, working in groups or as a whole group, to spot the motive of the parents. Notice if the parent is trying to be with the child in PACE, using curiosity to understand, accept and empathize, or if she is trying to use PACE coercively, in the hope of getting some behaviour change. Reflections on these scenarios are given in Handout 14.

Introducing PACE to children

As group members understand PACE and how this attitude or way of being can help children feel more secure, the facilitators can move to exploring how to bring PACE into their interactions with their children. By this time, they will understand that PACE is a way of being with themselves and with their children. Now they can reflect on whether their children are ready to join them in this discovery of their internal experience, or still need parents to do this on their behalf.

The facilitators might focus the group members on how the elements of PACE link together. Notice that there is not one place to start: it is a circular process.

The facilitators might find it helpful to illustrate this with a specific example. A group member might have shared a difficulty which she is prepared to explore with PACE in mind. Notice how ACE will always be present, starting with any of these elements, and P will come in and out as appropriate.

It can also be helpful to think about how curiosity can deepen acceptance and empathy. The parent responds to the child's mental state with acceptance and empathy; the parent's curiosity about the child's experience can then increase understanding, leading to a deeper A and E response. Again, an example here might be useful to illustrate, perhaps from one of the facilitators' own experiences.

The facilitators can prepare the group members for the different ways that children can respond to PACE. In particular, reflect on the developmental sequence of how children come to understand their internal experience. Understanding where their children are developmentally can help parents use PACE in a way that the children can manage.

Activity: If you want to explore this more deeply, consider the examples on Activity Sheet 13. Ask group members, in small groups or as a whole group, to consider how they might hold an attitude of PACE with these different children. This is another activity which could be explored by group members before the next session if time is limited. Help the group members to understand the different developmental stages and responses to PACE that these children display and how parents might respond to these. Reflections on these scenarios can be found in Handout 15.

This can lead into a discussion about how children will respond to PACE in different ways. Some children respond positively straight away and the parents experience a stronger connection with them. Other children might resist the feeling of closeness that PACE brings. It may feel too strange to them, not fitting their sense of who they are. Empathy in particular can expose the child to being known in a way that is unsettling. Older children might comment on how the parent is reading their mind. The parents will need to approach these children more slowly; lighter PACE can gradually deepen over time, allowing the children to get used to being known and to feel safe in this experience.

PACE with discipline

The facilitators now help the group members to explore PACE and how it can combine with discipline.

Activity: Explore the transcript of a PACE and non-PACE conversation with a child or young person (see Activity Sheets 14–17). Facilitators choose the most appropriate conversation depending upon the age and situation of the children the group members are caring for.

Possible questions for discussion

- What does the parent think is the child or young person's internal experience during the interactions?

- Does the parent show curiosity, acceptance or empathy for the child or young person's experience?

- Does playfulness help the interactions?

- What is the consequence of this as the interaction develops?

- How will the child or young person make sense of and learn to manage his inner life from this interaction?

- What are the main differences between the non-PACE and PACE dialogues?

Help group members to notice that PACE does not mean that parents will tolerate behaviour that is unacceptable to them. However, by using PACE before discipline the parent has a greater understanding of the child's experience; the child feels more understood and is more likely to respond to the discipline as a result. Discipline together with ongoing PACE becomes a way of supporting the child's behaviour, helping the child to behave in a way that is more comfortable for him as well as everyone else. PACE following the discipline can help ensure that the relationship continues to be strong, and the child experiences love as unconditional.

PACE at its best allows the child to feel that his emotional experience is fully accepted whilst there are also expectations about his behaviour. The connection that acceptance and empathy brings will help to regulate any shame the child is experiencing. This is more likely to lead to the experience of guilt for his behaviours, and the child will want to make amends. Consequences become collaborative rather than imposed by the parent, as the child is prepared to explore this and come up with suggestions himself.

Activity: Facilitators might suggest that parents have a go at being PACE-ful with their partners between sessions. Notice if this improves the relationship, and helps them to feel closer. Does it reduce or repair conflicts? How does it feel to give and receive comfort with PACE?

SESSION TITLE: SUPPORTING BEHAVIOUR

AIMS OF SESSION

- To explore traditional behaviour management and why this needs adapting for children with attachment insecurities.

- To increase understanding of what is meant by the term 'connection with correction' and to explore how emotional regulation using PACE and mind-minded parenting can be combined with behavioural support.

- To provide group members with a set of parenting principles for increasing security in the children.

- To provide group members with an understanding of how the ideas explored within Module Two fit together in a parenting sequence.

SUMMARY OF SESSION

This session follows closely on from the previous session. It explores how to combine the use of parenting skills to connect with the children, using mind-mindedness and PACE, with the important task of supporting the children's behaviour. Group members will have an opportunity to reflect upon the traditional behaviour management we use culturally and why this might be problematic with children who are emotionally insecure. This leads to a consideration of how 'connection' and 'correction' can be combined so that security can be built whilst helping children to learn to behave in ways that fit in to the family, community and society generally. The word 'connection' is used to reflect the importance of parents recognizing and accepting the emotional experience of the child, providing an emotional connection with her. This can help emotional regulation, allowing children to be more open to thinking about and adjusting their behaviour. It reduces the experiences of shame, allowing children to experience guilt and feel remorse: necessary experiences to allow them to learn and to make amends when things go wrong. The word 'correction' is used to reflect the importance of behavioural support: structure, supervision and discipline to help children adjust their behaviour in ways which are helpful for them and others who they are interacting with.

SESSION PLAN

Example session plan	
Catch-up and reflections	10 minutes
Exploring behaviour support instead of behaviour management	35 minutes
Discussion: Difficulties that can arise	15 minutes
Discussion and completing the connection and correction table	20 minutes
Break	20 minutes
Activity: Exploring behaviour vignettes	30 minutes
Exploring a set of parenting principles	20 minutes
Bringing it all together: Parenting in the moment	20 minutes
Parenting in the moment: A story	10 minutes

TRAINER NOTES[2]

DIFFICULTIES FOR DEVELOPMENTALLY TRAUMATIZED CHILDREN WHEN PARENTS USE TRADITIONAL PARENTING STRATEGIES

> **KEY POINTS**
>
> * Trust in parents leads to belief in parents' good intentions even when putting in behavioural boundaries.
>
> * Lack of trust and a need to be in charge within the relationship mean that developmentally traumatized children prefer to feel disconnected than connected.
>
> * Developmental trauma leads to lack of safety in the most normal of parental discipline and praise, reinforcing feelings of shame and not being good enough.
>
> * Difficulties in trusting in parental support lead to defensive responding and difficulties with emotional dysregulation.

Parenting children with experience of developmental trauma is especially challenging because the parents are trying to provide nurture, behavioural support, guidance and teaching to children who do not trust them or their good intentions. The trauma that these children have experienced has led to them developing ways of being that are organized around a need to be in charge within the relationships. They have developed a range of controlling behaviours to do this. These children have learnt to behave defensively to ward off the dangers of not being good enough and of the rejection that they are anticipating. They are more comfortable being disconnected to others than in experiencing connection.

Traditional parenting techniques, described as behavioural management, can be helpful when children experience themselves as unconditionally loved and can therefore believe in their parents' good intentions:

---

2   The accompanying online materials can be accessed at www.jkp.com/voucher using the code GOLDINGFOUNDATIONS.

- When they are distressed, perhaps because of the boundaries and consequences provided for their behaviour, they can manage this distress because they can let their parents help them with it.

- Over time they internalize the values that the parents are trying to instil, and can behave in acceptable ways.

- These children grow up well adjusted; they remain open to parents' support, even when they are going through the rebellion and risk-taking of adolescence.

- They become adults who are socially comfortable, can form healthy relationships and are open and engaged to connection with others.

When love feels more conditional, as in the experience of developmental trauma, this all becomes much more difficult:

- These children do not believe in the good intentions of others.

- They experience high levels of shame, not feeling good enough.

- Evaluation of behaviour through rewards and consequences is viewed as evaluation of themselves.

- Therefore, they perceive danger in the most normal of boundaries and they respond with highly defensive behaviours.

- When these children become distressed they cannot turn to parents for support so easily. Dysregulation therefore tends to increase as emotional arousal intensifies, without the ability to regulate or soothe this.

- These difficulties with relationships and with regulation make adolescence a much more dangerous time. They engage in rebellion and risk-taking without being able to use the adults for needed support.

- These children become adults who remain socially uncomfortable. They form adult relationships which continue to be organized around the need to control. They remain closed to social engagement and are more comfortable with disconnection than connection.

Behavioural management parenting advice can increase the anxiety of the child who does not trust and does not feel good enough. The parent needs to find different ways to support the child with their behaviour whilst reducing the child's feeling of anxiety.

EXPLORING BEHAVIOUR SUPPORT INSTEAD OF BEHAVIOUR MANAGEMENT

KEY POINTS

* Behaviour management which relies on parents using environmental contingencies to reward or provide negative consequences for behaviour increases anxiety in mistrusting children.

* Behavioural boundaries and consequences signal imminent abandonment.

* Praise and rewards also increase anxiety as the child fears evaluation.

* Parents need to connect before they can provide behavioural support.

* Children need supportive relationships in order to emotionally regulate and to put feelings into words via reflection.

Parenting based on social learning theory relies on parents managing environmental contingencies so that appropriate behaviour is rewarded and unwanted behaviour is ignored or meets with a negative consequence. This is likely to increase the anxiety an anxious child is already experiencing, leading to more dysregulated behaviours.

This is especially problematic for children who have had experience of conditional love in a developmentally traumatizing environment, especially when they have also experienced loss of parents. This combination can lead to core fears of not being good enough and anticipation that current parents will be lost too. Children can experience behavioural boundaries and discipline as being indicators that the parents recognize their badness and will get rid of them. Even rewards and praise can raise anxieties. These also represent an evaluation of the child, and the child anticipates being found wanting, if not this time then next time. In the face of these fears, children will dysregulate more quickly and move into the experience of shame. This only increases the challenge presented by their behaviour.

Parents need to attend to the regulation of shame and to emotional connection with the children before they will be able to help the children to adjust their behaviour. Emotional connection allows the parent to help the child to regulate. The emphasis on the regulation of the child's internal experience means that this approach to parenting is regulation based rather than behaviour based. This does not mean an absence of behaviour support, but behaviour support can only be successful once the child has been helped to regulate, and has experienced emotional connection with the parent. This is what Dan Hughes tried to capture in the expression he coined: 'connection with correction', which is used in this parenting programme.

Too narrow a focus on behaviour management can lead to a range of difficulties:

- The focus is on the behaviour, rather than the relationship. The lack of emotional connection within the relationship will not help children to develop trust and increase security.

- Behaviour management without a solid relationship can be shame-inducing. The children are more likely to experience shame. This prevents the experience of guilt and therefore children cannot feel remorse or learn to make amends.

- Behaviour management represents an evaluation. Children experience disapproval of self rather than their behaviour, triggering shame. Children also experience approval (praise, rewards) for behaviour that they believe they can't sustain. They become anxious in the face of the parents' pleasure, anticipating times when the parent discovers how bad they are. Thus, shame is triggered again.

- Behaviour management is based on consequences for behaviour. Consequences might feel like loss of relationship. Children experience this as a reminder that relationships are conditional – they can be lost. The child expects that the parent will stop loving her under specific conditions. Discipline therefore triggers fears of abandonment, greatly increasing anxiety.

- Behaviour management focuses on predictability and consistency, so that the child learns from cause and effect. If the child has lived in highly inconsistent and unpredictable environments, she may lack causal thinking. She can't make sense of cause and effect. When effect (consequence) is disconnected from cause the child experiences consequences as the parent just being mean or unreasonable.

The behaviour management strategies can be helpful when children experience being unconditionally loved, and have trust that their parents only have good intentions towards them. This is much more problematic for children who have had experience of conditional love, especially when they have also experienced loss of parents. This leads to core fears of not being good enough and anticipation that current parents will be lost too. Behavioural boundaries and discipline are indicators that the parents recognize their badness. The children will fear abandonment.

In the face of these fears children will experience high levels of stress and anxiety which:

- overwhelm their already fragile regulation abilities

- will lead to them dysregulating more quickly, often through displays of anger and temper

- confirm for them that they are bad kids, and their stress increases further.

The children do not want to behave this way, although it can seem that they do. They have lost control, and in doing so the shame that is always there is increased.

Now, when it seems furthest away, the children need the relationship with their parents most; a relationship that can help the child to regulate, and eventually to move from behaviour to reflection, being able to put feelings into words.

Relationship

It is at the hardest times, when parents are likely to be feeling at their most desperate, that the children need connection most. Parents need to be ready and waiting to connect as soon as the child can tolerate this. It is this openness to the relationship, even at these most difficult of times, that will help the children to trust in parents and gain the security of knowing that they are acceptable to their parents; they are unconditionally loved.

Regulation

Whilst children's behaviours can feel targeted, manipulative and intentional, many of these behaviours stem from dysregulated emotion. The child's emotional arousal has risen to a level where it is threatening to overwhelm her. Alongside this, levels of shame are increasing. Not being able to use parental support at these times, the child does the only other thing she can do: she uses the shield against shame. Her behaviour dysregulates as her emotion becomes overwhelming, but she turns this outwards, attacking others.

Notice also the child who dissociates rather than dysregulates: because these children are less challenging to others their struggles with emotion can be missed. They withdraw, become switched off, perhaps extra compliant, as they too try to manage without parental support.

Emotional connection allows the parent to help the child to emotionally regulate again.

Reflection

Connection helps the child to reach the point where she is ready to think about what has happened. This assumes that the child is developmentally able to reflect on her behaviour. A younger or more immature child will need the parent to do this on her behalf. For an older or more mature child, this can be done together. The child is regulated and has experienced the parent as supportive towards her. She is now able to sit with her parent and think about her experience. Using PACE and having a story-telling attitude at this point can further strengthen the connection between them.

REGULATION-BASED PARENTING WITH PACE

KEY POINTS

* Parents need to understand the arousal level of the child and adjust their parenting in line with this.

* This will guide the parents in using regulation and PACE to support the child.

* Some of the more traditional parenting strategies to support behaviour can also be used if these are adapted to take into account the need for regulation and connection via PACE.

Regulation-based parenting needs to take into account the arousal of the child. As stress increases arousal also increases and this will change what the child is open to. Bruce Perry suggests that there are five arousal states to be considered, each of which changes the way the child behaves. Each state is governed by a different part of the brain, with the lower arousal states drawing upon higher brain regions which are open to thinking. As arousal increases, lower and yet lower brain regions take over, leading to increasingly more instinctive behaviour (Perry 2006):

1. *Calm.* Arousal is low. The child is rational and is open to reflection. In this state a verbal child is likely to be able to join in PACE, being open to playfulness and curiosity as well as the connection that acceptance and empathy brings.

2. *Aroused.* As emotional arousal increases the child will appear younger and more concrete in her ability to think. She might still be open to PACE, but is less likely to engage with curiosity. Her reflection has reduced.

3. *Alarmed.* The child is getting increasingly emotional and this is reflected in her behaviour and increasingly young functioning. Dysregulation is increased. The child now needs her parent to be curious on her behalf, receiving genuine acceptance and empathy (A and E). She will not be able to reflect in this state.

4. *Fearful.* The child is now very reactive, as she responds to the increasing arousal experienced in increasingly immature ways. A and E might still reach her if kept clear and simple, with a high level of acceptance for her experience.

5. *Terror.* The child is now displaying a full fight/flight response. There is little more that the parent can do but hang on and keep both himself and the child safe. PACE via A and E is aimed at reducing the panic. Convey acceptance in your voice, but the words are less likely to reach her until the terror subsides and she starts to go down the arousal continuum again. Arousal will subside with time, and the child, emotionally spent, will be open to PACE again. This is

a time for a high level of nurture, aided by the PACE the parent is holding on to. This will reduce arousal further. Only later will the child be calm enough to engage with PACE again.

It might be helpful to think of this as a volcano as in Figure M2.S2.1. PACE can be effective in reducing arousal during the build-up. During the eruption, the child needs to be kept safe but will be open to PACE as it subsides. Keep to A and E to avoid further eruptions, only involving the child in playfulness and curiosity as you move away from the eruption.

Where do traditional behaviour management strategies fit in?

Behaviour support strategies can still be helpful, although may need some adaptation for this group of children.

Relationship

Some behaviour support strategies can help with the building of the relationship. Playfulness is part of PACE and positive time together is part of most behavioural parenting advice. Playfulness looks for moments of fun and joy; these can build towards finding positive activities and time together.

Regulation

Other behaviour management strategies can help with regulation. 'Time out' is a well-known strategy that is not helpful for traumatized children but can be adapted. For developmentally traumatized children 'time out' can increase the children's fear of abandonment. Margot Sunderland describes a simple adaptation of 'time out' to what she calls 'time in' (Sunderland 2008). The child is removed from a situation that she is struggling with, but is brought in closer to the parent. The parent is now on hand to co-regulate the child's emotional arousal, increasing regulation and allowing her to return to the situation successfully, perhaps with additional parental support. This is also a more helpful response than ignoring. Ignoring negative behaviour is a simple way of conveying to a secure child that the behaviour will not get her the desired attention. For the insecure child, it can convey that she is not worth bothering with. The child fails to distinguish between her behaviour as unacceptable and herself as acceptable. Ignoring can therefore increase shame and dysregulation.

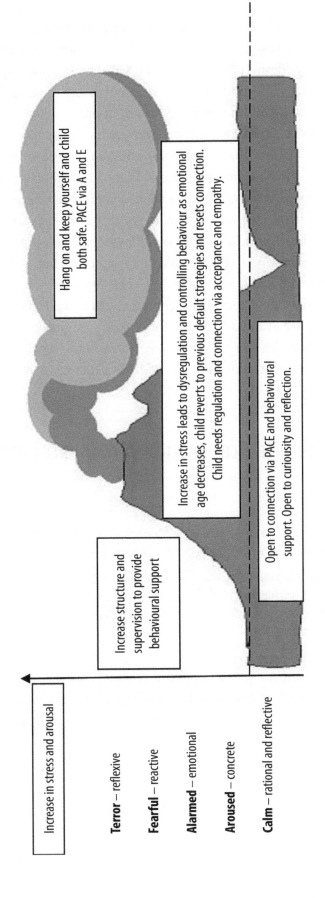

Increase in stress and arousal

Terror – reflexive

Fearful – reactive

Alarmed – emotional

Aroused – concrete

Calm – rational and reflective

Increase structure and supervision to provide behavioural support

Hang on and keep yourself and child both safe. PACE via A and E

Increase in stress leads to dysregulation and controlling behaviour as emotional age decreases, child reverts to previous default strategies and resets connection. Child needs regulation and connection via acceptance and empathy.

Open to connection via PACE and behavioural support. Open to curiousity and reflection.

Figure M2.S2.1 The volcano of arousal

Reflection

One very popular way of increasing the child's sense of accomplishment and therefore her self-esteem is using praise and rewards. Praise and rewards ultimately work because the children want and desire parental approval within a relationship. When this desire is absent, we see children responding very manipulatively to rewards. Similarly, praise is viewed as a trick; after all, the parent does not approve of them and so they cannot believe in this praise at face value. Global praise which tries to convince the children that they are good simply does not fit the children's sense of self and so must be rejected. Of course, we do want to help children to feel good about themselves, and to enjoy their accomplishments. We would like their self-esteem to increase. Praise and rewards are an important way of conveying this if we go cautiously. Praise needs to come from the heart and be a way of enjoying an accomplishment together. If it is used as a technique the child is likely to reject it, but if it is experienced as genuine joy in the child and what she has achieved then the child might be able to share in this. Rewards might be accepted if they are low key and descriptive. Praise and rewards are evaluative. They are making judgements about the children's worth. This is likely to lead to defensiveness. More than praise and rewards, children need stories: opportunities to make sense of their experience, rather than having this experience evaluated.

SOME PARENTING PRINCIPLES: 'CONNECTION WITH CORRECTION'

KEY POINTS

* The parenting ideas expressed in the phrase 'connection before connection' can be summarized in a series of parenting principles.

* These principles illustrate the use of PACE with behavioural support; regulation via the relationship; understanding the child's experience rather than trying to change this; and providing appropriate structure and supervision.

With an understanding of mind-mindedness and PACE, parents can combine this with behaviour support; in this way PACE plus discipline can build security for the insecure child. This can be conveyed through a series of principles which can guide DDP-informed parenting.

Principle one: PACE is a consistent feature and discipline is brought in as needed

PACE before discipline helps the child to feel emotionally connected and unconditionally loved. PACE with discipline helps to maintain this connection when the child is at her most vulnerable: experiencing shame and fear. PACE following the discipline provides the child with a continuing sense of being unconditionally loved, repairing any ruptures in the relationship.

Principle two: Authoritative parenting

Connection with correction via authoritative parenting includes:

- warmth and nurture

- provision of structure and boundaries

- allowing appropriate autonomy matched to developmental age.

This can be considered as having two hands for parenting.

Two hands of parenting

Hand one provides warmth and nurture, and allows children appropriate autonomy matched to their developmental age. In other words, children are supported to make choices and to develop independence but only at a pace that they can cope with. This hand also contains the curiosity, allowing the parent to wonder about and accept the child's internal experience. Hand one supports PACE.

Hand two provides structure and boundaries: the support from the parents that children need to be successful.

Two hands of parenting allow for:

- *Connection with correction.* Whilst they might need to give a consequence for behaviour (discipline, correction) this is likely to be more successful when the child feels understood by the parent (connection). This is not finding an excuse for behaviour; this still needs to be dealt with, but it is dealt with empathically.

- *No correction without understanding.* If the parent responds without understanding the child will feel less secure, and will not build trust in the parent. This is not an excuse, but an explanation. The explanation helps the parent to get the consequences right.

Principle three: Parenting sandwich

Misattunements are normal in any relationship, including between a parent and child. These ruptures present an opportunity to the parent for building trust with the child (Tronick 2007). If a parent can repair the connection with the child soon after the disruption, the child will feel more secure rather than less secure. Thus, parenting a child represents cycles of attunement–misattunement–repair which strengthen the relationship. One necessary form of rupture occurs when parents need to discipline the child.

Discipline, in the form of boundaries and consequences, is important, alongside warmth and empathy for the child. This happens when discipline is sandwiched between the attunement and relationship repair (see Figure M2.S2.2).

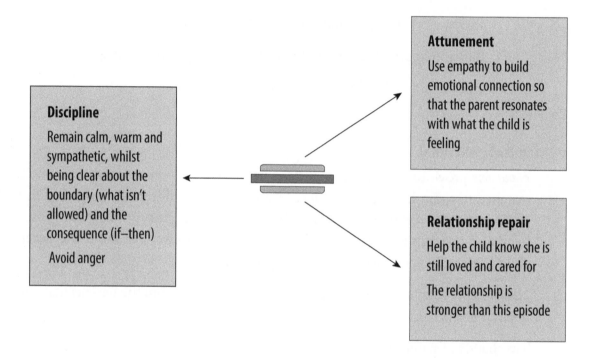

Figure M2.S2.2 The parenting sandwich

The child learns from these experiences that misattunement does not mean that she is about to be rejected or abandoned. Reparation is possible, even when the child moves into defensive behaviour. The repair restores the connected relationship, allowing the child to become open and engaged again. The parent attending to the repair is providing the social buffering the child needs to quieten her reactive state. He is also letting the child know that the relationship is more important than any conflict now, or in the future. This provides a platform on which trust is built. For the parents, it is important, although often tricky, to stay open and engaged to the child at the moments of misattunement. If the parents do move into defensive states also, the repair won't happen. At these times the parents need to take care of themselves so that they can move back to the open state that allows them to provide the necessary repair. An essential part of building trust is through the responsibility taken by the adults for repairing the relationship.

Principle four: Adult takes responsibility for the relationship offered to the child

Taking responsibility for the relationship means:

- *Don't punish with the relationship.* Children who are insecure are quick to assume that they are not good and that they are not loved. If the parent withdraws the relationship as a consequence or in anger, then the child is quick to confirm these beliefs (e.g. you're disappointed with me; your relationship with me is conditional on my behaviour). This increases insecurity further and moves the child even further away from developing a trusting relationship with the parent. Judgemental disciplinary methods are therefore ineffective.

- *Taking breaks when needed.* Parents need to look after themselves. This gives them the strength and resilience to keep going. The parent is looking after the relationship with the child by taking breaks before he reaches breaking point. The child can be helped to understand that the parent is protecting the relationship because it is important to him. The child needs to know that this is not a sign that she is being abandoned.

- *Adult takes responsibility for relationship repair.* It is the parents' job to let children know that the relationship is still there for them after a period of difficulty. There may be a consequence for the behaviour but this does not mean that love is conditional. Parents are only human and it is inevitable that they will get cross or frustrated at times. It is important that these times are also followed by relationship repair led by the adult. Parents needn't be afraid to acknowledge that they got it wrong, they are sorry and that they will continue to be there for the child. For example, 'I am sorry; I think I made you feel really bad; maybe you think I don't love you. I don't want you to feel bad about yourself but I do want to support you to manage things differently.'

Principle five: Understanding without lectures, premature problem solving and rushed reassurance

- *Don't lecture, and delay problem solving.* Children can rarely be talked into or out of behaviour. Remember that behaviour change comes from being understood within relationships, so that boundaries are experienced with warmth and empathy. Children might be able to join in with some problem solving – how they might have managed something differently – but they will not engage with this until they know that parents are understanding their experience.

- *Not rushing to reassure.* Reassurance that tries to talk children out of what they are experiencing is not helpful. This is not acceptance. It is effectively saying to the child that you understand what she is thinking and feeling, but she doesn't need to or shouldn't think or feel this way. Reassurance denies that thinking and feeling is neither right nor wrong, it just is. Later, the parent might reassure to give hope to the child. This reassurance is different, as it is about helping the child rather than making the parent feel better. For example, 'This has been a hard day, but we will get through this together.'

Principle six: Provide appropriate level of structure and supervision

Very often parental expectations of children are based on chronological age alone. This can lead to increased pressure for the children to manage a level of structure and supervision that is too low for them. Parents need to be mindful of children's emotional maturity, adjusting their expectations in line with this level of maturity. This is made more complicated because levels of immaturity can fluctuate depending upon the level of stress being experienced. We all act younger when under stress and this can be exaggerated in children who are emotionally insecure. Structure and supervision will therefore have to be adjusted in relationship to the child's current level of stress.

Notice that if the consequences are piling up, it is a sign that the child needs increased structure and supervision alongside empathy.

It can be helpful to think about this in terms of Vygotsky's zone of proximal development (see Figure M2.S2.3). Children will make developmental progress when the parent provides them with some scaffolding. The child can do so much on her own, and a little bit more with parental support. If parents' expectations are within the zone, they are holding the right level of expectations and the child is likely to progress. If, however, their expectations are outside this zone, the child is less likely to progress because expectations are too high (Vygotsky 1978).

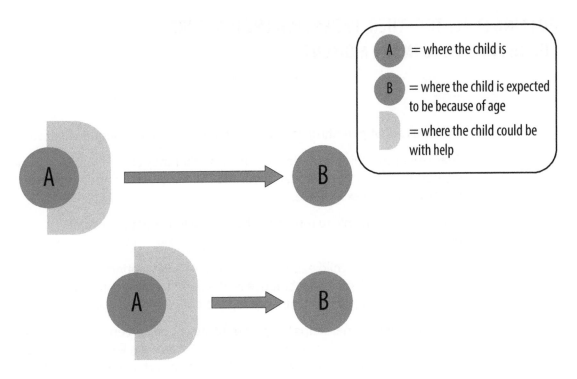

Figure M2.S2.3 Zone of proximal development

Principle seven: Help the child to manage shifts between playfulness and parental authority

One of the hardest things a mistrusting child can do is to accede to the authority of the parent. These children have learnt to control others as a way of maintaining their own safety. Giving up this control is not going to be easy. This means that at times when a parent needs to use his authority for keeping the child safe, providing a boundary and structuring the environment, the child will revert to her own pattern of controlling behaviours. Baylin and Hughes (2016) point out that the shift from what they call 'companionship mode' to 'parental authority mode' can be especially difficult. The child is much more able to connect with the parent when he is being playful; during these times the difference in power and authority between parent and child is at its smallest. As the parent moves back into being parental (e.g. 'It's nearly teatime, let's put this away now'), the child needs to adjust to the parent being back in charge. These relational transitions can lead to very rapid shifts in the child towards anger and meltdown. The parent needs to find a way to stay open and empathic to the child's struggles in letting parents have a benevolent authority over her.

PUTTING IT ALL TOGETHER, PARENTING THE INSECURE CHILD: PARENTING IN THE MOMENT

KEY POINTS

* The ideas about parenting can be brought together into a sequence of stages.

* These focus the parents on slowing down so that they ensure that they provide support for themselves, regulation for the child and understanding of the child's emotional experience.

* Children are then able to reflect on their behaviour and to consider other people.

* This can lead to the child experiencing remorse and wanting to make amends. Consequences become collaborative as the parent supports the child to do this. Along the way relationships are repaired or strengthened.

* Following these stages helps the parent to stay open and engaged rather than becoming defensive. This avoids the spiralling of anxiety, feelings of failure and increasing coercion that can occur between a parent and child when each is defensive.

Parenting a child with connection and correction can be understood by breaking it down into seven stages. By keeping these stages in mind, it is easier to stay open and engaged with the child rather than becoming defensive within parenting. This in turn helps to make an emotional connection with the child, whilst also providing some behavioural support. When a parent connects before correcting, the child will experience unconditional love and acceptance alongside the safety that empathic boundaries and discipline can provide. This is parenting by the long route. More attention is given to connecting with the child and providing regulation, whilst the focus on behaviour is delayed. The parents slow themselves down in providing the behavioural support, and end up getting where they want to be more quickly as a consequence. When parents stop trying to make behaviour change, trust increases and the children gradually start to shift the behaviours that they are displaying.

* *Stage one.* Notice what is happening. Do I need to step in? What immediate steps do I need to do to ensure everyone's safety?

* *Stage two.* Pause for a moment and think: 'What is the impact on me? Am I regulated? Can I stay open and engaged? Am I becoming defensive? If I'm becoming defensive, do I need a break or can I get back to being open and engaged? Can I be compassionate to myself?' Obviously in the midst of behaviour, the parent may not have much time to do this, but just taking a moment to notice this can help the parent to stay regulated. It may also be

helpful to notice reactions which can be reflected upon later with more time and with a trusted other.

- *Stage three.* Do I need to help regulate the child? Is the child open for some reflection? What part of the child's brain is activated at the moment? Do I need to provide sensory regulation? Do I need to emotionally regulate? Or can I help her to reflect?

- *Stage four.* Curiosity and understanding. Reflect with the child or, if this is not possible, on her behalf. Make sense of what's going on. What is my best guess of what the child's internal emotional experience is at this moment, remembering that internal experience is neither right nor wrong, it just is? I'm not going to judge it.

- *Stage five.* Demonstrate acceptance and empathy to connect with the child around the best guess of what her emotional experience is. How can I help her to know that I get it?

- *Stage six.* The correction. Do I need to do anything further? Do I need to provide a consequence? Do we need to do some problem solving?

- *Stage seven.* Repair the relationship. Let the child know she is loved unconditionally. It may have felt tough but the relationship is stronger. 'Together we have got through it.' Help the child to repair any relationships with others who may have been hurt during the difficulty. Often this repair is part of the logical consequence for the child. Many children who have felt supported through the connection with the parent will now be experiencing some guilt and remorse and will want to make this repair. The child might even have some ideas about how to do this.

In more traditional parenting the parent is likely to jump from stage one to stage six with stages two to five getting lost on the way. 'Connection with correction' is the longer route to parenting, as the parent works through all seven stages. It is this longer route that will allow trauma to be healed as the child can experience safety and build trust with parents.

Open and engaged parenting

This parenting helps the parent to stay open and engaged to the child. Any feelings of defensiveness are noticed and the parent uses curiosity to move out of, or avoid moving into, a defensive attitude. When parents don't take a moment to take care of themselves, and when they become overly focused on managing the behaviour without ensuring that they have a connection with the child, then defensiveness is likely to follow. The parents will have the best of intentions. They want the child to behave well, not just because this is easier for them, but also because they know this will ultimately be more helpful for the child.

When children misbehave, it is easy to become lost in the future, imagining the trouble the children might get into if they can't behave in a societally acceptable way. Concerns about such a future can lead parents to be overly defensive in their parenting approach. This can result in a more coercive approach with the child. The well-intentioned need to change the child's behaviour overrides any thought about connecting with the emotional experience of the child. Unfortunately, this move to coercion is experienced by the child as disapproval of her. This triggers her own feelings of blocked trust and she anticipates loss and abandonment. The child moves into a feared future too.

Alongside these fears, the child also experiences a reinforcement of her experience of not being good enough and her sense of shame increases. As we have previously explored, feelings of shame can be defended against through the shield against shame. The child moves into more behaviour which further triggers the parents' anxiety. As the child tries to cope with intense feelings of shame, the parents in turn are trying to cope with their own feelings of failure, with increased focus on behaviour. In this situation, behaviour management can become increasingly punitive as the parent tries even harder to get the child to change her behaviour. Punitive parenting is often a response to big fears in parents that they are failing and that the child is going to develop in ways that are unacceptable, for her and for society at large. This increases further when parents are feeling judged by others. The child's behaviour becomes a reflection upon themselves, and it is an image they do not want to look at.

Slowing down, taking time to care for self and maintaining an attitude of PACE alongside behaviour support can all increase the amount of time the parent can be open and engaged to the child.

SUGGESTIONS FOR ACTIVITIES

It is not anticipated that all these activities will necessarily be used in the delivery of this session. These are suggestions for facilitators to select from. An example of how these activities can be incorporated into the session is provided within the process notes.

Activities to support the exploration of supporting behaviour	
Group discussion	Reflect with the group on difficulties of using traditional parenting strategies with children who are insecure.
As a whole group or in small groups	Ask group members to reflect on what the goals of PACE are.
As a whole group	Return to the 'connection and correction' table written in the first session. What would group members like to add to the table?
Whole group or small groups	Use Activity Sheets 18 and 19 to explore supporting children and young people on the arousal continuum with PACE. Choose the example that is most appropriate for the group.
As a whole group	Consider what the advantages of using connection as well as behavioural support are for children who are insecure.
In small groups	Explore the behaviour scenarios in Activity Sheet 20 and reflect on how the parents can connect with the children as well as support their behaviour.

Activities to support the exploration of open and engaged parenting	
In small groups	Use Activity Sheet 21, the newspaper report of the Japanese boy lost in the forest, to consider defensive and open and engaged parenting.
Activities to support the parenting in the moment sequence	
In small groups	Provide each stage of the sequence separately and ask groups to explore how these might be put together.
As a whole group	Use the story in Activity Sheet 22 to explore the parenting in the moment sequence.

PROCESS NOTES

Begin the session with a general catch-up and opportunities for reflections following the last session.

EXPLORING BEHAVIOUR SUPPORT

Reflect with participants on behaviour management training they have done and the way they were parented. What is society's approved way of managing children's behaviour in our culture? Notice how much of this parenting advice is based on social learning theory.

Activity: Now reflect on some of the difficulties in using this approach with children who are insecure.

Guide participants to think about the difficulties that can arise because the focus is:

- on the behaviour and not the relationship, i.e. without emotional connection and shame-inducing

- evaluative – the child feels not good enough

- on consequences for behaviour – this reminds the child that the relationship is conditional

- on cause and effect – which is difficult for children who lack causal thinking.

It is now time to provide some deeper insight into the way that DDP principles and behaviour support can combine.

Begin with some reflections about PACE following the previous session. What have group members understood about PACE as an attitude, and how might they see it being combined with discipline?

Activity: Ask group members, as a whole group or in small groups, to reflect on what the goals of PACE are. In feedback notice any suggestions that imply that the goal is changing the child's behaviour. Notice how this reduces acceptance for the child and the emotional struggles she is having. Notice the more helpful goals of helping the child to become open and engaged, learning to trust, being more open to intersubjectivity, and being less shameful. Reflect on how these goals are more likely to be attained if PACE helps the parent to stay open and engaged, regulated, connected and less shameful. PACE is helping the parent to change rather than the child. If these goals are attained, then behaviour change in the child is likely to follow, even though this is not the immediate goal.

Now facilitators will think back to the last session and the ideas explored about mind-mindedness and PACE. Revisit how these parenting skills can be used alongside behaviour support. Explore how PACE plus discipline can build security for the insecure child, leading to a set of parenting principles for behaviour support.

Activity: Facilitators can now return to the exercise carried out in the first session. What do participants want to add or change in the table based on what has been explored since? For example:

Connection	Correction
Mind-minded parenting	Time in
PACE	Bringing child close
Open and engaged	Help child to understand cause, effect and consequences
Relationship, regulate, reflect	
Understanding reasons for behaviour	Descriptive praise
Meet hidden and expressed needs	Low-key rewards
Help child to regulate feelings of shame, weaken the shield	Distraction, diversion
	Positive activities
Connection first	Guidance, suggestions
Attunement and relationship repair	Structure and supervision for developmental age
Stories	
Safety	Explaining, reasoning
Hand one	**Hand two**

Facilitators now reflect on the importance of relationship, regulation and reflection, helping group members to become more sophisticated in their understanding of how to connect with the children at different stages of the arousal continuum, bringing in behavioural support when it is relevant.

Activity: This can be explored in an activity which explores one simple episode and how a child might respond depending on where she is on the arousal continuum

(Activity Sheets 18 and 19). This uses a simple scenario of a child who has to visit her gran instead of watching the television. Ask the group to order the different scenes in increasing level of arousal. This could be done by putting the numbers which are against each scene onto the volcano. Reflect on how Mum might use PACE to support the child. There is an alternative scenario (Activity Sheet 19) of an adolescent who is not able to go out and meet her friends which can be used if this is more appropriate for the group.

Handouts 18 and 19 show the scenes in order of arousal level, together with reflections about these.

CONSIDERING CONNECTION WITH CORRECTION

It is now time to return to the theme of 'connection with correction'. Group members have now met this idea several times and will be able to reflect on the importance of connection and regulation before providing support for behaviour.

Activity: A whole-group discussion focused on the question of what the advantages of using connection with correction are

Help group members to think about children with trauma who lack security and the ways that connection can build this security.

This discussion can lead into an activity which helps group members to explore this with some examples of children's behaviours.

Activity: Exploration of behaviour scenarios (see Activity Sheet 20)

These vignettes can be considered in relation to how parents can provide connection and regulation before correction. Some reflections on these scenarios are given in Handout 20.

PARENTING PRINCIPLES

At the end of this exercise, facilitators can bring the understanding gained so far in this session into a set of parenting principles to guide parenting that will build security.

- *Principle one:* PACE is a consistent feature and discipline is brought in as needed

- *Principle two:* Authoritative parenting

- *Principle three:* Parenting sandwich

- *Principle four:* Adult takes responsibility for the relationship offered to the child

- *Principle five:* Understanding without lectures, premature problem solving and rushed reassurance

- *Principle six:* Provide appropriate level of structure and supervision

- *Principle seven:* Help the child to manage shifts between playfulness and parental authority.

Facilitators will work through these principles, which should make sense to group members following on from the previous session as well as this one. Allow discussion as these principles are described.

OPEN AND ENGAGED PARENTING

Notice with group members how these parenting principles will help them to stay open and engaged in their parenting. Explore how easy it is to become defensive when dealing with behaviours that are challenging, alongside coping with judgement of others and self, and fears of the future. Defensive parenting quickly becomes coercive, even building to being punitive, as correction dominates and connection with the internal experience of the child is lost.

Activity: the newspaper story of the Japanese boy lost in the forest can be explored to consider how good intentions can become punitive parenting when parents are more defensive than open and engaged (see Activity Sheet 21).

PARENTING IN THE MOMENT

The final part of the session brings the thinking of both sessions in Module Two together as facilitators work through the stages in the 'parenting in the moment' cycle. Whilst this is set out as a series of stages, remember that parents might need to go back and forth between these as they support their children.

- *Stage one:* Notice what is happening.

- *Stage two:* Pause for a moment and think: 'What is the impact on me?'

- *Stage three:* Do I need to help regulate the child?

- *Stage four:* Curiosity and understanding.

- *Stage five:* Demonstrate acceptance and empathy to connect with the child.

- *Stage six:* The correction. Do I need to do anything further?

- *Stage seven:* Repair relationships.

Activity: During the pilot work on this programme, one group adapted this into an exercise that provided all the steps separately and asked group members to think about how to order these into a sequence before showing the full model. They found this to be helpful for discussion and reflection.

Activity: This sequence of parenting stages can also be explored through the story in Activity Sheet 22. Talking through the principles, the 'parenting in the moment' handout (Handout 17) and then reading the story can be helpful for bringing the parenting ideas explored within this programme together.

PACE: FREQUENTLY ASKED QUESTIONS

In this section, a range of common questions which parents ask when discovering and exploring PACE will be considered. These might come up at any time during the lifetime of the group and beyond. They are collected here for convenience. Advice is given on how to respond to these questions, always remembering to model PACE when responding.

Why do I need to use PACE in my parenting? I parented my other children as I was raised and they have turned out okay.

The facilitator will acknowledge that this is a good question. It can feel frustrating to be given different parenting advice and might even lead a parent to question what he has done before. Secure children will do well with the parent's well-intentioned parenting of them. However, PACE is an attitude which can strengthen any relationship. We all want to be understood and accepted for who we are. When a child experiences safety in relationships she will develop resilience. A PACE attitude from a parent will increase wellbeing even when the child is not needing to heal from trauma and a fear of relationships. A traumatized child can only start to heal when she begins to feel a level of safety within the relationship; safety which is taken for granted by the more secure child. PACE is an essential part of the parenting experience which can give this sense of safety. The relationship needs to be experienced by the child as more important to the parent than attending to her behaviour; only in this way can the child start to develop trust and thus can become open to relationship and the comfort and joy that this can offer. With this trust, she will accept necessary restrictions on her behaviour. Without trust she is likely to be non-compliant and oppositional when restrictions are applied.

I am trying to use PACE, but it is so difficult. What can I do?

The facilitator will acknowledge that PACE is hard, but also encourage the parent to reflect that it is worth the effort as she notices her child growing in security with her. Some parents use PACE very intuitively; it comes naturally to them. Many of us, however, have to really work at this. With commitment and practice we can improve in our ability to maintain the attitude of PACE. The dual capacities for emotional regulation and mentalization will support the use of PACE. If the parent has weak capacity for emotional regulation and struggles to be mind-minded towards her child she will be weak in PACE. The effort to use PACE will, however, help her to strengthen these capacities. The facilitator can notice that we all have to start somewhere. By making the effort to adopt an attitude of PACE the parent will find that she grows in her ability to regulate and mentalize. Good self-care, social support and self-understanding will also help parents to strengthen their emotional regulation and capacity for mentalization. Attending to their own needs will strengthen their attitude of PACE. The final module will provide guidance about how parents can look after themselves.

I am using PACE but my child is not changing.

The facilitator will first acknowledge with PACE the parent's motivation to help the child and be accepting and empathic of the parent's experience of feeling that this is not working. This might be a feeling of frustration, failure, hopelessness or anger. Then the parent wonders what the long-term goal might be for the child. This is likely to be around the child being successful, healthy, and able to have good relationships. Notice that to achieve this, the child will need to be able to trust, connect, enter intersubjective relationships and not experience high levels of shame. A narrow goal of behaviour change, even if it can be realized quickly, is not likely to achieve this for the child. Parenting by the long route is needed to help the child with 'connection' as well as 'correction'. PACE will help the parent to stay regulated, connected and open and engaged to the child. This ultimately will help the child to change in positive directions. This is not a quick fix but a journey that the parent is going on with the child.

When I use PACE my child gets angry and tells me to stop it.

The facilitator will empathize with how difficult this is. The parent is working hard to help the child and to apply the ideas learned during the programme but this is being thrown back in his face. Acknowledge and accept the parent's fear that this is not going to be helpful after all; maybe his child needs something different. PACE is an attitude that connects emotionally with the child. Children with developmental traumas have learnt to defend against such connections because of the pain and fear they have experienced when they have been emotionally open to parents in the past. PACE can therefore evoke the child's vulnerability, and the child resists this, anticipating more pain and fear. For example, she does not experience safety in feeling sad, and being open to comfort. The anger is a way of defending against this emotional vulnerability. As the child develops safety over time she will begin to feel greater trust in the parents and allow herself to be vulnerable, confident in their support at these times. If the parent can maintain the attitude of PACE and accept the child's feelings of anger she will, over time, feel less angry and be more open to emotional connection. The parent might also be curious about the child's regulation at the point at which the parent is expressing empathy and curiosity towards the child. Does the parent need to find ways to help the child feel calmer and more soothed? What works for this child: staying close but giving the child some space; giving the child a hug; perhaps something more active, such as a walk, food, drink? When the child is more regulated she may then be open to some gentle PACE or some wondering aloud near to her.

I am trying to have a PACE attitude but my child seems to be getting more distressed.

Acknowledge that this can feel like a step backwards to the parent. However, as was explored in Module One, children who have experienced a lack of comfort early in life adapt by blocking the experience of social pain; this is pain that arises from within a relationship. When a child begins to find safety in a relationship with a parent she does not need this adaptation any more. It is safe for the child to experience pain and sadness because she now trusts a parent who can offer comfort. The child will begin to allow herself to be more vulnerable, to experience pain and distress that she had previously blocked and to turn to the parent for comfort with these experiences. The child will be more emotionally distressed because she trusts the parent to help her with this. She no longer needs to suppress this distress behind anger and oppositionality. Commonly, the first tentative explorations into distress are brief and the parent might notice an oscillation between vulnerability and anger as the child moves towards and then retreats from these experiences. The parent might want and hope that the child can be happy, but it is also important that he can stay open to emotional distress. When parents experience distress in their child as a sign of failure or as PACE not working, they will become defensive. This is a sign to the children that their trust was misplaced. When this happens the parent needs to attend to the relationship again, providing a repair to the rupture his defensiveness might have caused. Without such a repair the child is likely to suppress the emotional distress again and revert to previous adaptations to the anticipation that parents will not be available or comforting.

I thought that my child was responding to my PACE attitude but then she will do something which just spoils it and it feels like we are back at the beginning again.

This is so hard; to feel you are making progress and then to see it moving backwards can make any parent doubt what he is doing. However, progress is rarely straightforward and ups and downs are likely to be common. The facilitator can help the parent think about how when he has developed a new habit or skill, progress could feel very inconsistent. It is with practice that the new becomes habitual. Any new learning requires new neural pathways to be formed within the brain. As the skill or habit is practised these pathways strengthen, or in neurological terms, become myelinated. Consistency only comes with practice. An analogy might help the parent to understand this. Imagine taking a daily walk through a field: if you walk across the field in the same way a number of times a path will begin to form. At first this path will be unstable; if you walk a different way for a few days the grass will grow back and the emerging path will disappear. The more that you take the same path, however, the more stable it becomes.

Parents can find the ups and downs of the child's functioning harder to cope with than when no progress is being made. When the child is doing well the parent can relax and start to enjoy the relationship he is offering to the child, and which is now being received. The child then feels a need to retreat from the warm feelings that comfort and joy in relationship can bring. She is still uncertain that she deserves this and fears that she might lose what she is starting to like. She does something to create distance again. This might be a way of testing the parent: is this a part of me that will drive you away? Alternatively, she might be ensuring that she can still manage without the thing that she believes she doesn't deserve. At these times, it is easy for the parent to lose confidence. He might doubt that any progress observed was real. He might despair, unsure that he can go through it all again. This can be experienced as a 'dopamine crash'. The warmth and connection that was present in the relationship with the child leads to increased dopamine, allowing the parent to feel good about this. The disruption to the relationship as the child retreats again can lead to a crash, as dopamine rapidly reduces. This can feel worse than not experiencing the dopamine reward at all. It is hard to continue offering PACE with the discouragement and pain that this can bring.

My child seems to manage me being curious but hates it when I am empathic.

The facilitator will explore the parent's experience of this. Sometimes parents will use empathy as a technique without feeling it. As the facilitator explores the parent's feelings of frustration, anger, or sense of failure, and how this makes genuine empathy difficult for him, he might be able to be more curious and accepting of his child's experience. This will increase understanding and elicit deep feelings of empathy for the child which can be communicated with genuine feeling. Parents may try to 'fake it until they make it', but this will not be helpful for expressing PACE, which needs to come from the core of the self. Instead, suggest parents find helpful people in their life who can have PACE for them and their experience of the child; as the parent feels connected and emotionally supported by others he will be able to 'make it' without any need for fakery.

Wonder too whether the child is struggling with the intensity of the relationship that is provided with PACE. Some children who have high levels of mistrust may be helped to experience empathy more indirectly initially. Allow them to hear the empathy without having to respond to it. Talk to another person, a family pet, a soft toy. When the child is ready to respond, she will let the parent know. The facilitator can help the parent to think about when direct empathy is provided and how this is conveyed. When we communicate empathy we tend to be quite animated and musical in our communication. We use intonation and rhythm in speech to convey what we are feeling. This is called prosody. Children who struggle with empathy will need to hear less prosody in the voice. This means parents being more matter-of-fact in their speech. Prosody can increase as the child becomes more tolerant of empathy, but for a while she might need this lighter empathy.

For my child empathy is helpful but curiosity just isn't accepted. She calls me a freak and a witch.

PACE from the facilitator will help the parent to acknowledge and feel accepted for his experience of this. He is likely to be feeling quite rejected by the child and need acceptance for this. Then the facilitator can wonder about the child's early experience of others making sense of her feelings and thinking. If the child is not likely to have experienced much of this, wonder what it must be like as an older child to have a parent who appears to know what she is thinking and feeling. Wonder how the parent might express acceptance for the strangeness and perhaps fear of this that the child is experiencing. Bigger empathy and lighter curiosity might be helpful as the child becomes used to others talking about her inner experience. Express curiosity less often and more tentatively. The child might also be helped by hearing family members wonder about each other's inner experience. Let her witness this without the intensity of having to hear it about herself. Watching TV programmes and films together can also be a way of noticing what others might be thinking and feeling.

When I ask my child what she is feeling, she just shouts at me that she doesn't know.

Again, the facilitator will begin with PACE for the parent, and then gently explore how he is talking with the child. Is he expecting the child to know, without acceptance that the child might not know? Is he losing the story-telling in his well-meaning effort to question the child? Is he mindful of the child's emotional maturity and early experience? Does he need to help the child to know what she is experiencing without expectation that she will be able to tell him?

When I am playful with my child she just gets over-excited, or spoils it in some way; it all ends in tears.

PACE for the parent can lead to some exploration of how he is being playful and whether he is mindful enough about regulation as well. Is he expecting too much from the child? Is he over-arousing? Tickling, for example, can be too intense for children. Is he planning activities which are too much for the child? Large days out can be too exciting and challenging, and trigger worries for the child that she does not deserve these. PACE is much more about joy in relationship than activities, and small playful moments are equally if not more important than sustained experiences. In fact, children can experience a strong need to put distance back into the relationship after a long period of connection. Small moments, on the other hand, can be accepted without anxiety.

I can't always find ways to be playful with my child. Sometimes it doesn't feel right to be playful.

Sometimes parents want to be playful in every interaction, or even think that they need to start with playfulness each time. The facilitator notices how hard the parent is trying to make this work and gently reminds him that playfulness comes in and out. A background of ACE is always helpful but the P comes and goes as suits the moment.

I just can't be PACE all the time. When I get cross or start nagging I feel so disappointed with myself.

The facilitator needs to be careful not to jump straight to reassurance here. We want the parent to hear that it is all right to get it wrong sometimes. It is human to move from open and engaged to defensive, but first the parent needs to be heard by us that he has strong feelings about not 'getting it right'. Then he will be ready to explore how normal this is, and to have compassion for himself. Also, a gentle reminder about relationship repair can remind the parent that there is something he can do to restore the relationship even after the most difficult of times.

PACE just isn't working.

When parents stress that PACE is 'not working' they can be experiencing a mixture of feelings: a sense of failure; disappointment that this isn't the answer they were looking for; hopelessness that nothing seems to make a difference. It will be important to understand and accept these difficult feelings before gently wondering if the parent had focused enough on the relationship, the child's feelings of shame, fear of connection, and need for regulation. Has the focus become a bit too narrowly on the behaviour? If this is the case it might be that in 'using' PACE, the parent may have wobbled with acceptance. His well-meaning desire to help his child to feel happier, less troubled, better behaved, etc., means that it is hard to accept where she is right now. When acceptance reduces, it can make curiosity more intrusive and empathy more misattuned, not matched to how the child is feeling.

How can I have PACE with two or more children?

It is difficult to advise, especially if there are fewer parents than there are children and so all the children cannot be attended to at the same time. Sibling rivalry can be very intense for children who have developmental trauma because of the fears of abandonment that the children experience. Parents need enormous empathy based on a good understanding of how challenging this can be. Parents will need to deal with any immediate threats to safety for the children and then decide which child to focus on whilst helping the other child(ren) to know that they are not forgotten.

Typically, a parent will support the most dysregulated child first but this can leave a less dysregulated child who is equally struggling unsupported, perhaps reinforcing the self-reliance that she has learnt to help her survive. Wonder how the parent might let all children know that they are being thought about whilst also focusing on the child who needs immediate regulation. Empathize with how emotionally exhausting this can be, but ensure that the other child(ren) will get some supportive time with the parent as well, even if later in the day.

What about when we are in a public place and my child is having a meltdown?

The facilitators will acknowledge how difficult this can be and notice with the parent how fear of judgement by others can move them away from being open and engaged and towards defensive responding. This can prolong the meltdown. The focus needs to be on the child, and the responses and disapproval of others can be ignored. With strangers, it can be helpful to remember that you are not likely to see them again. With familiar people, the parent equally needs to block out their judgement, but then will decide whether this is a person he feels he could have on his side. Is it worth investing in helping him to understand the struggles the child is having? Family members can be equally unhelpful as they try to give good advice or outright criticism. Again, a decision needs to be made about how much to invest in trying to help them to understand. The parent's resilience and confidence in what he is doing will be helpful, and so it is important to have people in his social network who do get it and support him in what he is trying to do. This can maintain resilience in the face of less helpful people.

My child has learning difficulties; will PACE still be helpful for her?

All children, whatever their ability or disability, will benefit from parents who want to connect emotionally with them. Gently explore with the parent what expectations he holds for parenting the child. Does he have realistic expectations of what he might achieve or is he looking for PACE to somehow fix the child? Empathy and understanding for his desire to make life different for the child can lead to some exploration of what is realistic. PACE can build connection and security, but it will be a slower process. The child is likely to find life more stressful and therefore progress can feel like it is going backwards at times. The child is dealing with a double blow of trauma and disability and so the journey will be longer. Good support and an understanding school will both be important to help the parent stay with the attitude of PACE and to notice improvements, however small.

MODULE THREE
LOOKING AFTER SELF

SESSION TITLE: UNDERSTANDING ATTACHMENT HISTORY

AIMS OF SESSION

- To reflect on the previous modules and to explore the importance of looking after self.

- To reflect on the importance and relevance of early relationship experience when parenting children.

- To provide time for self-reflection, relating this to strengths and vulnerabilities for own parenting.

- To relate this self-exploration back to the idea of defensive responding to children and how to move back to being open and engaged.

SUMMARY OF SESSION

This session moves the focus in this module away from the children to the self. Group members are helped to reflect upon themselves in a way that relates this to their own parenting of the children. This session specifically focuses on an exploration of past attachment and other relationship history. This is likely to be an emotive session for parents and therefore it is important that facilitators are on hand to provide support as needed. It might also be helpful to know of local services that parents could be referred to if this session reveals a bigger need for therapy or support because of past history.

SESSION PLAN

Example session plan	
Catch-up, reflections and introduction to Module Three	20 minutes
Introducing the importance of early relationship experience	30 minutes
Discussion: How might this impact on parents?	10 minutes
Attachment state of mind	10 minutes
Break	20 minutes
Self-reflection exercises	60 minutes
Discussion: Moving from defensive to open and engaged	30 minutes

TRAINER NOTES[1]

EXPLORING PAST RELATIONSHIP AND ATTACHMENT HISTORY

KEY POINTS

* Past relationships, and especially past attachment relationships, can influence current parenting.

* Parents can be triggered to respond defensively to a child who reminds them of a past relationship.

* Unconscious parenting influenced by past relationships is linked to the attachment state of mind that earlier attachment patterns mature into.

* Parents will be helped to avoid this if they can reflect on current behaviours and past relationships with compassion for themselves.

* Reflection helps parents to stay open and engaged to themselves and to the child.

Past relationship history can have a big impact on the way parents relate to their children. Parents may unconsciously parent in response to the way that they were parented. For example, a parent may have experienced authoritarian parenting. Independence may have been frowned upon and she may have been expected to stay at home and help with household chores. Such a parent may do one of two things. The parent may adopt the same parenting style when parenting a child who is trying to establish his own autonomy and develop independence. She may be authoritarian in approach, stifling the child's attempts to be more autonomous. Alternatively, the parent may consciously try to parent very differently, perhaps over-compensating for experiences of childhood. In this example the parent may allow the young person too much freedom, failing to provide the boundaries that are needed for this youngster to feel safe.

This becomes even trickier if a child reminds the parent in some way of a past relationship. Parents might find themselves unconsciously reacting to the child in line

---

1   The accompanying online materials can be accessed at www.jkp.com/voucher using the code GOLDINGFOUNDATIONS.

with their feelings about the past relationship. For example, parents like the one above may struggle when the child is quite needy of them, perhaps restricting what he can do. This might be because of the age of the child or because of difficulties the child has. Parents might feel angry when they can't go out or do things they want or need to do because of the demands of the child. The unconscious anger towards their own parents' restrictions upon them might spill over into their feelings towards this child. Without good self-awareness and understanding the parenting becomes invaded by the experience of being parented.

It is not only historical experience of parents that can have this influence. Memories of any past relationships can be triggered by a parent–child relationship, whether it is parents, siblings, extended family, work colleagues or romantic relationships. For example, a parent may have escaped a relationship characterized by domestic abuse, or have left a job because of a bullying boss. If the child starts to become demanding or threatening to the parent in some way, this past relationship may come back into the present, and the parent experiences fear or anger towards the child that belongs in the past with this historic relationship.

This unconscious parenting in response to past relationships is linked to the parents' attachment state of mind. The way they learnt to relate to others from childhood, beginning with their attachment relationships, initially impacted upon how they related to later relationships. As adults, this is translated into a general state of mind linked to attachment experience; a way of orienting to all relationships.

Autonomous attachment state of mind

The secure attachment pattern of childhood becomes an autonomous attachment state of mind. These adults have a balanced view of their childhood. They recognize and value the strengths it has given them, but can also acknowledge any difficulties they encountered. They are aware of how this experience has made them the adult they are today. These experiences mean that as parents they can cope well with their children's negative as well as positive emotional states. This makes them sensitive and responsive parents who are able to stay regulated when their children express distress or dysregulation.

Preoccupied attachment state of mind

An ambivalent attachment pattern in childhood becomes a preoccupied attachment state of mind. When parenting the child triggers this state of mind, parents becomes absorbed or preoccupied with the past relationships. The feelings they have towards the person in the past become enacted in their parenting of their child. This preoccupation is generally unconscious; the parents experience themselves as responding to the child and not to the leftover feelings from their past. Being unaware of this influence the parents will struggle to alter or adapt their parenting responses to be attuned to the child's needs.

Dismissing attachment state of mind

Alternatively, an avoidant attachment pattern in childhood becomes a dismissing attachment state of mind. When parenting the child triggers this state of mind, the parents tend to withdraw from the emotional experience that the child is triggering within them. An emotional avoidance means that the parents cannot be aware of how the child is currently feeling as they unconsciously endeavour to remain unaware of how they felt at the time of their own past experience. Again, parents will struggle to care for the child in an attuned way.

Unresolved attachment state of mind

Most difficulty is posed when the parents have unresolved relationship trauma in their past. Distress in the child triggers a dysregulated response in the parents, as the unresolved attachment trauma from the past prevents the parents perceiving and meeting the child's need for safety and comfort. This is frightening for the child, and thus traumas are perpetuated.

Exploration of past relationship history, including early attachment experience, is therefore an important part of understanding current parenting challenges. Being able to reflect on past relationships with compassion for self is helpful. These relationships were difficult and understanding how they influenced the adult they have become is important. This can help parents to integrate this experience, helping them to distance themselves from it. In this way, current experience does not keep taking them back to their old struggles.

Moving from defensive to open and engaged

As the parents notice how their responses to their children are linked to their responses to previous relationships they will be able to consciously change the way they are responding in the present, remaining open and engaged to their child rather than becoming defensive with him.

This might include:

- Noticing in the moment and reflecting later with a trusted other. This will increase self-understanding and increase resilience to these moments with their child.

- Taking a break. If they can't physically take a break because there is no one else to care for the child, they can take a break from dealing with the issue at hand. Ensure safety but do not worry about discipline right now. This might be a time to do something regulating, including the child if they are open to this.

- When the parent can become open and engaged again, and if the child is sufficiently regulated, it might be helpful to reflect together upon what happened, remembering to begin with the child's experience and only later to expect him to think about anyone else involved, as in the 'parenting in the moment' experience.

- Be compassionate to self; know that parenting is a hard job and parenting this child has its challenges.

SUGGESTIONS FOR ACTIVITIES

Activities to support the exploration of early relationship experience, including attachment history	
As a whole group	Reflect on how earlier relationships can impact on parenting.
In small groups or pairs	Give group members an opportunity to reflect on their attachment histories, using Activity Sheets 23 and 24, if these are helpful.
Activities to support the exploration of defensive or open and engaged	
As a whole group	Revisit open and engaged parenting by thinking about the differences from defensive parenting, and how to move back to open and engaged from defensive.

PROCESS NOTES

Time will be needed at the beginning of this session for a general catch-up and reflection on the previous two modules, with their focus on understanding and parenting the children.

As we move into Module Three, the focus moves from the children to the parents, and to looking after themselves. The importance of this cannot be stressed enough. In many ways, these final two sessions could be placed at the beginning of the programme, such is their importance. The decision to place them at the end was made because it was felt that a deeper understanding of the challenges of parenting children with emotional insecurities is important first. Attempting to parent the children in different ways will probably highlight for the parents why looking after themselves is so important, making the importance of this last module very evident.

In addition, it is hoped that the time spent in the previous sessions will have built up safety and comfort within the group so that group members will be prepared to do some self-exploration. The facilitator explains to the group why this is important and how it can help to reduce the challenges of parenting the children that were explored in Module One. This will increase the capacity to provide 'connection with correction' as explored in Module Two.

This session can be emotionally intense, and experience of supporting parents in emotional distress will be important. Extra facilitators can be helpful for this session because group members might need support with this endnote exercise. However, it is not helpful to bring in a new person at this stage when feeling safe within the group is so important. A way around this might be to include student mental health or social care practitioners for the group. This will contribute to their learning and they will be able to support the facilitators in giving emotional support as needed. Graduate group members might also have an interest in coming back to help facilitate future groups. Their insight and experience can be helpful throughout the programme. They will also be on hand to give emotional support in this session.

Facilitators will also need to be alert to parents who are struggling to an extent that they may need further help. They can be signposted to services that can provide them with help from therapists and mental health practitioners with experience in working with parents caring for traumatized children.

REFLECTING ON EARLY RELATIONSHIP EXPERIENCE

The facilitator now discusses the importance of early relationship experience and how it impacts upon the way we develop and therefore its influence in determining the person we become.

Activity: Ask the group to reflect on ways that this might impact upon them as a parent.

The facilitator then links this to an understanding of attachment theory, noticing how patterns of attachment develop into adult attachment states of mind, which can influence the way we parent.

Activity: Group members are now encouraged to reflect upon their past relationship experience. Group members can be given the choice of doing this alone, in pairs or in small groups, depending on what they feel most comfortable with. Activity Sheets 23 and 24 can be used to guide this exploration. Encourage group members to notice resilience and strengths that they have developed as well as areas where they feel more vulnerable. This can be an emotive exercise so facilitators need to be on hand to provide support as needed.

MOVING FROM DEFENSIVE TO OPEN AND ENGAGED

This session ends with a further focus on building trust and security within the child by learning to parent in an open and engaged way. These ideas were met earlier in the programme but are revisited here.

Activity: Ask group members to recall the difference between being open and engaged and being defensive, with answers being flipcharted.

Now ask the group to reflect on things that might move them from open and engaged to defensiveness. For example, this might be things that the child does, things that are going on externally leading to increased stress, or things that the parent is doing. Again, these responses can be flipcharted.

The facilitator draws this together by noticing how past experiences can act as triggers for current experience. Help group members to think about what their trigger points might be as identified in their earlier reflections. Notice how children who are insecure will often seek out these 'buttons to push', and think about reasons why they might be motivated to do this.

Finally, the facilitator helps the group to reflect on what they might do when their buttons are pushed. It is important to reduce feelings of guilt about this by demonstrating that this is a normal part of parenting, and all of us will succumb at times. Remind group members of the 'parenting in the moment' sequence explored earlier in the programme and encourage group members to:

- Notice, so that they can reflect upon this later with a trusted other. This will increase self-understanding, increasing their resilience to these moments with their child.

- Take a break, if possible, when they can feel themselves becoming defensive. If they can't physically take a break because there is no one else to care for the child, they can take a break from dealing with the issue at hand. Ensure safety but do not worry about discipline right now. This might be a time to do something regulating, including the child if he is open to this.

- When the parent can be open and engaged again, and if the child is sufficiently regulated, it might be helpful to reflect together upon what happened, remembering to begin with the child's experience and only later expect him to think about the parent or anyone else involved, as in the parenting in the moment experience.

- Not be too hard on themselves if they feel like they 'blew it'. Encourage them to be compassionate to themselves; know that parenting is a hard job and parenting this child has its challenges. Whatever happened, focus now on feeling better in themselves and repairing the relationship with the child. If the child remains angry and/or rejecting they should be accepting that this is how he is feeling right now and let him know that they will continue to love him no matter what and that they have a strong belief that the relationship will survive this difficulty.

SESSION TITLE: SELF-CARE AND BLOCKED CARE

AIMS OF SESSION

- To check in with group members after the emotive self-reflection of the previous session.

- To consider the importance of self-care to maintain resilience as a parent.

- To explore the concept of blocked care and to provide an opportunity to reflect on this in relation to the self.

- To explore ways to care for the self and to make a self-care plan.

- To review the Foundations for Attachment Model and have a preview of the House Model of Parenting.

SUMMARY OF SESSION

This is the last session of the group and the focus is very much on looking after self. The importance of self-care is emphasized if group members are to maintain their resilience as parents. Group members will leave this session with the beginning of a self-care plan. The importance of this is reinforced by the exploration of blocked care. Group members will be introduced to the risk of blocked care when parenting children who experience blocked trust. They will consider how to recognize that they are experiencing blocked care and what to do to protect themselves from this, as well as how to recover from episodes that they might experience.

The session ends with a quick revision of the whole Foundations for Attachment Model of parenting, and when relevant a preview of the House Model of Parenting that group members might go on to explore. This might be through a future group experience or by reading the book *Nurturing Attachments* (Golding 2008), which explores this model.

SESSION PLAN

Example session plan	
Catch-up and reflection	15 minutes
Reflection on self-care	30 minutes
Exploration of blocked care	25 minutes
Break	20 minutes
Self-reflection with reference to blocked care	20 minutes
Protecting self from blocked care	20 minutes
Mindfulness practice	15 minutes
Developing a self-care plan	20 minutes
Review of Foundations for Attachment Model and introduction to House Model of Parenting	15 minutes

TRAINER NOTES[2]

SELF-CARE

Self care builds resilience

KEY POINTS

* * The importance of self-care for building resilience as a parent.

* * Self-care which allows others to help increase the emotional support that the patient is receiving.

* * Self-care reduces the feeling of being emotionally overwhelmed.

* * Building in activities to improve mental health and wellbeing allows more time and energy for building the relationship with the child.

Self-care is a critical part of parenting children with relationship difficulties. Staying open and engaged with someone who is behaving defensively begins here. Self-care builds emotional resilience and enhances the ability to move out of defensive responding.

Self-care involves:

* ensuring that the parent gets a good level of emotional support

* building emotional reserves; time and space to recharge emotional batteries

* reducing feelings of being emotionally overwhelmed through time for self and good social support.

As will be explored within this session, self-care is also a protection from blocked care, and can help with the recovery from blocked care.

Dan Siegel and his colleague suggest a 'healthy mind platter' for self-care (Rock and Siegel 2011). They suggest that parents attend to:

* *physical health:* aerobic exercise increases heart rate and improves physical health

* *focus:* periods of focusing on one thing at a time

---

2   The accompanying online materials can be accessed at www.jkp.com/voucher using the code GOLDINGFOUNDATIONS.

- *down time:* allowing time in the day when nothing needs to be attended to

- *connecting:* time to connect with others and receive social support

- *sleep:* getting enough good-quality sleep

- *play:* time to be spontaneous and have fun

- *time in:* reflecting on inner world.

It can feel quite daunting when this list is reviewed. All this and parenting too! However, attention to this can improve mental health and wellbeing, allowing more time and energy for building the relationship with the child.

BLOCKED CARE

> ### KEY POINTS
>
> * Blocked trust in children can lead to blocked care in the parents, as biological systems for caregiving shut down in the face of defensive behaviours from the children.
>
> * The strength of the parent's executive system within the brain will determine how safely he can parent when in a state of blocked care.
>
> * There is a range of ways of experiencing blocked care linked to past and current circumstances.
>
> * PACE, relationships, ability to regulate and reflect and therapy can all be helpful in recovering from blocked care.
>
> * Mindfulness is an intervention that has been shown to be helpful in preventing or recovering from blocked care.

Parenting developmentally traumatized children can be challenging. These children tend to withdraw from the relationship with their parent rather than approaching it. They are in a state of 'blocked trust', fearing and mistrusting relationships and not experiencing security in the parenting they receive. Parents who are used to children trusting them, and feel confident in their abilities to offer a safe home and relationship to the child, can have the rug pulled from under them when trying to care for a child with blocked trust. Baylin and Hughes (2016) describe how a parent can be blindsided by intense negative reactions to his offers of love and care. This rejection can be intensely painful: a pain which the parent will reasonably try to protect himself from. The child's habitual defence against anyone trying to parent her can feel very personal when the parent becomes the target.

Continually offering a relationship without this being reciprocated can have a profound impact upon the parent. As illustrated in Figure M3.S2.1 (see page 171), Dan Hughes describes how the parent's caregiving systems within the nervous system can be active as the parent tries to provide the experiences the child needs. However, when the child consistently fails to respond with appropriate attachment responses, i.e. to be care receiving, this is experienced as stressful and the parent's own caregiving systems become weak or unstable. The functioning of the caregiving systems in the brain are suppressed, which moves parents into defensive responding and impairs their ability to attune to and connect with their children. In other words, the parents experience 'blocked care' in response to the child's 'blocked trust' (Hughes, in Alper and Howe 2015).

Hughes and Baylin (2012) describe the five caregiving systems functioning within the brain which allow parents to care sensitively and responsively to their children.

Approach

The hormone oxytocin is released in parents to prime them for caring for their children. This facilitates the parent staying open and engaged with their children instead of becoming defensive. The drive to approach and care for the child is activated whilst the drive to avoid is deactivated. When caring for the child is very difficult, less oxytocin is released, and the drive to avoid is more likely to be activated.

Reward

Social engagement with the child leads to the release of dopamine. This sustains the caregiving process as the parents enjoy interacting with and caring for their children. This is a reciprocal process as each enjoys being with the other; the relationship is experienced as pleasurable. When this reciprocal process does not happen, there is less dopamine and thus no feelings of pleasure. This leads to disengagement.

Child reading

The attuned relationship with the child facilitates the parents' deep interest in the child, and a desire to make sense of her experience. The parents can use their powers of empathy and mind-minded abilities to understand the child's feelings and needs. When the attuned relationship fails, this empathy and mind-mindedness declines. The parents become defensive and thus are not open and engaged to the child's experience. High levels of stress reduce mind-mindedness, impacting upon this ability to make sense of the child's experience; parenting becomes focused narrowly on changing behaviour, whilst empathy and compassion are reduced.

Meaning making

Parents are drawn to make meaning of their experience with the child. At its best, the parents will construct positive narratives (stories) about their children and about themselves as parents. This links with their past history of attachment and relationships, i.e., we make meanings through the lens of past relationships. When the parent–child relationship is under stress, parents tend to make negative meanings, as memories of past relationship stresses are activated. Under stress parents are more likely to hold negative narratives about their child or themselves which increases their defensiveness. For example, they may view their child as 'bad' or 'naughty' and/or themselves as failing.

Executive system

This is the integrative centre of the brain that co-ordinates the functioning of all the parts of the brain. The executive functions allow for integrated brain functioning so that cognitive and emotional parts of the brain work well together. These processes are responsible for guiding, directing and managing cognitive (thinking), emotional and behavioural tasks. Executive functioning allows purposeful, goal-directed and problem-solving behaviours. Parents can regulate their emotions and maintain a caring state of mind towards the child. This functioning is less dependent upon the child's influence upon the parents. Executive functioning will reduce under stress. If the parents have developed reasonable executive function they will be able to care for the child but, without the other caregiving systems working well, the joy in this parenting is lost. The parents do the job, but experience no pleasure in this.

When not in a state of blocked care parents can stay open and engaged to their children. Inevitably there will be times when they become self-defensive, but they do not get trapped here. Shifting between open and engaged and defensive responses is a normal part of parenting, depicting the usual give and take of parent–child relationships. Blocked care, on the other hand, represents the parent being unable to shift out of a negative state of mind towards the child. The parent remains defensive as a protection against the pain of rejection that she is experiencing from the child (Baylin and Hughes 2016). As blocked trust suppresses the pain of loss, neglect and abuse a child has experienced or anticipates experiencing from parents, blocked care suppresses the pain of rejection a parent is experiencing from the child.

Blocked care can develop in a range of ways.

- *Chronic blocked care.* This can occur when parents have experienced very high levels of stress beginning early in life. In this case the ongoing stress means that the care system and the self-regulation system are poorly developed. Thus, the caregiving process is difficult to activate and this, combined with an underdeveloped executive system, makes parenting attuned to the child's needs very difficult.

- *Acute blocked care.* This can occur when the parents experience a period of more acute stress. This overwhelms the parents' ability to cope and caregiving is suppressed. Support at this time is essential so that this temporary state of blocked care does not become more enduring.

- *Child-specific blocked care.* This can occur when children have difficulties which mean that they do not respond in the way the parents are expecting. This is especially difficult when the children do not respond in a positive, reciprocal way to the parents' care of them. The violation of expectations leads to more defensive responding from the parents as they feel rejected by and/or angry towards their children. This results in blocked care. Parents can be especially sensitive to this reaction to a child if that child reminds the parent of someone in their past that they had a difficult relationship with.

- *Stage-specific blocked care.* Children and adolescents can go through stages of being more argumentative and less open to their parents' caring behaviours. Some parents do well when the child is engaged and receptive to them but struggle during these stages of more challenging behaviours, especially when they experience this as rejection from their child.

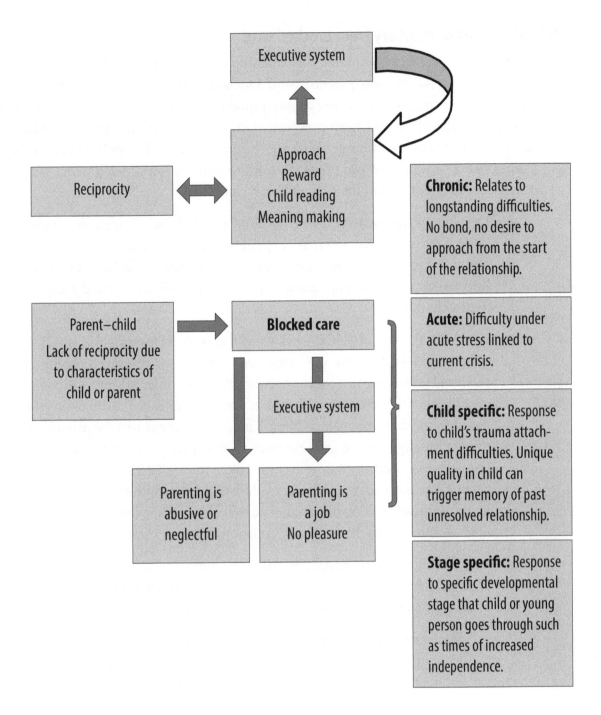

Figure M3.S2.1 Blocked care

Protection from or recovery from blocked care

Many of the ideas being explored for parenting children with developmental traumas will contribute to helping parents avoid blocked care. Support to return to these when experiencing blocked care can additionally aid recovery. This begins with the parent understanding and having compassion for her own internal experience and then extends to the attention given to the children. Good self-care has been explored earlier in the session. This can provide a solid foundation on which parents can apply the DDP principles within their lives. This includes:

- Developing the capacity for being mind-minded. Being open to noticing and understanding own internal experience can increase parents' empathy and compassion towards themselves. This can reduce feelings of failure and hopelessness, allowing parents to stay in touch with the internal experience of their children.

- Practising the use of PACE towards self as well as towards the children. The attitude of PACE allows the caregiving systems to work well, strengthening them and improving integration between them. At times of stress the parents can avoid becoming defensive and remain open and engaged to themselves and to their relationship with their children. This in turn strengthens the parents' abilities to emotionally regulate and increases their capacity for reflection. Regulation and reflection both further reduce the likelihood of defensive responding and so an open and engaged attitude to the child is strengthened further. This can have a positive effect on the child, who will also become less defensive and more open to entering an intersubjective relationship with the parent.

- This use of PACE requires the parent to embrace the mistrust the child is presenting her with. This has been variously described as hugging a porcupine or a cactus (Baylin and Hughes 2016, pp.90–91). As these authors note:

> We believe that the most powerful intervention for helping mistrusting children learn to trust trustworthy caregivers is to help caregivers embrace the child's mistrust. Rather than trying to redirect the child and eliminate the mistrust, the caregiver who can approach and welcome the child's mistrustfulness, greeting this part of the child with empathy and compassion, can create a window of new learning for the child, an opportunity to experience the crucial difference between past experiences with caregivers and the experience of being with a truly safe caregiver.

- Being surrounded by strong social relationships. It is especially helpful to experience PACE from another. Intersubjective relationships with trusted others can be very protective. Parents need good social support from others: friends and relatives who are able to understand and accept the parents' emotional experience, to communicate this through empathy, and can engage in a playful, mutually enjoyable relationship. These relationships help the parents to increase their capacity to withstand the stress of parenting a challenging child, and to be able to stay with their own use of PACE towards the child.

- By developing and strengthening abilities to emotionally regulate and to reflect on self and others. This means being open to both emotional experience and thinking about this emotional experience. When emotion and reflection work well together the parental brain is integrated and thus strengthened. This allows more resilience to stress.

- Parents can use their attachment history exploration to notice if they tend to try to avoid feeling things, preferring to rationalize and intellectualize, as in the dismissing attachment state of mind. Alternatively, they may find that they are easily overwhelmed by emotional experience without being able to reflect on this experience, as in the preoccupied attachment state of mind. In either case the parent will benefit from support to correct the balance. The dismissing parent can learn to become more open to her emotional experience. The preoccupied parent can learn to reflect on this experience from a distance, so that she is less caught up in her immediate emotions. Supportive relationships can help. Regular mindfulness practice has also been shown to be useful for restoring balance in the brain, strengthening healthy reflection and regulation.

- Therapy can also provide support for parents in, or at risk of developing, blocked care. Therapeutic support which offers the parent a non-judgemental, intersubjective relationship with the opportunity to experience PACE from another can strengthen emotional regulation. This also provides the parent with support to reflect on current and past experience and to make sense of how she is responding to this.

Mindfulness

Mindfulness is the ability to deliberately focus attention on feelings, thoughts and experiences in the present moment and in a non-judgemental and accepting way (e.g. Kabat-Zinn 2004). Mindfulness improves the capacity for compassion and intersubjectivity both interpersonally and intrapersonally (*The Mindful Therapist*, Siegel 2010). The mindful parents notice their here-and-now experience without evaluation. Mindfulness therefore has a strong resonance with PACE. This allows the parent to notice and understand her child's emotional experience without judgement, evaluation or attempts to change it, and to convey this understanding to the child through the intersubjective relationship. PACE therefore facilitates a mindful approach to parenting.

Training in mindfulness has been found to significantly reduce parenting stress and can increase the use of social support, improve the relationship with the child and reduce the child's behavioural difficulties (see Harnett and Dawe 2012, cited in Alper and Howe 2015).

Hughes and Baylin (2012) describe evidence suggesting that the practice of mindfulness can increase sensitive, attuned parenting. Mindful parental attention helps children to feel cared about and deeply connected with, and therefore can improve the relationship between parent and child.

SUGGESTIONS FOR ACTIVITIES

Activities to support the exploration of self-care	
As individuals or in a small group	Use Activity Sheet 25 to reflect on current levels of self-care.
Activities to support the exploration of blocked care	
In small groups	Use Activity Sheet 26 to reflect on risk of blocked care.
Activities to support the exploration of preventing and recovering from blocked care	
In whole group	Provide group members with an experience of a simple mindfulness practice.
Small-group work	Use Activity Sheet 27 to start constructing individual self-care plans.

PROCESS NOTES

It is important to allow time for a catch-up and reflection following the previous session. This will both remind group members where they had got to last time, whilst also giving the facilitators an opportunity to check that group members are okay following the self-reflection that is likely to have continued between sessions.

SELF-CARE

This session builds on the previous one, in which parents were encouraged to know themselves more deeply. In this session, the focus shifts to an emphasis on ways of taking care of self.

Activity: Start with a self-reflection exercise. Using Activity Sheet 25 ask individuals to reflect on how well they are currently taking care of themselves. This will lead into some discussion about the relationship between parenting and self-care. Often there is an inverse relationship between these with an imbalance between caring for others and caring for self. The group can reflect on what gets in the way of caring for self.

Now shift the discussion to a focus on why self-care is important and how this can be achieved. Consider the importance of building emotional resilience and reducing feelings of being emotionally overwhelmed. Dan Siegel's 'healthy mind platter' (Rock and Siegel 2011) suggests a range of activities that can improve self-care.

One risk of parenting a child with challenges that impact on the parent–child relationship is the danger of developing blocked care.

WHAT IS BLOCKED CARE?

The facilitator provides an overview of blocked care.

Review the caregiving systems:

- approach

- reward

- child reading

- meaning making

- executive system.

Notice that blocked care can develop in a range of ways:

- chronic blocked care

- acute blocked care

- child-specific blocked care

- stage-specific blocked care.

Allow discussion, especially focusing on any experiences group members have had with blocked care.

Activity: This can lead into some work in pairs reflecting on any risk factors individuals might have which increase their chance of developing blocked care. Using Activity Sheet 26, group members can reflect upon past experience, current experience and challenges that the child currently or potentially presents. Also, ask individuals to reflect on how they might notice they are moving into blocked care.

Protecting self from and moving out of blocked care

The facilitators now outline the various things that are protective against blocked care.

- *Self-care.* This relates back to the earlier part of this session; notice how self-care can increase general resilience, making it easier to manage the particular risks that parenting challenging children can present.

- *PACE.* This has been explored in earlier sessions and is therefore familiar to group members. Explore the way that PACE can be protective as it increases emotional regulation and reflection whilst allowing the parent to remain open and engaged to the child when the parent is at risk of becoming defensive.

- *Relationships.* Explore the importance of relationships, and the characteristics of relationships that are particularly protective. Notice that experiencing PACE from others is an important part of what makes other relationships supportive.

- *Strengthening regulation and reflection.* Explore the importance of these and notice how relationships can help to strengthen them. The facilitator can also talk about mindfulness and how this can be a protective practice because it strengthens regulation and reflection.

- *Therapy.* A little bit of time can be spent discussing how therapy can be a source of support. Outline the ingredients of therapy which will be most useful for parents who are experiencing blocked care.

Activity: If there is time following this discussion the group could be introduced to a mindfulness practice. Explain why mindfulness is a helpful practice supporting noticing and acceptance of experience. Introduce an exercise that will give some experience of this such as a breathing practice.

This can be followed by some discussion about how mindfulness can provide a practice that helps to notice and accept the child's emotional experience without getting caught up in defensive responding to it. This will help the parent make any discipline or gentle correction for the child more compassionate, increasing connection, as was explored earlier in the programme.

Activity: Allow time at the end of the session for individuals to begin to construct a self-care plan using Activity Sheet 27. This will help them to reflect upon what changes they would like to make in the way that they care for themselves.

CONCLUSION: REVISITING FOUNDATIONS FOR ATTACHMENT MODEL

As this is the last session time is needed before finishing to bring the group to a successful conclusion. The Foundations Model can be revisited to remind group members of everything they have covered and to encourage them to continue to reflect on their parenting using what they have learnt.

If there are opportunities for these group members to go on to a Nurturing Attachments group it might also be relevant to introduce the House Model of Parenting, to illustrate how they can develop their attachment-focused parenting further if they would like to. Group members can also be referred to the book *Nurturing Attachments* (Golding 2008) if they would like to explore this model by themselves.

Glossary

Abandonment

Children who do not receive the physical or emotional care that they need experience this as abandonment by their parents. This leads to continuing fears that this abandonment will be repeated in the future from significant people in their life.

Arousal state

Our arousal state describes how physiologically alert we are. As arousal increases, a person moves from calm and reflective to increasingly reactive.

Attachment theory

Psychiatrist John Bowlby developed attachment theory to describe the bond that develops between a child and parent. This bond is a response to the degree to which a parent helps a child to feel safe and secure.

Attachment is dependent upon an *attachment behavioural system*. Children have an innate predisposition to display attachment behaviours when they are feeling insecure or distressed in some way. The attachment behavioural system is activated leading to the child seeking proximity to the attachment figure, protesting separation from that person and therefore seeking to use the caregiver as a secure base. This behavioural system works together with the *exploratory behavioural system*. This is also an innate predisposition, this time to seek novelty and new experience. It focuses attention onto exploration and learning. These two behavioural systems are complementary: as one is activated the other deactivates dependent upon current circumstances.

The way that parents respond to the cues or signals that children give about their need to attach or explore represents the degree to which they are sensitive or insensitive to these signals. From this experience children develop attachment patterns.

- *Secure.* The attachment that children develop when a parent is experienced as sensitive and responsive to their emotional needs. The child learns trust in others and appropriate self-reliance.

- *Ambivalent-resistant.* Also called anxious attachment, this is the attachment pattern or style of relating that develops when attachment needs are triggered but the child has experienced the parent as inconsistent and unpredictable. The child maximizes the expression of attachment need in order to maintain the availability of the parent.

- *Avoidant.* This is the attachment pattern or style of relating that develops when attachment needs are triggered but the child has experienced the parent as rejecting. The child minimizes the expression of attachment need in order to maintain the availability of the parent.

- *Disorganized-controlling.* This is the attachment pattern or style of relating that develops when attachment needs are triggered but the child has experienced the parent as frightened or frightening. The child has trouble organizing his behaviour at times of stress. As they grow older, children with these patterns of relating under stress learn to control relationships to force predictability. Controlling relationships develop instead of reciprocal relationships.

Within the insecure patterns children develop ways of hiding and expressing needs in line with their expectations of their parents.

This attachment experience leads to the development of an *internal working model.* This is a cognitive model of the relationship (i.e. a memory or template) that the child has experienced. This model influences how the child will respond to future relationships.

Children develop multiple models of attachment influenced by the range of relationships that they have experienced. The model guides the behaviour that they will display within the different relationships that they go on to encounter.

Through adolescence and into adulthood, these attachment patterns based on multiple models transform into an attachment state of mind, based on the way the multiple models combine to give the adult a single more complex model to guide behaviour. Four states of mind are described which can be linked to the childhood patterns:

- *Autonomous attachment state of mind* emerges from secure patterns. The individual with this model is likely to have experienced a secure attachment relationship or to have resolved difficult experience with attachment figures. This experience will help the individual to be a sensitive and responsive parent.

- *Dismissing attachment state of mind* emerges from avoidant patterns. This individual is likely to have learnt to distrust emotional expression and to value self-reliance. As a parent, this experience will make it harder for the individual to recognize the child's attachment needs, will increase discomfort with the child's distress and will lead to a valuing of independence in the child.

- *Preoccupied attachment state of mind* emerges from ambivalent patterns. This individual is likely to have learnt to coercively use expression of emotion to keep others engaged. As a parent, this individual is likely to find the child's needs to be overwhelming, and will quickly feel emotional and angry towards the child.

- *Unresolved attachment state of mind* emerges from disorganized-controlling patterns. Past loss and frightening experiences remain a source of trauma. As a parent, the child's distress can trigger memories of this early trauma, meaning that the parent is unavailable to the child when needed most.

Attunement

An emotional connection between two people in which one person mirrors or matches the rhythm, vitality and affect (externally displayed mood) of the other.

Authoritative parenting

Parenting that provides a child with a high degree of warmth and nurture alongside clear and appropriate boundaries. The child is enabled to develop autonomy (independence) in line with the developmental stage he is at.

Autonomy

This represents the degree of personal independence an individual possesses.

Behaviour management

Behaviour management (sometimes called behaviour modification) provides a set of strategies for parents to use with the focus on changing the behaviour of the child. The aim is to reduce challenging behaviour and to increase prosocial behaviour: the behaviours we want to see children using. This is achieved through the use of consequences, sanctions, praise and rewards. In this programme I use the term *behaviour support* to describe an approach that has a focus on relationship, building connection and helping regulation; the support for the behaviour is then provided in the context of this relationship. This is captured in the expression *connection with correction* (see also **social learning theory**).

Blocked care

In a healthy parent–child relationship, caregiving in the adult synchronizes with care-seeking in the child. This is supported by five regions in the brain which, when working well, will help the adult to be a caregiver. These systems are:

- *Approach.* The parent seeks connection with the child.

- *Pleasure.* This is a reciprocal process as each enjoys being with the other.

- *Child reading.* The parent wants to make sense of the child.

- *Meaning making.* The parent seeks to understand the child. This links with past experience of attachment and relationships. Parents make meaning through the lens of past relationships.

- *Executive system.* This integrative centre of the brain makes all of this work but is less dependent upon the child's influence.

A state of blocked care can result when the child is unable to engage in a reciprocal relationship with the parent. The brain regions 1–4 above deactivate, leaving only the executive system working.

Blocked trust

Blocked trust is a failure in social relatedness. It develops as a response to frightening and painful relationship experiences with caregivers. The innate need for comfort and companionship is suppressed, leading to chronic defensiveness and a lack of social engagement. The child strives to be self-sufficient, keeping the caregiver at a distance through controlling rather than reciprocal relationships. This adaptation means that the child is not getting the social buffering needed to manage stress and alarm in the world.

In blocked trust, five systems in the brain have adapted to living in a harsh social world.

- The *stress system* is chronically activated, easily triggered and hard to switch off.

- The *social switching system* does not move easily between social engagement and self-defence, as appraisal of threat and danger during interactions is set very high.

- The *social engagement system* is suppressed.

- The *self-defence system* is activated.

- The experience of *social pain* is blocked.

Co-construction

Within DDP this describes the joint discovery of a story or narrative about the person's experience. Through the relationship the story emerges, helping the individual make sense of current or past experience.

Consequences

Any piece of behaviour is followed by consequences. These consequences will to some extent determine what we do in the future. Consequences therefore can be used to help someone to behave differently. In this programme I have called this use of consequences *coercive consequences*, as they are used in an effort to change the behaviour of the other. When the child is supported in a relationship he comes to understand his behaviour and the impact it has had on another. This can lead to feelings of remorse and a desire to make amends. The child seeks a consequence which can help him to repair. The parent can support him with this and thus the consequence becomes part of a collaborative process of planning for and making this repair. Thus, in this programme I have called these *collaborative consequences*.

Controlling behaviours

Controlling behaviours represent a need to feel in charge within the relationship. This is generally because the person fears a relationship which is reciprocal. She feels vulnerable being open to the influence of the other, so she seeks to coercively influence instead.

DDP

Dyadic Developmental Psychotherapy was originally developed by Dan Hughes as a therapeutic intervention for families who were fostering or had adopted children with significant developmental trauma and insecurity of attachment. The therapist facilitates the child's relationship with his parents through the development and maintenance of an affective-reflective (a-r) dialogue which explores all aspects of the child's life: safe and traumatic, present and past. The therapist and parent's intersubjective experience of the child provide the child with new meanings which can become integrated into his autobiographical narrative, which in turn becomes more coherent. In this way the child experiences healing of past trauma and achieves safety within current relationships. The conversations and interactions (verbal and non-verbal) within the therapy room are all based upon PACE and have a quality of story-telling. Dyadic Developmental Psychotherapy therefore is an approach within which the child and parents work together with the therapist. The child gains relationship experience which helps him to grow and heal emotionally as family members develop healthy patterns of relating and communicating.

DDP has a broader application as Dyadic Developmental Practice (see Figure Glossary 1). This provides a set of principles that can support networks, inform and enrich parenting, and support the child outside of the home, for example in residential settings and at school.

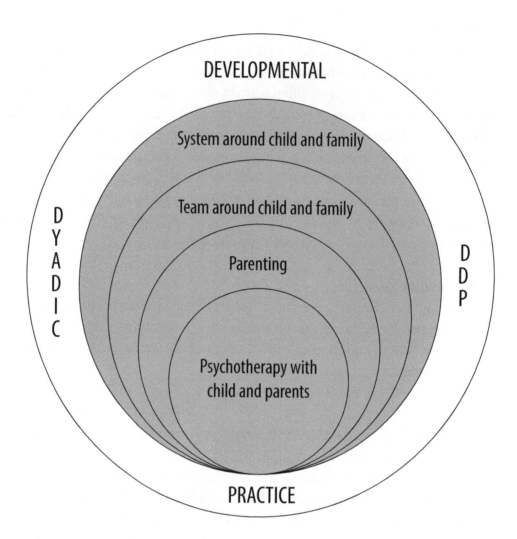

*Figure Glossary 1: Model of Dyadic Developmental Practice
and its relationship to Dyadic Developmental Psychotherapy*

DDP is theoretically based on the models of attachment theory and intersubjectivity, and is consistent with the needs of children and young people who have experienced developmental trauma.

Defensive

When we experience physical or psychological threat, we instinctively move to defend ourselves, through a range of fight/flight behaviours. If these options are not available to us we will move into shut-down responses (dissociation) as a means of survival. These defensive reactions are governed by the nervous system which can be sensitized to react more quickly for individuals whose earliest experience has been frightening.

Discipline

Discipline means giving another skills and knowledge through teaching. In childhood parents use discipline to teach children about their expectations of them and to give them guidelines and principles they can use to live their lives. These are based on the parents' morals and values.

Dissociation

This describes the process by which a person defends against overwhelming stress by cutting off from conscious awareness what is being sensed or felt. At its extreme, the person cuts off from contact with others or the world, becoming numb, unfeeling or unaware. Dissociation reduces the ability to make sense of self or others.

Intersubjectivity

In child development, intersubjectivity describes the relationship that develops between infant and parent. The infant has an innate ability to co-ordinate his actions with that of his parent so that they are both synchronized. This is necessary experience for social interactions. Children are able to emotionally connect with others, with their responses contingent on the response of the other. This is a bit like a game of tennis, when a ball is hit backwards and forwards between two players. Each player is influenced by the other.

Mentalization

Mentalization describes the ability to predict responses based on an understanding of the inner experience of others. For example, an understanding that someone is upset by an event might lead to an expectation that the other person will cry. This is dependent on the ability to take the perspective of the other person (*perspective-taking*). Mentalizing and perspective-taking rest upon the ability to think about our own mind and the mind of others, i.e. to have *theory of mind*. This in turn leads to a capacity for *reflective function*, which is the ability to understand why things happen and why people behave as they do.

Mentalization involves the parents holding their child's mind within their own mind and helping the children to experience the parent's mind within theirs.

One aspect of mentalization is the ability to be *mind-minded*, i.e. to be able to understand and take into account the mental state of another person, what the person might be thinking, feeling, wishing, believing, desiring, etc. When a parent can understand the internal experience of the child it is easier for her to emotionally connect with him.

Mindfulness

Mindfulness is the process of bringing attention to experiences occurring in the present moment. Attention can be directed to internal experience, for example our internal world of thinking and feeling. Alternatively, it can be directed to external experience, for example, to what we are seeing, hearing, smelling, tasting or sensing. When we are mindful, we are living fully in the present. It is therefore difficult to be mindful when feeling depressed, as this tends to take our attention to the past, or when anxious, as this tends to focus attention on to the future. Regular practice of mindfulness has been found to improve mental health.

Narrative

A narrative is a cohesive story of real or imaginary events. The narrative is at the heart of story-telling. Discovering the story is an important part of DDP, as we make sense of the experience of the other.

PACE

PACE is the therapeutic attitude that is used within the DDP model to facilitate emotional connection. The attitude of PACE offers an unconditional relationship expressed through playfulness, acceptance, curiosity and empathy.

Regulation

This represents an individual's ability to control and modulate his level of emotional arousal. This ability to regulate is influenced by the experience of *emotional co-regulation*. This is the experience children need when parents help them to manage their emotional arousal. *Emotional dysregulation* represents a lack of regulatory ability. This occurs when an individual fails to control and modulate his level of emotional arousal. The emotional experience overwhelms the individual.

Relationship repair

This is a psychological term used to describe the process whereby one person in a relationship repairs a rupture that has occurred within the relationship. A parent can re-establish a positive emotional connection between herself and a child (attunement) following a time when the relationship was ruptured, either because of the behaviour of the child or of the parent.

Self-esteem

This describes how people perceive themselves and their abilities. It represents their sense of their own worth. High self-esteem suggests that an individual perceives himself positively whilst low self-esteem represents a low opinion of self and worth to others.

Shame

A complex emotional state within which a person experiences negative feelings about herself; a feeling of inferiority, not feeling good enough.

Social engagement

Social engagement is the capacity to engage in social relationships, being open to responding to, as well as influencing, others in the relationship. Biologically, we are innately prepared to engage with others, but when we experience fear and trauma such engagement reduces. Within the DDP model the phrase *open and engaged* is used to describe a relationship where partners within the relationship are open to social engagement with each other. This is the opposite state to *social defensiveness*, when social engagement is reduced.

Socialization

Socialization is a developmental process of helping children to acquire the skills that they will need to engage in social relationships. This includes learning cultural norms and values so that the children are equipped to live within their own communities. This socialization process goes on through childhood and into adulthood, influencing behaviour, beliefs and the way that people make relationships.

Social learning theory

In behavioural psychology (social learning theory) the term 'reinforcement' refers to the consequence to behaviour. This consequence can be a *negative reinforcer*. This is experienced as unpleasant. The person behaves in a certain way in order to avoid the negative consequence. For example, a parent may buy a child some sweets to stop him crying. The sweet-buying behaviour in the parent has been negatively reinforced. Alternatively, it can be a *positive reinforcer*. This refers to a consequence to a behaviour that is experienced as pleasant and thus rewarding. The person behaves in a certain way in order to gain the pleasant consequence, for example, the child cries because the crying has been rewarded by sweets. The child's crying behaviour has been positively reinforced. Reinforcement, which is strengthening of behaviour, can be contrasted with *punishment*, which is weakening of behaviour. In behavioural psychology, punishment refers to a consequence to a behaviour that is experienced as unpleasant. The person stops behaving in order to avoid the unpleasant consequence. For example, if a child was smacked when crying for sweets, the child's crying behaviour would be punished, leading to the child stopping crying. As punishment also leads to shame and feelings of low self-worth and doesn't teach the child what behaviour is acceptable, it is generally considered to be a poor parenting technique. Parents are advised to reward good behaviour rather than punish bad behaviour.

Social learning theory has less focus on relationship and emotional connection and therefore is not attachment focused.

Therapeutic parenting

Therapeutic parenting is a general term to describe any parenting approach that aims to heal the child as well as to parent the child. There are lots of different parenting ideas described as therapeutic parenting. In this programme, a DDP-informed therapeutic parenting approach is described.

Trauma

In this context we are reflecting on psychological trauma rather than a physical trauma, such as a break to a bone, although both can overlap. Trauma is an experience of an event or events that involves actual or threatened death or serious injury to self or witnessing such an event to another person. Learning about unexpected or violent death, serious harm or threat of death or injury to family or friends can also represent a trauma. For the event to be traumatizing, the response by the individual is of intense fear, helplessness or horror. In other words, it is the experience of the event that determines whether it is a trauma for the individual. An event is traumatic if it is extremely upsetting and at least temporarily overwhelms an individual's internal resources. Such traumas can include extreme emotional abuse, major losses or separations, degradation and humiliation.

Complex trauma occurs when an individual is exposed to multiple traumatic events with an impact on immediate and long-term outcomes (e.g. war, ethnic cleansing).

When complex trauma occurs through childhood with early onset, is chronic and prolonged, occurs from within the family, and impacts on development, it is described by some researchers as *developmental trauma*. This is a useful description of the experience of children who develop attachment difficulties, blocked trust and fear of relationship. The children can become trauma organized in a pattern of highly controlling behaviours. When parents are trauma informed they can help the children to discover other ways of being.

Unconditional love

Unconditional love represents a love which will be given 'no matter what'. When love is only given if certain circumstances exist it is described as conditional: 'I will love you only if…', instead of 'no matter what'.

Verbal and non-verbal communication

Verbal represents the use of words to communicate, whereas non-verbal is the way we communicate without words. Communication is generally a mixture of verbal and non-verbal behaviours.

Zone of Proximal Development (ZPD)

Russian psychologist Lev Vygotsky suggested the zone of proximal development to describe how children can achieve more when the adults or older peers provide them with support to do this. He describes the ZPD as 'the distance between the actual developmental level as determined by independent problem solving and the level of potential development as determined through problem solving under adult guidance, or in collaboration with more capable peers' (Vygotsky 1978, p.86). In this programme, I am using this idea as a helpful way for thinking about the structure and supervision that children need to support their emotional development as well as their cognitive development. Expectations that are beyond the child's abilities are outside his ZPD, whilst low expectations mean that the child is not in the zone and doesn't make progress. If the parent provides support within the zone the child is likely to make emotional progress.

References and Reading List

REFERENCES

Alper, J. and Howe, D. (2015) *Assessing Adoptive and Foster Parents: Improving Analyses and Understanding of Parenting Capacity.* London: Jessica Kingsley Publishers.

Ainsworth, M.D.S., Blehar, M.C., Waters, E. and Wall, S. (1978) *Patterns of Attachment: A Psychological Study of the Strange Situation.* Hillsdale, NJ: Erlbaum.

Baylin, J. (2016) 'Mistrust to trust: The neurobiology of attachment-focused therapy.' Presentation to the DDP Conference, Glasgow, UK.

Baylin, J. and Hughes, D.A. (2016) *The Neurobiology of Attachment-focused Therapy: Enhancing Connection and Trust in the Treatment of Children and Adolescents* (Norton Series on Interpersonal Neurobiology). New York: W.W. Norton.

Blaffer Hrdy, S. and Sieff, D.F. (2015) 'The Natural History of Mothers and Infants: An Evolutionary and Anthropological Perspective.' In D.F. Sieff (ed.) *Understanding and Healing Emotional Trauma: Conversations with Pioneering Clinicians and Researchers.* East Sussex: Routledge.

Bloom, S.L. (2013) *Creating Sanctuary: Toward the Evolution of Sane Societies.* New York: Routledge.

Bowlby, J. (1988/1998) *A Secure Base: Clinical Applications of Attachment Theory.* London: Routledge.

Dozier, M. (2003) 'Attachment-based treatment for vulnerable children.' *Attachment and Human Development 5,* 3, 253–257.

Erikson, E.H. (ed.) (1963) *Youth: Change and Challenge.* New York: Basic Books.

Fonagy, P., Gergely, G., Jurist, E.L. and Target, M. (2002) *Affect Regulation, Mentalization, and the Development of the Self.* New York: Other Press.

Golding, K.S. (2008) *Nurturing Attachments: Supporting Children who are Adopted or Fostered.* London: Jessica Kingsley Publishers.

Golding, K.S. (2014) *Nurturing Attachments Training Resource: Running Parenting Groups for Adoptive Parents and Foster or Kinship Carers.* London: Jessica Kingsley Publishers.

Golding, K.S. and Hughes, D. A. (2012) *Creating Loving Attachments: Parenting with PACE to Nurture Confidence and Security in the Troubled Child.* London: Jessica Kingsley Publishers.

Hughes, D.A. (2009) *Attachment-Focused Parenting.* New York: W.W. Norton.

Hughes, D.A. (2011) *Attachment-Focused Family Therapy: The Workbook.* New York: W.W. Norton.

Hughes, D.A. and Baylin, J. (2012) *Brain-based Parenting: The Neuroscience of Caregiving for Healthy Attachment.* New York: W.W. Norton.

Hughes, D.A. and Baylin, J. (2014) 'From mistrust to trust: A brain-based therapy model.' Presentation to the DDP UK Conference, Birmingham, UK.

Kabat-Zinn, J. (2004) *Wherever You Go, There You Are: Mindfulness Meditation for Everyday Life.* London: Piatkus.

Main, M. and Solomon, J. (1986) 'Discovery of a New, Insecure Disorganized/Disorientated Attachment Pattern.' In T.B. Brazelton and M. Yogman (eds) *Affective Development in Infancy.* Norwood, NJ: Ablex.

Perry, B.D. (2006) 'Applying Principles of Neurodevelopment to Clinical Work with Maltreated and Traumatized Children: The Neurosequential Model of Therapeutics.' In N. Boyd Webb (ed.) *Working with Traumatized Youth in Child Welfare.* New York: The Guildford Press.

Porges, S. (2011) *The Polyvagal Theory: Neurophysiological Foundatons of Emotions, Attachment, Communication, and Self-Regulation.* New York: W.W. Norton.

Porges, S. (2014) 'Social connection as a biological imperative.' Conference presentation, Melbourne: Australian Childhood Foundation.

Rock, D. and Siegel, D.J. (2011) *The Healthy Mind Platter.* Available at www.drdansiegel.com/resources/healthy_mind_platter/, accessed on 07 December 2016.

Sieff, D.F. (2015) *Understanding and Healing Emotional Trauma: Conversations with Pioneering Clinicians and Researchers.* East Sussex: Routledge.

Siegel, D.J. (2010) *The Mindful Therapist: A Clinician's Guide to Mindsight and Neural Integration.* New York: W.W. Norton.

Sunderland, M. (2008) *The Science of Parenting.* London: Dorling Kindersley.

Trevarthen, C. (2001) 'Intrinsic motives for companionship in understanding: Their origin, development, and significance for infant mental health.' *Infant Mental Health Journal 22,* 95–131.

Tronick, E. (2007) *The Neurobehavioural and Social-Emotional Development of Infants and Children.* New York: W.W. Norton.

Vygotsky, L.S. (1978) *Mind in Society: The Development of Higher Psychological Processes.* Cambridge, MA: Harvard University Press.

ADDITIONAL READING

Archer, C. (1997) *First Steps in Parenting the Child who Hurts: Tiddlers and Toddlers.* London: Jessica Kingsley Publishers.

Archer, C. (1999) *Next Steps in Parenting the Child who Hurts: Tykes and Teens.* London: Jessica Kingsley Publishers.

Archer, C. and Gordon, C. (2006) *New Families, Old Scripts.* London: Jessica Kingsley Publishers.

Bailey, B. (2000) *I Love You Rituals.* New York: Harper Collins Publisher Inc.

Bombèr, L.M. (2007) *Inside I'm Hurting: Practical Strategies for Supporting Children with Attachment Difficulties in Schools.* London: Worth Publishing Ltd.

Bombèr, L.M. (2011) *What about Me? Inclusive Strategies to Support Pupils with Attachment Difficulties Make It through the School Day.* London: Worth Publishing Ltd.

Bombèr, L.M. (2016) *Attachment Aware School Series: Bridging the Gap for Troubled Pupils.* London: Worth Publishing Ltd.

> *Book One: The Key Adult in School*
>
> *Book Two: The Senior Manager in School*
>
> *Book Three: The Key Teacher in School*
>
> *Book Four: The Team Pupil in School*
>
> *Book Five: The Parent and Carer in School*

Bombèr, L.M. and Hughes, D.A. (2013) *Settling Troubled Pupils to Learn: Why Relationships Matter in School.* London: Worth Publishing Ltd.

Cohen, L.J. (2001) *Playful Parenting.* New York: Ballantine Books, The Random House Publishing Group.

Davis, J. (2015) *Preparing for Adoption: Everything Adopting Parents Need to Know About Preparations, Introductions and the First Few Weeks.* London: Jessica Kingsley Publishers.

Donovan, S. (2013) *No Matter What: An Adoptive Family's Story of Hope, Love and Belonging.* London: Jessica Kingsley Publishers.

Donovan, S. (2015) *The Unofficial Guide to Adoptive Parenting: The Small Stuff, the Big Stuff and the Stuff in between.* London: Jessica Kingsley Publishers.

Elliott, A. (2013) *Why Can't my Child Behave? Empathic Parenting Strategies that Work for Adoptive and Foster Families.* London: Jessica Kingsley Publishers.

Forbes, H.T. (2012) *Help for Billy: A Beyond Consequences Approach to Helping Challenging Children in the Classroom.* Boulder, CO: BCI.

Gerhardt, S. (2004) *Why Love Matters: How Affection Shapes a Baby's Brain.* East Sussex: Brunner Routledge.

Golding, K.S. (2014) *Using Stories to Build Bridges with Traumatized Children: Creative Ideas for Therapy, Life Story Work, Direct Work and Parenting.* London: Jessica Kingsley Publishers.

Howe, D. (2011) *Attachment across the Lifecourse: A Brief Introduction.* Hampshire: Palgrave Macmillan.

Hughes, D.A. (2012) *It Was that One Moment: Dan Hughes Poetry and Reflections on a Life of Making Relationships with Children and Young People.* London: Worth Publishing Ltd.

Hughes, D.A. (in preparation) *Building the Bonds of Attachment: Awakening Love in Deeply Troubled Children*, Third Edition. Lanham, MD: Jason Aronson.

Karr-Morse, R. and Wiley, M.S. (1997) *Ghosts from the Nursery: Tracing the Roots of Violence.* New York: Atlantic Monthly Press.

Lloyd, S. (2016) *Improving Sensory Processing in Traumatized Children: Practical Ideas to Help your Child's Movement, Co-ordination and Body Awareness.* London: Jessica Kingsley Publishers.

Music, G. (2011) *Nurturing Natures: Attachment and Children's Emotional, Sociocultural and Brain Development.* London: Psychology Press.

Perry, A. (ed.) (2009) *Teenagers and Attachment: Helping Adolescents Engage with Life and Learning.* London: Worth Publishing Ltd.

Siegel, D.J. and Hartzell, M. (2003) *Parenting from the Inside Out.* New York: Tarcher/Putnam.

Silver, M. (2013) *Attachment in Common Sense and Doodles: A Practical Guide.* London: Jessica Kingsley Publishers.

Staff, R. (2016) *Parenting Adopted Teenagers: Advice for the Adolescent Years.* London: Jessica Kingsley Publishers.

Sydney, L., Price, E. and AdoptionPlus (2014) *Facilitating Meaningful Contact in Adoption and Fostering: A Trauma-informed Approach to Planning, Assessing and Good Practice.* London: Jessica Kingsley Publishers.

Szalavitz, M. and Perry, B.D. (2010) *Born for Love: Why Empathy is Essential – and Endangered.* New York: HarperCollins Publishers.

Tangney, J. and Dearing, R. (2002) *Shame and Guilt.* New York: Guilford Press.

Taylor, C. (2010) *A Practical Guide to Caring for Children and Teenagers with Attachment Difficulties.* London: Jessica Kingsley Publishers.

ACCOMPANYING RESOURCES

The following materials can be accessed at
www.jkp.com/voucher using the code
GOLDINGFOUNDATIONS

ACTIVITY SHEETS

UNDERSTANDING A CHILD/YOUNG PERSON

Child characteristics	Developmental experiences (as any child)

Parent characteristics	Life experiences (specific to a child)

Additional complexity

UNDERSTANDING A CHILD/YOUNG PERSON
(BLOCKED TRUST AND FEAR OF CONNECTION)

Signs that my child might mistrust (blocked trust) *Reflect on early experience as well as current behaviour*	
Signs that my child is reluctant to engage intersubjectively with me	
What controlling behaviours does my child demonstrate?	
What behaviours suggest that my child is open to my influence?	
What can I do to help my child build trust and feel safe being open to my influence?	

UNDERSTANDING A CHILD: CASE STUDY*

Carmel's very earliest experience was of an emotionally absent birth mother and a frightening birth father. Many people came in and out of the house and fights would break out at regular intervals. Sometimes Carmel's eldest sister, Siobhan, would take her out of the house when things were really bad.

Carmel and Siobhan were eventually moved in an emergency to a temporary foster placement. They were removed by the police during a violent fight that had broken out within the house. At this point Carmel was two and a half years old. This was a first placement for the foster carers. They provided a quiet and well-ordered home, but struggled to manage Siobhan's difficult and testing behaviour. They were very fond of Carmel who was quiet and easy to manage.

A care order was secured and, following a range of assessments of family members, it was decided that Carmel would be placed for adoption whilst Siobhan would move to live with her grandmother. Carmel was moved to a new foster placement to prepare her for adoption. Her initial foster carers struggled to see her moved. They applied to keep her as a long-term foster child, but this was declined based on her young age and suitability for adoption. She continued to have weekly contact with her sister and grandmother. She additionally had monthly contact with her birth mother. Her foster carers declined to have contact with Carmel as they found this too distressing.

The foster placement that Carmel moved to was a busy home. Carmel was one of three foster children, and the foster carers' grandchildren visited regularly. Carmel was a placid child, who made few demands on her carers. It was noticed that Carmel found it much easier to play with the younger grandchild, whilst she struggled to connect with the grandchildren similar to her age. During this time Carmel had goodbye contacts with her birth mother, grandmother and Siobhan.

Carmel came to live with Chris and Paula when she was four years old. She is their first child and she has now lived with them for nine months. They are about to put the order in to legally adopt her. She is settling well into her new family, with some positive signs that she can seek comfort from her parents. Although initially very quiet and withdrawn, she is now becoming more outgoing. In the last three months, she has become highly attention needing, especially with Paula, who she does not like to have out of her sight. Carmel is developing a stubborn streak and a strong need to be in charge at times. She can be very distressed, for example, after a social work visit or following a contact visit with her foster carers. At these times, she becomes more withdrawn again and does not want Chris or Paula near her. Chris and Paula are also puzzled that Carmel can make a huge fuss over a minor cut on her finger, but when she had a nasty fall from her bike she acted as if nothing had happened. She also had a tooth abscess for several weeks before anyone realized.

Developmentally, Carmel appears behind her peers. Her speech is good, but she does not always understand what is said to her. At school her academic attainment is low and she is struggling to learn to read. She does not yet play symbolically with toys, preferring the sand tray and painting (mainly with her fingers!). Professionals are unsure whether her development is delayed because of the early neglect she experienced or if she has a degree of learning difficulty. It is known that she has a birth aunt with a significant learning difficulty.

---

*   This case study can be used for group members not currently parenting a child throughout the programme.

UNDERSTANDING AN ADOLESCENT: CASE STUDY*

Jacob spent his first five years living with his 16-year-old mother and much older father. His mother had grown up in foster care from the age of seven, and residential care from when she was 14. She met Jacob's father shortly after leaving care, and he got her involved in drugs. Pregnancy was difficult and Jacob was born prematurely. He was described as a fractious baby who was hard to soothe. He was presented to hospital on two occasions during his first year when non-accidental injury was queried although never substantiated. This couple went on to have two further children; Jacob had brief episodes of foster care around the birth of these children. There were concerns about neglect of the children's needs, and the home conditions were described as chaotic and dirty. However, Jacob's mother would respond to support workers coming in and helping her, and improvements would be sustained for a time. When Jacob was four and a half there was a serious domestic incident in which the youngest child also sustained injuries. The children were all removed and placed together into foster care.

The foster carers described Jacob as wild and unruly. He was oppositional, would have major tantrums and slept poorly. After six months, it was decided to place Jacob into a different short-term foster placement. His younger siblings remained in their placement until they were adopted a year later. Jacob responded well to an experienced foster carer, and some of his behaviours improved, although sleeping continued to be poor and he would also steal and gorge on food whenever he could. He stayed in this placement for 18 months before being moved into a long-term placement as a single child. He lived with this same-sex couple until he was 14. During this time, he had monthly contact with his mother, now in a healthier relationship and successfully parenting two further children. Jacob's behaviour always deteriorated leading up to these contacts.

As he reached adolescence, Jacob became increasingly hard to support. He would leave the house, and hang around with a group of children in the town. He had many exclusions from school, generally because of rudeness, absconding and verbal aggression. At home, he had a particularly confrontational relationship with one of his foster mums, although related better to his other foster mother. He was frequently verbally aggressive towards her, and had also begun stealing money from them both. When verbal aggression escalated to physical aggression, they decided they could not continue. Jacob rapidly moved through two more foster placements. An allegation towards his last foster carer led to him being placed within a residential home. He was nearly 15 years old.

Within the home, Jacob is described as very self-reliant. He does not engage with staff easily and is quick to become oppositional and verbally aggressive, especially towards the female staff. He is a little more compliant with the male staff. He likes to appear tough and uncaring, although with one member of staff with whom he has started to form a relationship he has occasionally shown a more vulnerable, scared side. He does not get on with the other two young people within the home, who feel rather scared of him.

Jacob is not in education as all attempts to reintegrate him back into school have failed. He is now being provided with an alternative curriculum. He is interested in cars and it is hoped he might be able to join an apprentice programme with a local garage.

---

*   This case study can be used for group members not currently parenting a child throughout the programme, including residential workers.

HANDOUTS

FOUNDATIONS FOR ATTACHMENT MODEL

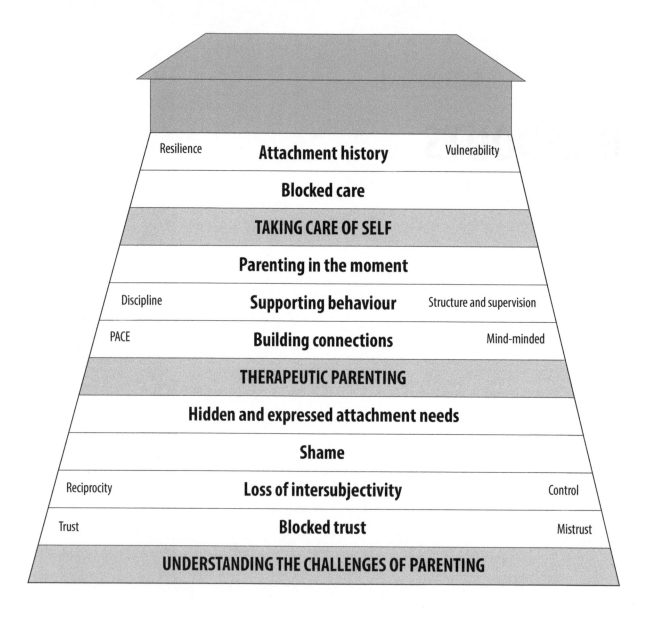

Resilience	**Attachment history**	Vulnerability
	Blocked care	
	TAKING CARE OF SELF	
	Parenting in the moment	
Discipline	**Supporting behaviour**	Structure and supervision
PACE	**Building connections**	Mind-minded
	THERAPEUTIC PARENTING	
	Hidden and expressed attachment needs	
	Shame	
Reciprocity	**Loss of intersubjectivity**	Control
Trust	**Blocked trust**	Mistrust
	UNDERSTANDING THE CHALLENGES OF PARENTING	

PARENTING CHALLENGE ONE: LOSS OF TRUST IN INFANCY

Good-enough parenting	
Connection	**Correction**
First year of life	*Second year of life*
Attuned parenting matched to emotional needs of young child	Child begins to develop autonomy and to assert independence
Provide experience of intersubjective relationship	Structure and supervision become important
Offer attachment security by offering comfort and facilitating exploration as needed	Parent also becomes rule maker and limit setter as boundaries are put in place: 'agent of socialization'
Development of **trust**	Trust allows child to believe in parents' good intentions and to know that the relationship remains unconditional
Experience of unconditional relationship – child is loved 'no matter what'	Accepts limits on behaviour because knows loved no matter what

Frightening parenting	Different parenting
No connection	**Connection plus correction**
First year of life	*Through childhood*
Poor and frightening parenting experience	Child is provided with improved parenting via fostering, adoption, kinship care
Poor experience of attunement and intersubjectivity	These parents have missed the sequential opportunity to build trust and then set boundaries
Insecure/frightening attachment experience	Parent tries to offer an unconditional relationship whilst also setting limits on the behaviour.
Loss and separation	
Multiple caregivers	
Development of **mistrust**	Parent needs to provide parenting that builds trust and provides socialization at the same time rather than sequentially. This can strengthen mistrust leading to blocked trust.
Relationship is conditional – child is loved 'only if'	Without trust, ordinary parenting can trigger ancient fears of abandonment. 'You do not love me. I am not good enough. You will hurt me and leave.'
Development of mistrust sensitizes the nervous system	Child learns to resist authority and to oppose parental influence
Social monitoring system is alert for signs of rejection, anger, neglect	Does not trust in parents' good intentions or in unconditional support and love
Social engagement system becomes inactive	Child trusts in himself rather than others and thus is controlling in his behaviours.
Social defence system becomes active	Control means they are not open to reciprocity. They influence without being open to influence and this feels safer.

BRAIN, BIOLOGY AND MISTRUST

DEVELOPMENT OF THE NERVOUS SYSTEM (ADAPTED FROM PORGES 2014)

> **Social monitoring system**
> (Am I safe or unsafe?)

Primitive nervous system
(old vagal system)

⟷

Modern nervous system
(new vagal system)

Safe:
Open to social engagement
but remain vigilant

Safe:
Socially engaged

Danger:
Mobilization via freeze, fight, flight

Safe:
Mobilization able to play, explore, learn

Life limiting:
Immobilization via faint, dissociation

Safe:
Immobilization via loving
behaviours, hugs

= **Defensive**

= **Open and engaged**

BLOCKED TRUST AND THE BRAIN (ADAPTED FROM HUGHES AND BAYLIN 2016)

Caregiving environment
Non-nurturing; distress met with pain, fear and/or silence

Inner life: terror and shame

Stress response system
High alert

Bottom-up reliance on self via heightened **self-defence system**

Tiger/opposum/chameleon

Chronic hypervigilance

Curiosity and new learning suppressed

Social switching system
Biased for danger

Suppress **social engagement system**

Can't experience comfort or joy in relationship

Inhibit **social pain system**

Lack of top-down social buffering to provide regulatory support

PARENTING CHALLENGE TWO: FEAR OF INTERSUBJECTIVE RELATIONSHIPS

INTERSUBJECTIVITY

Primary intersubjectivity

An attuned relationship within which the infant and parent discover each other and in the process discover more about themselves.

- Infant discovers he can influence the parent – beginning of autonomy.

- Infant is open to influence from the parent – beginning of capacity for reciprocal relationships.

Children experience emotional regulation within the relationship: a precursor for the development of self-regulation. Children develop a sense of self, reflected in the responses to her from the parents.

Secondary intersubjectivity

The child learns about the world of people, events and objects. The child and parent together focus their attention outwards. This shared attention helps them both to explore the world and learn about the impact of this world on each other. The child learns about the world through the meaning the parent gives it. As the adult helps him to make sense of the world he develops the capacity to think. In this way children learn that the world, themselves and other people make sense. This in turn allows children to reflect upon, process and learn from experience (see Trevarthen 2001).

Autonomy without reciprocity = controlling

Intersubjective experience = reciprocity. Children are open to influence and enjoy influencing. Lack of intersubjectivity leads to sense of shame and social defensiveness. Need to take control of relationships rather than engage in mutual influence.

- Children who experience neglect lack early intersubjective experience. They feel not special and not loveable.

- Children who experience anger, fear or rejection experience terror and shame.

Children learn to avoid intersubjective experience.

Impacts on caregiver

Living with alternative parents, the child avoids intersubjective experience and this can impact on the parent's beliefs about self as a parent – they feel that they are failing as parents and therefore do not feel safe with the child. They too withdraw from intersubjective experience.

Comfort, curiosity and joy

Sadness is the hardest emotion to experience for traumatized children.

They are afraid to feel sad, anticipating no comfort.

Help child to feel sad and become open to comfort again, i.e. help child to feel safe to be sad and need comfort; to be able to cry in parent's presence.

Need to recover the capacity for sadness

Open and engaged.

Safe to be curious and share in a state of wonder.

Ask you, 'Why...?'

Need to recover the capacity for curiousity

When children resist relationship they cannot experience joy within relationship.

Help child to shine in the delight of the other and to mirror joy in being with them.

Note: 'manic happiness' as a defence against sadness is not relational.

Need to recover the capacity for relational joy

ACTIVITY SHEETS

CASE EXAMPLE: ANDREW AND JOSEPH

It has been a fraught day in school. The children in Year 5 are all getting tired as the end of term approaches, and on top of this the rain has kept the children inside. Andrew and Joseph have been provoking each other all day. The teacher, Mrs Jones, and teaching assistant, Miss Smith, have tried to keep them apart, but during the last break time, whilst they are dealing with other children, a fight breaks out between them. Both children are removed from the classroom to wait for their parents to collect them.

At home time, Mrs Jones records the incident in the home-school book as agreed with Andrew's parents. She takes Andrew out to meet his mother. She briefly tells her that Andrew has had a hard day today, and expresses the hope that tomorrow will be better.

In the meantime, Miss Smith escorts Joseph out to his mother. She lets her know of the fight between the children, and again expresses the hope that tomorrow will be better.

Andrew and his mother walk home together. Judging that it isn't the right time to talk about school, instead Mum engages Andrew in a favourite game, making up words based on the car licence plates that they pass. Andrew is soon laughing as he makes up strange and funny words. They arrive home and Andrew has a drink and snack. He wants to watch television, but Mum suggests they figure out what was difficult at school today first. Andrew protests, but Mum gently talks to him:

Mum: It sounds like today has been hard. Maybe we can figure out what went wrong. (Andrew hides under the cushion, but listens.)

Mum: I wonder if you were worried about something at school today?

Andrew: No. I was just tired. (Andrew comes out from the cushion and looks at Mum.)

Mum: Ah, it's hard to manage school when you are tired, isn't it? It sounds like maybe you were feeling cross too?

Andrew: I was cross with Joseph; he was being really annoying.

Mum: That sounds difficult. You guys usually get on so well. I wonder why it was hard today?

Andrew: He was being a pain. He got more spellings right than me, and he kept reminding me. I told him to shut up, but he wouldn't.

Mum: That does sound irritating; no wonder you got angry with him. You tried so hard to learn your spellings this week. Were you upset that you got some wrong?

Andrew: Yes, I wanted to get them all right like last week. Joseph had his name on the board and I didn't. He wouldn't let me forget it.

Mum: I can understand that you felt cross with Joseph if he was teasing you like that. I wonder why he did that. It doesn't sound like Joseph.

Andrew: He was really pleased he got his spellings right.

Mum: I expect he was. He finds spellings harder than you, doesn't he?

Andrew: Yes, and I was cross when he got more than me. (Andrew looks embarrassed.) I told him he was thick and he must have cheated.

Mum: Ah, you were cross and so you said those mean things to him?

Andrew: Yes, I was really cross. And then we started fighting. I guess it was my fault, wasn't it?

Mum: It does sound like it. I guess Joseph was upset and then he got mad.

Andrew: Yes, and then we fought. Do you think he will stay mad with me?

Mum: He might for a while. I wonder what might help?

Andrew: Do you think I can phone him? What if he won't come to the phone?

Mum: Yes, it might be hard for him to talk to you just now. I wonder what else you could do.

Andrew: I know, I could give him one of my trading cards. I know which one he needs. When Dad gets home do you think you could take it round to him?

Mum: I tell you what, I need to take Bracken out for his walk later. You can help me and we can post it through their letter box if we go that way around. You'll have to miss television tonight, but it would be a help to me with Bracken, and Joseph would know you are sorry tonight.

Andrew (looking a bit doubtful): Okay, I guess.

In the meantime, Joseph and his mum have left the school. Mum asks Joseph why he was fighting. Joseph looks down at the ground and doesn't answer.

Mum: I am really not happy, Joseph. I don't like to be met by the teacher telling me you have been fighting. What on earth got into you? I thought you and Andrew were friends.

Joseph: I hate him. I'm never going to be his friend again.

Mum: What has got into you today?

Joseph doesn't answer as they get into the car. As they drive home Mum tries to find out what went wrong.

Joseph: It was Andrew; I didn't do anything. I hate him.

Mum: It usually takes two to fight, something must have happened.

Joseph: He called me thick.

Mum: Well, that doesn't sound like Andrew. What did you do to make him say that?

Joseph (shouting): I DIDN'T DO ANYTHING!

They arrive home and Joseph jumps out of the car and runs up to his bedroom. Mum reflects that maybe she hasn't handled this very well. She decides to leave him whilst she makes tea and then she will have another chat with him.

REFLECTION

What signs were there that either boy was experiencing shame?	What signs were there that either boy was experiencing guilt?
What did either mum do that made shame more likely?	**What did either mum do that made guilt more likely?**

UNDERSTANDING A CHILD/YOUNG PERSON
SHAME AND EXPRESSED/HIDDEN NEEDS

Shame Signs that my child might be experiencing shame	
Shame Has my child had experiences of shame regulated by me?	
Shame Are there things that have made it hard for my child to experience shame being regulated because of difficulties with attunement and/or relationship repair?	
Hidden and expressed attachment needs How does my child express need for comfort? How does my child express need to explore?	
Hidden and expressed attachment needs Are there any needs for comfort which are hidden away? Are there any needs to explore which are hidden away?	

EXPLORING THE DDP PRINCIPLES IN PARENTING

Scenario	DDP principle
Sarah has woken up late and is in danger of missing her train. She is very stressed as she tries to get ready. Her mum has offered to give her a lift to the station. Mum is getting impatient waiting for her to be ready. She shouts up, reminding her of the time. Sarah storms down, shouting at her to stop nagging and get off her back. Later that day when Sarah is home again Mum quietly talks to her. She apologizes for not realizing how stressed she had got and acknowledges that reminding her of the time was not the most helpful thing to do.	
Sienna has chicken pox, but is feeling better. She is bored, missing school, and it has been raining all day. Mum suggests that they put on coats and wellies and go out and splash in puddles. They have a lovely time splashing down the lane, getting wet and muddy in the process. They are soon laughing together as they find deeper and deeper puddles to jump in. The afternoon passes quickly and soon it is time to go home for a bath and tea.	
Keisha has moved into a short-term foster placement. She is frightened as she does not know what is going to happen. Her foster mum walks into the living room to find her tearing up her school books. Foster mum: Keisha, you sure look cross with those books. Keisha: I hate these stupid books and I hate school. Foster mum: You haven't been back to school since you came to live here, have you? I wonder why you are feeling cross about school right now? Keisha: I don't want to go. School is stupid! Foster mum: It feels like school is stupid so you thought you would tear those books up. Perhaps it is making you feel better, but I am wondering if you are worried about going to school tomorrow? Keisha: Everyone will look at me. I hate their stupid faces. Foster mum: Ah, it is so hard to go to school when so much has changed and you don't know what is going to happen. You must be so worried about what everyone will think when I take you to school instead of your mum. Keisha: I know what they will think. They will think I have done something really bad. I hate them. Foster mum (pulls Keisha into a hug and gently strokes her hair): It is so hard to leave your mum and not know what is going to happen. I am guessing you are worried that maybe you have done something bad too? It is so hard to understand why this has happened and so scary not knowing what is going to happen next. Keisha (crying): I just want my mum. Foster mum: I know you do, love, I know.	

Yadon has just been brought back to the residential home by the police, having been missing all night. Staff are concerned that he has been hanging out with local kids who are dealing drugs. Once the police have gone his key worker, Mark, sits down to chat to him. Yadon is acting like there is nothing wrong. He becomes angry and abusive towards Mark when he is reminded of the consequences for being out all night. Mark comments that although Yadon is saying he is fine and there is nothing to worry about, he can see that he is looking pretty scared right now. Perhaps it was being brought home by the police, or maybe something that happened overnight? Yadon denies this and continues being abusive for quite some time, but later admits that it was pretty scary the night before when one of the boys threatened him with a knife.	
Joshua has just had a visit from his social worker. He has been doing some early life exploration with him. Joshua is now sitting with his grandmother. He is feeling upset and wonders why his mum locked him in his room. Grandmother: I don't know, Josh, I wonder if your mum just didn't know how to look after you. Perhaps she was trying to keep you out of the way when your dad was drunk, I just don't know. All I do know is that you were such a little boy, and it must have been so scary for you all alone in that room. I expect you could hear all sorts of noises going on in the house, and you had no idea when anyone was going to come. What a scared little boy you were. Your mum has had a hard life, and one day I will help you to understand that, but she should not have looked after you like that. No little boy should be locked in a room with no one to cuddle him.	
Daniel has had a friend around, which was clearly a struggle for him. He found it difficult to share his toys and wanted to be the boss in any game they played. Now he is being bossy with his dad, refusing to eat the tea, which he suddenly doesn't like, and generally being unco-operative. Dad decides not to get into an argument with him. 'Come on', he says, 'you and I are going to take the dog out.' Fortunately, Daniel agrees. As they walk up the hill Dad quietly chats to him about how sometimes friends can be quite tricky. Daniel doesn't answer, and Dad doesn't pressure him to. They reach the field and Daniel enjoys throwing the ball for the dog. By the time they get home, Daniel is ready for his tea which he eats almost as fast as the dog eats his!	

Robyn is really angry with her mum. She wants to go on a school trip but has been told she isn't allowed to. Unreasonably she is shouting at her mother that it is her fault. Mum (with intensity and animation): I can see you really, really wanted to go on that trip. It seems so unfair that you can't go. Robyn: You told them, didn't you? That I shouldn't go? Mum: You think I told them because the last trip didn't go well? Well, I can see that would make you mad if you thought I had told them behind your back. Robyn: You must have, why else wouldn't they let me go? Mum: I don't know, Robyn. This school was meant to be a fresh start and now they are telling you that you can't go on the trip. I can see why you would be angry about that. Maybe it feels like they don't trust you at all. Robyn: Well, if you didn't tell them then they can't trust me? Why don't they trust me, Mum? I know I could do that trip. Mum: I think maybe you could too. I don't know why they have said you can't go, but I am happy to go and talk to them about it. Robyn: Thanks Mum. Mum does talk to the teachers, and discovers that Robyn has misunderstood. Two trips have been arranged so all the children aren't taken out at once. It was the first trip that Robyn couldn't go on!	
Ivy's stress has been building up all weekend. She had a family contact on the Friday and then her birthday on the Saturday. It is now Sunday evening and she has blown up over having her bath. She is now trashing her bedroom, but won't let her foster carer, Sandra, in. Sandra sits outside the door and tries talking to Ivy. This seems to be making things worse. The cat has come to sit with Sandra and so she talks quietly to the cat. She tells the cat that Ivy is really upset right now and doesn't want to come out. She has had such a lot to cope with, seeing her family and then having a birthday. She wonders whether not being with her family on her birthday was pretty hard. Sandra continues chatting to the cat whilst Ivy gets quieter. After about 15 minutes she comes out of her bedroom and cuddles with Sandra.	

HANDOUTS

PARENTING CHALLENGE THREE: LIVING WITH SHAME

When children are not helped to manage shame by their parents they become overwhelmed by these feelings. This impacts on their emotional development.

Things can go wrong at each of the three parts of the socialization process:

- *Little experience of attunement.* The child does not experience emotional states shared or contained by the parent.

- *Discipline occurs with rejection, humiliation or anger.* The experience of shame is excessive.

- *No or delayed interactive repair.* The experience of shame is not integrated. The child is unable to develop a capacity for shame regulation. The child develops a sense of self as bad.

Without parental support the child must find alternative ways of managing the overwhelming sense of shame that she is experiencing. The child develops defences against the feelings. Whilst these are adaptive in the short term, if stretched too far these adaptations start to become maladaptive, interfering with the child's emotional development and ability to relate positively to others.

These defences can be explored as a shield against shame (Golding and Hughes 2012).

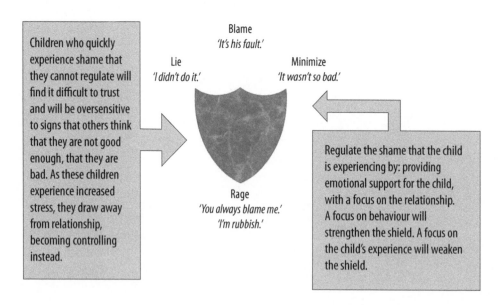

For children with insecure attachment relationships the experience of shame is disintegrative. These children do not experience the attunement–shame–reattunement cycle but instead they experience unregulated shame that overwhelms them. Many experiences of disintegrative shame lead to shame becoming part of the core identity: 'I am a shameful child.' This child becomes chronically angry and controlling of others.

PARENTING CHALLENGE FOUR: MISCUING THROUGH HIDDEN NEEDS

Attachment pattern	Expressed need	Hidden need	Head or heart
Secure	*Exploration and attachment* *Child:* I will tell you when I need comfort and reassurance I will enjoy you helping me to explore *Parent:* Offers comfort and reassurance when needed Helps the child to explore and learn in the world	None	Can use head and heart E A Attachment and exploration needs are in balance
Avoidant	*Exploration* *Child:* I will act like I want to explore even when I need comfort I will not show my need for comfort and reassurance *Parent:* Help child to feel comfortable needing and being helped by parent	*Attachment* *Child:* I will do it by myself I fear my need of you I will push you away *Parent:* Help to feel comfort and safety with the parent Support to accept nurturing Co-regulation of emotion that is hidden Help to trust emotion and to know that it will be acceptable to others	Uses head, ignores heart E A Exploration needs appear high; attachment needs appear low

Attachment pattern	Expressed need	Hidden need	Head or heart
Ambivalent	*Attachment* *Child:* I can't trust in your availability I need you to attend to me all the time *Parent:* Reassure about availability to the child Provide predictability and consistency Provide structure and routine Co-regulate expressed emotion	*Exploration* *Child:* I will not show my need to separate and explore I will pull you in and push you away to keep you noticing me *Parent:* The child needs to learn to be apart and to feel secure in parent's reliability Support to trust in parent's reliability and not just to rely on his feelings	Uses heart, ignores head Exploration needs appear low; attachment needs appear high
Disorganized-controlling	*To be in control* *Child:* I will not need you I must be in control *Parent:* Help child to trust in your ability to meet her needs Help child to trust in your ability to keep her safe	*Attachment and exploration* *Child:* I can't explore the world I can't seek comfort I am too busy keeping myself safe *Parent:* Help child to feel safe Provide a low-stress environment Help child to trust feeling and thinking Help child to develop emotional regulation and reflective function abilities	Can't use head or heart Need to control overrides attachment and exploration

DDP PRINCIPLES AND PARENTING DEVELOPMENTALLY TRAUMATIZED CHILDREN

The relationship:

- *Intersubjective.* Past experience has led the children to fear the intersubjective relationships they need in order to feel safe, to trust and for healthy emotional and social development. Children use controlling behaviours as a way of avoiding reciprocal interactions. They influence but are not open to influence. Connect with the child to help her to feel safe in relationships within which she is open to influence.

- *Attitude of PACE.* Hold an attitude of PACE to offer an unconditional relationship that is expressed through playfulness, acceptance, curiosity and empathy. Maintain a curiosity in the inner life of the child and accept this without judgement or evaluation. This acceptance is communicated with empathy for the struggles this experience can bring. PACE also offers the child fun and joy within the relationship, moments of healthy relationship and respite from the day-to-day struggles.

- *Open and engaged.* Be open and engaged by using PACE to connect intersubjectively. Often the children respond by being closed and defensive. Try to avoid joining them in this closed, non-engaged, defensive state. These responses will close down the relationship. Of course, you will at times lose the attitude of PACE and will become defensive, evaluative or judgemental. At these times, you can avoid the relationship being damaged through relationship repair as described below.

The relationship helps the child to:

- *Feel safe and secure.* Notice the child's verbal and non-verbal communications and whether these signal that the child is feeling safe or not. Safety can be increased by accepting and acknowledging the child's experience with PACE, and providing co-regulation as needed.

- *Co-regulate affect.* The child feels emotion which is expressed bodily through her affect. Match the vitality, intensity and rhythm of the affect. You can then respond with empathy, verbally and non-verbally. This helps the child to feel understood and aids regulation.

- *Co-construct meaning of experience.* Help the child to make sense of both present and past experience. When the child responds to PACE and her attention is held by your attentive stance there is an opportunity to put words to experience. This increased understanding can provide the child with flexibility to respond to events verbally and not just through behaviour. The world is explored in new ways, creating new meanings from within the relationship.

You can help the child by:

- *Discovering the narrative or story.* Instead of trying to change the child through reasoning, lecturing or reassuring, try to engage your child in understanding what is happening. In other words, discover and tell the story of the moment as it is occurring in the present and influenced by the past. The immediate aim is not to change the child but to be genuinely interested in understanding his experience.

- *Affective-reflective dialogue.* As in any good story, talk with the child in a way that is affective (expressing emotion) and reflective (providing the content through the narrative). This will involve both verbal and non-verbal communication. It is the interweaving of curiosity and empathy that carries the narrative forward.

- *Follow–lead–follow.* To connect with a child, you need to start where she is at. The child experiences being understood. Now you can lead her into deeper understanding. The child will respond to this; you follow again. In this way, you set a rhythm to the telling which allows the story to emerge.

- *Talking with and about.* This way of communicating is emotionally intense, especially for children who have found ways to exist without connection in their past. You can help the child to tolerate this without becoming overwhelmed by it. This can be helped by not always talking directly to the child. At times, it can be helpful to talk about her. This can be a wondering out loud or perhaps sharing a thought with another person. The child may quietly listen, but if she joins the conversation again you can resume talking with her.

- *Attending to verbal and non-verbal communication.* Every communication is non-verbal; some are also verbal. Noticing discrepancies between verbal and non-verbal can help you to understand the experience of the child. When verbal and non-verbal again match, the communication becomes deeper and more open.

- *Relationship repair.* You will notice ruptures in your relationship with the child. You may have become defensive, or the child may have misunderstood. It is important that as the more mature person in the relationship, you, the parent, take responsibility for repair at these times. With mistrusting children, relationship repair will need to occur much more frequently as the child seeks signs of rejection and abandonment. As the child experiences connection, she may experience remorse and want to make amends. At these times, you can support the child, helping her to repair the relationship with anyone hurt by what has happened.

REFLECTIONS ON THE SCENARIOS USING DDP PRINCIPLES

Scenario	DDP principles
Sarah has woken up late and is in danger of missing her train. She is very stressed as she tries to get ready. Her mum has offered to give her a lift to the station. Mum is getting impatient waiting for her to be ready. She shouts up, reminding her of the time. Sarah storms down, shouting at her to stop nagging and get off her back. Later that day, when Sarah is home again, Mum quietly talks to her. She apologizes for not realizing how stressed she had got and acknowledges that reminding her of the time was not the most helpful thing to do.	*Mum is staying open and engaged, not getting cross because Sarah's stress is being expressed as anger towards her.* *Mum is able to repair the relationship with Sarah, realizing she added to the stress, and this will increase Sarah's safety and security.*
Sienna has chicken pox, but is feeling better. She is bored, missing school, and it has been raining all day. Mum suggests that they put on coats and wellies and go out and splash in puddles. They have a lovely time splashing down the lane, getting wet and muddy in the process. They are soon laughing together as they find deeper and deeper puddles to jump in. The afternoon passes quickly and soon it is time to go home for a bath and tea.	*Sienna is experiencing secondary intersubjectivity with her mother, with some nice playful moments.* *This is increasing Sienna's safety and security, as she experiences influencing and being open to influence.*

Keisha has moved into a short-term foster placement. She is frightened as she does not know what is going to happen. Her foster mum walks into the living room to find her tearing up her school books.

> Foster mum: Keisha, you sure look cross with those books.
>
> Keisha: I hate these stupid books and I hate school.
>
> Foster mum: You haven't been back to school since you came to live here, have you? I wonder why you are feeling cross about school right now?
>
> Keisha: I don't want to go. School is stupid!
>
> Foster mum: It feels like school is stupid so you thought you would tear those books up. Perhaps it is making you feel better, but I am wondering if you are worried about going to school tomorrow?
>
> Keisha: Everyone will look at me. I hate their stupid faces.
>
> Foster mum: Ah, it is so hard to go to school when so much has changed and you don't know what is going to happen. You must be so worried about what everyone will think when I take you to school instead of your mum.
>
> Keisha: I know what they will think. They will think I have done something really bad. I hate them.
>
> Foster mum (pulls Keisha into a hug and gently strokes her hair): It is so hard to leave your Mum and not know what is going to happen. I am guessing you are worried that maybe you have done something bad too? It is so hard to understand why this has happened and so scary not knowing what is going to happen next.
>
> Keisha (crying): I just want my mum.
>
> Foster mum: I know you do, love, I know.

The foster mum is staying open and engaged, demonstrating acceptance, curiosity and empathy in PACE. This is intersubjective and Keisha's emotion is co-regulated whilst her experience is being co-constructed. As foster mum talks with Keisha, they discover the story of Keisha's experience, with the foster mum providing an affective-reflective dialogue with some follow–lead–follow.

Whilst Keisha is unlikely to feel safe with such uncertainty the foster carer's support will be giving her some temporary security.

Yadon has just been brought back to the residential home by the police, having been missing all night. Staff are concerned that he has been hanging out with local kids who are dealing drugs. Once the police have gone, his key worker, Mark, sits down to chat to him. Yadon is acting like there is nothing wrong. He becomes angry and abusive towards Mark when he is reminded of the consequences for being out all night. Mark comments that although Yadon is saying he is fine and there is nothing to worry about, he can see that he is looking pretty scared right now. Perhaps it was being brought home by the police, or maybe something that happened overnight? Yadon denies this and continues being abusive for quite some time, but later admits that it was pretty scary the night before when one of the boys threatened him with a knife.

Mark is noticing verbal and non-verbal discrepancies, which is helping him to connect with Yadon and increase his safety. Mark's open and engaged stance helps Yadon to confide in him about his frightening experience.

Joshua has just had a visit from his social worker. He has been doing some early life exploration with him. Joshua is now sitting with his grandmother. He is feeling upset and wonders why his mum locked him in his room. Grandmother: I don't know, Josh, I wonder if your mum just didn't know how to look after you. Perhaps she was trying to keep you out of the way when your dad was drunk, I just don't know. All I do know is that you were such a little boy, and it must have been so scary for you all alone in that room. I expect you could hear all sorts of noises going on in the house, and you had no idea when anyone was going to come. What a scared little boy you were. Your mum has had a hard life, and one day I will help you to understand that, but she should not have looked after you like that. No little boy should be locked in a room with no one to cuddle him.	*Grandmother is able to develop a narrative, or story, of Joshua's experience which is helping him to make sense of this (co-construction).* *Joshua is coping with Grandmother talking with him using PACE. They are intersubjectively connected.*
Daniel has had a friend around, which was clearly a struggle for him. He found it difficult to share his toys and wanted to be the boss in any game they played. Now he is being bossy with his dad, refusing to eat the tea, which he suddenly doesn't like and generally being unco-operative. Dad decides not to get into an argument with him. 'Come on', he says, 'you and I are going to take the dog out.' Fortunately Daniel agrees. As they walk up the hill Dad quietly chats to him about how sometimes friends can be quite tricky. Daniel doesn't answer, and Dad doesn't pressure him to. They reach the field and Daniel enjoys throwing the ball for the dog. By the time they get home Daniel is ready for his tea, which he eats almost as fast as the dog eats his!	*Dad remains open and engaged and this enables him to co-regulate Daniel's emotion both at a sensory level (exercise, food) and emotionally, connecting with PACE, but not expecting Daniel to join in. This is likely to increase safety and security.*

Robyn is really angry with her mum. She wants to go on a school trip but has been told she isn't allowed to. Unreasonably she is shouting at her mother that it is her fault.
 	
    Mum (with intensity and animation): I can see you really, really wanted to go on that trip. It seems so unfair that you can't go.
 	
    Robyn: You told them, didn't you? That I shouldn't go?
 	
    Mum: You think I told them because the last trip didn't go well? Well, I can see that would make you mad if you thought I had told them behind your back.
 	
    Robyn: You must have, why else wouldn't they let me go?
 	
    Mum: I don't know, Robyn. This school was meant to be a fresh start and now they are telling you that you can't go on the trip. I can see why you would be angry about that. Maybe it feels like they don't trust you at all.
 	
    Robyn: Well, if you didn't tell them then they can't trust me? Why don't they trust me, Mum? I know I could do that trip.
 	
    Mum: I think maybe you could too. I don't know why they have said you can't go, but I am happy to go and talk to them about it.
 	
    Robyn: Thanks Mum.
 	
Mum does talk to the teachers, and discovers that Robyn has misunderstood. Two trips have been arranged so all the children aren't taken out at once. It was the first trip that Robyn couldn't go on!
	Mum does well here not to become defensive. Her open and engaged stance and use of PACE brings them into an intersubjective connection. Robyn's affect is co-regulated, and she feels safe enough to allow Mum to try to sort this out for her.

Ivy's stress has been building up all weekend. She had a family contact on the Friday and then her birthday on the Saturday. It is now Sunday evening and she has blown up over having her bath. She is now trashing her bedroom, but won't let her foster carer, Sandra in. Sandra sits outside the door and tries talking to Ivy. This seems to be making things worse. The cat has come to sit with Sandra and so she talks quietly to the cat. She tells the cat that Ivy is really upset right now and doesn't want to come out. She has had such a lot to cope with, seeing her family and then having a birthday. She wonders whether not being with her family on her birthday was pretty hard. Sandra continues chatting to the cat whilst Ivy gets quieter. After about 15 minutes she comes out of her bedroom and cuddles with Sandra.

Sandra tries talking with Ivy, but this is not helping so she talks about her. This co-regulates Ivy's escalating arousal, whilst also making some sense of her experience (co-construction).

PACE and being open and engaged are important to help Sandra to do this. This will help Ivy to feel a little safer.

MODULE TWO, SESSION ONE

ACTIVITY SHEETS

DIALOGUES

PARENT–INFANT DIALOGUE*

Typical parenting

'Oh you have woken up, have you? You do choose your moments! Come on then, Miss Awkward, let's get you fed. We must hurry as Rosie is going to be here soon, I want you settled when she gets here. What is wrong with banana – you liked it yesterday? You have got it in for me today. Now you are getting it everywhere. All I ever do is clean up after you. Here, let me wipe your hands. Now stay there in your play pen whilst I put the kettle on.'

Take two

'Oh you have woken up, have you? Ah, that's a nice smile, are you feeling happier now that you have had a sleep? Come on then, time for dinner. Are you feeling hungry? No, you don't want to sit in your high chair, I think you want to play more than you want to eat. Here you are, sit here and play with this whilst I get your banana. Is that better? You like that toy, don't you? Right, here is your dinner. Oh, what does it feel like? Are you enjoying squashing it? You are getting it everywhere, whatever will Rosie think when she gets here? Come on, let's clean us up. Oh, you really don't like having your hands wiped, did you prefer the banana? Now let's pop you in the play pen whilst I put the kettle on.'

PARENT–TODDLER DIALOGUE

Typical parenting

'Here you are; you can use these crayons. Can you colour in this picture? The pizzas are taking a long time to come. No, you mustn't draw on the tablecloth. Here, can you colour this train red? I wish the food would hurry up. No, you can't get out of the highchair. Now, stop making a fuss – we won't be able to stay if you can't wait nicely.'

Take two

'Here you are; you can use these crayons. Can you colour in this picture? The pizzas are taking a long time to come. Are you feeling hungry? I am too. Yes, it is horrible having to wait when you are hungry. No, you can't draw on the tablecloth. Come on, I will help you, let's see if we can colour the train red? Oh, would you prefer to use the green? I like the green smoke coming out of the train! I know you want to get down, but you have to sit in the chair nicely. Do you remember that song you like? Let's see if you can remember the actions? That's it; you love the swish, swish of the windscreen wipers best, don't you? I think that's your favourite. Ah, here is food at last. I know you are hungry but just give me a minute to cut it up for you.'

---

*   This parent–infant dialogue is also used in *Nurturing Attachments* (Golding 2014).

PARENT–CHILD DIALOGUE

Typical parenting

'Mark, you cannot hit Ashleigh like that. Now, tell him you are sorry. You will not be able to have a friend to play if you can't share with him. Can't I leave you for five minutes whilst I get you both some lunch? Now, give Ashleigh that train and you play with the cars. Stop crying for goodness sake, you can play with your train any time. Well, if you won't stop crying you'll have to come with me, I can't trust you to play nicely at the moment. Ashleigh's mum will not be happy with me if I let you hit him.'

Take two

'Oh Mark, it looks like you are feeling very cross with Ashleigh. You mustn't hit him but help me understand why you are so cross? Hang on, slow down a bit, I can't make out what you are saying. Here, come and sit with me and take a big breath. So, you have just put all the train track together and Ashleigh was putting the train on to it when he knocked the bridge over. Ah, I see, and that broke up the train track. That sounds like a big accident. Oh, you think Ashleigh did it on purpose? Why would you think that? You think he doesn't like you? That sounds like a big worry. Why do you think he doesn't like you? Because he was cross with you for putting the track together? Oh, I see, was Ashleigh upset because you didn't let him help put the track together? Then he tried to put the train on before you could do that too? Well, I can understand that you were both feeling a bit cross with each other. I wonder if Ashleigh was bored just watching you do the track, especially if it took a long time. You think he might have been? It's like when your brother wouldn't let you help him with his Lego, isn't it? Yes, you did feel cross with him that day, didn't you? Do you think that was how Ashleigh was feeling today? You do? What shall we do to sort this out? Yes, of course I can help you both fix the track and then you can have five minutes using it together whilst I get your lunch ready.'

PARENT–ADOLESCENT DIALOGUE

Typical parenting

'I have told you a million times, Rebecca, you are not having a mobile phone. You are too young and you will just get into trouble with it. Of course they haven't, there will be lots of 13-year-old girls who do not have phones. You are not as hard done by as you think. Well, that isn't going to change my mind. I have spent all afternoon ironing your clothes, now they are all going to need doing again. Why are you always so ungrateful? Well, I care how you look; I don't want anyone thinking I don't look after you properly.'

Take two

'Let's sit down and have a talk about this. I can see you want a mobile phone really badly, but I am still not sure you are ready for one. I know you think you are, and I can see you are cross with me for not trusting you. Why not tell me why you want one so badly? You think all the other girls have one? That would make you feel left out, I guess. I am worried that you will get into difficulties like you did when you opened that Facebook account. Yes, I know it feels like I always bring that up. I guess right now it seems like I do not trust you. Yes, you are right, I don't trust that you will be able to use it sensibly until you are a bit older; you kind of do things without thinking them through. You will get better at this though as you get older. Oh, I see, you are cross that I let Shelley have one when she was your age. Yes, I can see that; I love you very much and am trying to protect you, but for you it just feels like I love Shelley more. That would make me pretty upset if I thought I wasn't loved as much as my sister. I will protect you as best I can and I know that doesn't feel fair, but fairness isn't about treating you and Shelley the same, it is about making sure you both get what you need. I guess you are going to feel cross with me right now, but I promise as soon as I believe you are ready I will get you a phone.'

HOW WOULD YOU MAKE THESE CONVERSATIONS MIND-MINDED?

For each conversation re-write the dialogue to help the parents be more mind-minded.

Mum has just gone out and Mark is standing by the front door crying.
 	
  Dad: Come on Mark, let's get your dinosaurs out.
 	
  Mark continues crying.
 	
  Dad: Tears won't bring her back, now do you want to play?

Mum is trying to hurry Kristen up so they can get to school on time.
 	
  Mum: Come on, Kristen, you haven't even got your socks on yet. Hurry up; we don't want to be late again.
 	
  Kristen: Can you put them on, Mummy? I can't do it.
 	
  Mum: Of course you can, you did it yesterday. You are a big girl now, you know.

Raj has been out playing with some local children. He arrives home dirty and dishevelled.

Mum: Goodness, whatever have you been doing? I'm never going to get that shirt clean again.

Raj: It was Jack. He was calling me names again. I hit him and then he pushed me over!

Mum: Oh Raj, why can't you just play nicely with them? You are always fighting.

Carol is due to go camping with her friend, but she is having second thoughts.

Carol: I'm not sure about going. I hate camping!

Dad: Well you liked it last month when we went! Anyway, you don't want to let them down. It is very nice of them to ask you to go.

A DAY IN THE LIFE ROLE PLAY: CHILD

Roles

Narrator

Foster mother

Foster father

Child (Amy, 10 years old)

Social worker

Teacher

Teaching assistant

Narrator

It is a school day and the parents are trying to get the children up and themselves ready for work. Amy is tired as she has been awake in the night with nightmares. She is dawdling, and has become distracted when she should be getting dressed.

Foster mother

Ordinary response: Amy, for goodness sake, will you get a move on? You don't want to be late for school again. Five minutes and breakfast will be ready.

PACE response: Amy, I think you are feeling tired. It was hard last night, wasn't it? I expect you wish you did not have to go to school today. Come on, I will sort your clothes out. See if you can get them on in five minutes and then breakfast will be ready.

Narrator

Amy is down for breakfast. Cereals are ready on the table for her. Amy gets angry. She wants toast, not cereals.

Foster father

Ordinary response: Well, it is cereals or nothing. Eat up or you will be going to school hungry.

PACE response: Amy, you are feeling cross today. You would really prefer to be back in bed, wouldn't you? What a shame you have school today. Now, eat your cereal and I will put a piece of toast on for you.

Narrator

Amy has got to school and has had a reasonable start to the day. They have just had a break and now it is time for some number work, something she tends to struggle with. Amy has a meltdown and has to be removed from the classroom.

Teaching assistant

Ordinary response: Well, what was that all about? You know I am here to help you if you find it difficult. You just have to call me. Now, sit here for five minutes and then come back into the classroom.

PACE response: Are you feeling calmer now? That was tricky, wasn't it? What do you think was wrong? Were you worried about the work? Fractions can be a bit difficult. Tell you what, why don't we find something from your calm box to help you and then we will sit together and look at it.

Narrator

It is the afternoon and the children have been doing some painting. It is break time but Amy wants to finish her painting rather than go out to play.

Teacher

Ordinary response: Come on, Amy, there is no more time. You can finish it tomorrow. Now leave it to dry and get out to the playground.

PACE response: You really want to finish this, don't you? What a shame that there is no more time. I like the way you have used the blue and yellow colours together. You need to get some fresh air on the playground. How about if I look after this for you and I will make sure you have some time to finish it tomorrow.

Narrator

It is end of school and Amy is being picked up by her social worker for a contact meeting with her birth mother. Amy hangs back, tidying up in the classroom. The social worker who has been waiting for her comes in to the classroom to find her.

Social worker

Ordinary response: Hurry up, Amy, we don't want to keep Mum waiting, do we? Come on, my car is just outside.

PACE response: Here you are, Amy. I see you are tidying up. I wonder if you forgot I was waiting for you, or maybe you are worried about seeing Mum today? You are worried. I am guessing that you might be worried about whether she will turn up or not. She doesn't always come, does she? I tell you what, let's go over to the contact centre. If she isn't there, I will take you for a milkshake and we can think about what you want to say to Mummy.

Narrator

Mum was there and contact went well. Amy is home and has a calm evening. At bedtime she finds that her foster carer has put up a dream catcher for her. They plan what she will do if she wakes up with a nightmare again and Amy settles down to sleep.

A DAY IN THE LIFE ROLE PLAY: ADOLESCENT

Roles

Narrator

Kate: key worker or foster mother, whichever is most appropriate

Dimitri: residential support worker or foster father, whichever is most appropriate

Young person (George, 15 years old)

Mr Frank: tutor

Mrs Phipps: learning support tutor

Gary: social worker

Narrator

It is a college day for George, but he's reluctant to get out of bed. He is lying in bed fully clothed and there are a couple of empty cans of lager on the floor. Kate is trying to get him out on time to catch the bus.

Kate

Ordinary response: George, will you get a move on. You don't want to be late for college again. They are not going to keep your place if you keep on skipping your classes. Fifteen minutes or you will miss the bus.

PACE response: Oh, George, not ready for college then? What's up? Are you worried about college, or maybe you're tired after last night? Looks like you were up late; tell you what, I'll make you a coffee and you get into some clean clothes. There is still time to get there and save that college place. Oh, maybe you are not sure about going to college? I'm sorry I didn't have time to talk to you yesterday. Tell you what, let's have a chat now and I will drive you to college.

Narrator

George gets up but is not making any move to leave for the bus or to talk to Kate. He gets angry with another young person who has been winding him up.

Dimitri

Ordinary response: Will you two cut it out now? George, shouldn't you be on your way? Come on now guys, you both have places to be.

PACE response: Heh guys, what's up with the two of you? Jack, come and help me with the bins; I need some muscle! How are you doing, George, tough to get out, heh? I think Kate's waiting for you.

Narrator

George lets Kate take him to college. On the way he tells her that he doesn't think he is up to the course. He feels so behind in the course work.

Kate

Ordinary response: Oh George, is that what this is about? You can do this, you know. You have brains; you just need to apply them.

PACE response: Oh, that sounds tough. It's hard to get the work done when you are worried about failing. No wonder you didn't feel like getting up this morning. Is that what the lager was about as well – drowning your worries? I guess college is bothering you more than I realized. Can I help? Okay, well let me know if you change your mind.

Narrator

George goes into college. He makes his first class, but then gets side-tracked by some of the other lads. They're messing about when Mr Frank, one of the tutors, walks past.

Mr Frank

Ordinary response: Shouldn't you lads be somewhere? Come on now, you're not going to get far in life if you can't even get to class on time. Now, don't let me see you here again today.

PACE response: Heh lads, how's it going? Oh George, I'm glad to see you. I noticed you haven't got that essay in yet. Are you having problems? You know where my office is; drop in if you want me to go through it again with you.

Narrator

It's the afternoon and George has a free period. He heads for the library, but as he gets to the door he changes his mind. He backs out quickly, bumping into Mrs Phipps, the learning support tutor.

Mrs Phipps

Ordinary response: Will you look where you're going! Are you going into the library or not? Come on, I've got work to do even if you haven't.

PACE response: Whoops, that was close! Have you forgotten something? No? Oh, it is a bit daunting isn't it, I don't think you come to the library often, do you? Well, it's good to see you here. I tell you what, you can sit in my office if you like, have some quiet space to work. I need to go and see someone, so it is all yours for the next half an hour.

Narrator

College has finished for the day and George heads back to the home. He is feeling a bit pleased with himself. He made a start on the essay, and it wasn't so bad. He's looking forward to letting Kate know. As he enters the house he sees Gary, his social worker. He had completely forgotten he was coming to see him today. He ignores him and heads to his room.

Gary:

Ordinary response: George, wait a minute. I have come to see you. I need to talk to you about seeing your dad. Don't go up to your room. I have driven over especially to see you, have the courtesy to talk to me.

PACE response: George, I will wait in the dining room, pop down and see me when you have dropped your stuff off, will you? (George comes down, but won't look at or speak to Gary. Kate smiles sympathetically at him as Gary chats to her.) I'm sorry, Kate, I think I've taken George by surprise. I should have reminded him that I was coming. I wanted to let him know that his dad has written to me. (Turning to George) George, this is big news, I know. I am guessing you are going to be a bit worried about what he has said. I can stay for a bit and go through it with you or I can leave it with Kate and she can go through it instead. Let me know what works best for you. Either way I will need to know what you want me to say back to him. This is a big thing; you can take your time. We can figure this out together.

Narrator

George chooses not to talk with Gary but he does let Kate show him the letter his dad has written. He decides to write back to his dad, but not today. He has a tense evening, winding up the other young people.

SPOT THE MOTIVE: PACE TO DO OR TO BE?

For each example reflect on whether the parent is seeking to understand the child or to change the child. What might the parent do differently, if using PACE to try to change?

Twelve-year-old Karen is with her older brother whilst Mum attends to some chores. When she returns to them they are both arguing. When Mum tries to intervene Karen turns on her and starts shouting.

Mum (with intensity and vigour): You are having a hard time today. I can see you are really angry.

Karen: I hate you, you always take his side. Always, Always!

Mum (Trying to be playful, but feeling a bit frustrated): And here I am helping you right now.

Karen: I hate Paul and I hate you. (Tries to hit Mum)

Mum: I am not going to let you hurt me, Karen. I will sit with you, but I am going to keep us both safe. Now, why not tell me what the problem with your brother is?

Nine-year-old Pascal has been kicking his football in the garden. He stomps back into the house.

   Pascal: I hate that stupid ball; it's not fair!

   Mum: Has it gone over the fence again?

Pascal collapses to the floor in what looks like a toddler tantrum. This takes Mum by surprise. She reassures Pascal that they can sort it out. He continues to tantrum. Mum realizes that talking with him is not going to help now. She also knows that if she tries to hold him he is likely to attack her. She therefore sits quietly near to him. She talks quietly to herself as she sits there: 'This is so hard for Pascal. All he wanted to do is kick his football. Then it went and flew over the fence. I wonder if Pascal is thinking that he is a bit rubbish at kicking that ball. It is so hard for Pascal when things go wrong. He always worries that he must be rubbish. So hard for Pascal. So hard for him to believe that I love him even when that stupid ball does go over the fence.'

Pascal crawls into Mum's lap. She sits quietly hugging him. 'I am here Pascal, I am here.'

Geoffrey is looking after his six-year-old granddaughter, Jamile. They have been playing all morning, but now he wants to sit and read the paper for a while. Jamile is not pleased. She tries to tempt him back into playing and when this doesn't work she starts aggravating him; pulling at his paper, and touching ornaments she is not allowed to touch. Geoffrey wearily puts down his paper and pulls her to him.

Geoffrey: Well, young lady, it looks to me like you don't want me to read my paper.

Jamile: Will you play with me now? You never play with me!

Geoffrey: It feels like I never play with you, eh! That must be a bit tough having a granddad who doesn't play with you.

Jamile: You do play with me sometimes, but I want to play now.

Geoffrey: Ah, I see. You remember me playing with you this morning, but you want to play this afternoon too. I wonder what it's like when I read my paper and don't play with you?

Jamile: It's boring!

Geoffrey: Boring is it, even with those jigsaws to do?

Jamile: Yes, you don't like me when you won't play with me.

Geoffrey: Oh, I'm sorry about that. There are lots of times when I don't have time to play with you. If it feels like I don't like you at those times that sounds kind of hard. Maybe you worry that I won't ever play with you again, if I don't like you. Perhaps that's why you don't want me to read my paper.

Jamile snuggles in to Geoffrey for a few moments. She then gets her jigsaw and starts to do it at his feet.

Geoffrey: Well, what a clever idea. Now I can read my paper, and keep an eye on what you are doing. You will know I like you because I am right here!

★

Module Two, Session One: Activity Sheet 12

Fifteen-year-old Jamie is becoming distant from his foster carers. They are trying to re-engage him back into the family, but he does not appear to be interested in any of their suggestions. Foster mum is keen to use PACE to see if this can reach him and she is looking for opportunities to have a go. She wonders with him about how he is feeling and tries to show him empathy when things have gone wrong. This just appears to be pushing him further away, however, as he angrily tells her to stop trying to get into his head.

HOW MIGHT THE PARENT RESPOND WITH PACE TO THESE CHILDREN?

For each example, reflect on where the child is developmentally. How might the parent maintain an attitude of PACE with these children?

Robert is nine years old, and very controlling. He struggles when his parents try to make sense of his experience, tending to get hyperactive and silly. Sometimes, however, when they have helped him to calm down, he can be more mature and tell them what is going on for him. If they accept and empathize with him, so he feels understood, he can think about how he has behaved, recognizing and having empathy for others he may have hurt. He wants to make amends.

Noah is 14 years old. He is struggling with school, and has few friends. At home he tends to stay close to his parents, ensuring that they are attending to him by talking to them all the time. He can get emotionally aroused very quickly and will have major outbursts of temper which can be prolonged. He can also get over-excited very quickly, and potentially nice events can get spoilt as a consequence. Noah struggles to talk about how he is feeling. When they try, he tends to shout at his parents or become very silly.

Eloise is 11 years old. She has always struggled with her mother and will reject her attempts to connect, aiming physical and verbal abuse at her. She quickly experiences shame, and so any attempt to correct her generally ends in a major outburst or her running away. When Mum expresses empathy for how hard Eloise is finding things, Eloise will shout at her to go away and leave her alone. At times, Eloise can be quite perceptive, noticing, for example, that her brother was upset about not being allowed out to meet his friends because he was worried that they wouldn't invite him another time.

Five-year-old Rachel is living with her aunt following the death of her mother. When she cries, she allows her aunt to comfort her and she has been able to tell her that she has a big worry that maybe her mum died because she was naughty. When her aunt expressed how sad it was to have a big worry, Rachel snuggled into her.

NON- PACE AND PACE DIALOGUE: YOUNG CHILD

Four-year-old Hussan is struggling with visitors to the home. He has been attention-needing all afternoon. Dad has been able to occupy him whilst Mum spends time with their visitor, but he has now had to go out. Hussan is now asking endless questions and trying to insert himself between his mother and the visitor.

Non-PACE dialogue

Mum: Come on now, Hussan, you have been playing with Daddy all afternoon. Sit down with your toys now.

Hussan: I want a drink.

Mum: Here you are, now go and play.

Hussan: What is this? (Holding out a toy cow)

Mum: It is a cow. Put it with the other animals.

Hussan: What is this? (Holding out a toy horse)

Mum: You know what that is. Now go and play. No, Hussan, you can't sit here. Go on, you like playing with your farm.

Hussan: I want a drink.

Mum: Now that is enough. Come on, I'll put the TV on for you.

Take two: PACE dialogue

Mum: Hussan, you have been playing with Daddy all afternoon. It is going to be hard to play on your own now. Here are your animals, see if you can make a farm and we will come and have a look at it.

Hussan: I want a drink.

Mum: I haven't forgotten you. I am just talking to my friend. Here you are, here's your drink. How is that farm coming along?

Hussan: What is this? (Holding out a toy cow)

Mum (taking Hussan in her arms): This is really hard for you, sweetheart. You don't like Mummy talking to her friend. I think it worries you. Here, let's bring your animals closer so that I can watch you whilst I talk.

Hussan: What is this? (Holding out a toy horse)

Mum: Still not close enough, eh? You are really worrying that Mummy is going to forget about you today. Here is your animal alarm clock. I think you can play for five minutes. When the alarm goes, we will look at your farm.

Mum (five minutes later): Heh, you did it! Now, let's see where you have put the animals, and then we will see if you can do eight minutes.

PACE AND NON-PACE DIALOGUE: OLDER CHILD[*]

Bryana is 12 years old. She has asked to spend the weekend at her friend Jenny's house. Jane is agreeable to Bryana spending most of Saturday with Jenny but not the whole weekend.

Non-PACE dialogue

Bryana: That's so unfair! You never let me have any fun!

Jane: Who is being unfair here? No fun – you are so wrong about that!

Bryana: You don't! You always say that I have to stay home, get my work done, and hang out with the family!

Jane: Well, you are a member of this family you know.

Bryana: Yeah, if it's what you want then it's for the family. If it's what I want I'm being selfish.

Jane: You better watch what you're saying.

Bryana: But it's true! You always seem to think that when I want to do something for myself, I am being selfish, that I don't want to do my share at home!

Jane: You're only 12, Bryana. You're not ready yet to be independent and come and go as you want.

Bryana: I don't ask to. I just want to spend one weekend with Jenny. This is the first time I've asked to do that in a couple of months.

Jane: And I said 'no' so you should just accept it and quit feeling sorry for yourself and thinking that I'm a horrible mother.

Bryana: I'm not feeling sorry for myself! You're so mean to say that!

Jane: You have no right to say I'm mean. I'm being very reasonable. You're the one who is being mean about this.

Bryana: Of course it's always my fault.

Jane: You're the one who got all upset over a reasonable denial of your request.

Bryana: I wish that you'd just listen sometime and not always try to run my life! If I don't agree with you, I'm some kind of ungrateful daughter.

Jane: It does seem a bit ungrateful to me that I do so much for you and I let you do so much that you want to do. You are just never satisfied. You think I'm mean when I'm probably one of the best mothers in the neighbourhood!

Bryana: Yeah, you should get a medal!

Jane: No more of your sarcasm! You need to start facing the fact that you are the unreasonable one here, not me. This is your issue, not mine.

Bryana: Like I said before, you always think that it's my fault and that you're never wrong.

---

[*]   Based on extract from *Creating Loving Attachments* (Golding and Hughes 2012, pp.105–110).

Jane: You don't really believe that. I admit it when I make a mistake. You're just saying that to try to make me feel guilty so that I'll give in to you. It's not going to happen.

Bryana: Now you know what my motives are better than I do. I'm trying to make you feel guilty. And if I say that you're wrong, I'll be wrong again, and unreasonable!

Jane: This conversation is a waste of time. You don't want to listen to me at all. You'll argue forever because you want your own way and you're not going to get it.

Bryana: You never listen! Know-it-all!

Jane: You've crossed another line, Bryana. Now you're not going to her house on Saturday either.

Bryana: Great! You're meaner than every other mother I know. All my friends feel sorry for me that I got stuck with you.

Jane: Go to your room. I don't want to talk with you.

Bryana: Being alone in my room is a lot better than being with you.

Jane: And stay there until I call you for supper!

Bryana: Don't bother, I'm not hungry.

Jane: That's fine with me.

Take two: PACE dialogue

Bryana: That's so unfair! You never let me have any fun!

Jane: It seems to you now that I never let you have fun?

Bryana: Well, maybe sometimes, but why can't I stay overnight?

Jane: The whole family has been so busy lately. I thought this weekend would be a good time to have some family time.

Bryana: Could we do that on Sunday night?

Jane: Well, I was thinking more like Saturday night and then an early start Sunday to go for a walk up by the lake.

Bryana: But I really want to see Jenny!

Jane: I understand that, love. You can spend most of Saturday with her.

Bryana: We'll just start having fun and then I'll have to leave!

Jane: It's hard, Bryana, to juggle the things that we all like to do separately with what I think we need to do as a family. I'm sorry that it makes you unhappy that I want us to focus more on family time this weekend.

Bryana: I'm not being selfish!

Jane: I know. I'm sorry if it sounded like I thought you were being selfish. I meant that it is hard for all of us to give up some things that we want to do, not just you. And I get it that you'd rather be with Jenny this weekend. I'm sorry if it seems that I'm asking you to give up more than the rest of us.

Bryana: Well, it does seem that way, like I'm the one who has to make the sacrifices for the good of the family. I don't see you, Dad or Julie giving up much.

Jane: So it does seem to you that I'm asking more of you than the rest of us. If it seems that way to you I can understand why you'd be angry about it.

Bryana: Well, you don't want to go away on your own this weekend. I'm giving up Jenny, it doesn't seem like anyone else is giving up much.

Jane: You're right about that, Bryana. I don't think the rest of us had any big plans.

Bryana: Then why am I the one that has to give up the most?

Jane: You are giving up the most this time, so it is harder for you. Other times it has been harder for someone else and it will be that way in the future too. But this time it is harder for you. I can understand your disappointment, and how it seems unfair. I can see why you might be angry with me.

Bryana: It does seem that way, Mum.

Jane: I can see where it might, love. Anything I can do to help?

Bryana: Let me spend the weekend with Jenny.

Jane: I can't, love. Anything else?

Bryana: Just don't expect me to be all happy and cheerful up at the lake.

Jane: That's a deal.

PACE WITH AN UNCOMMUNICATIVE ADOLESCENT IN FOSTER CARE

Belinda is fostering 14-year-old Lottie. This is a long-term placement and Lottie has been living with her and Frank since she was ten years old. The last year has proved stressful as Lottie is managing the demands of high school and coping with early adolescent changes. She struggles with friendships, being emotionally younger than her peers. Her organizational difficulties are also getting her into trouble at school as she is struggling to be in the right place at the right time with the right things. In the last six months Belinda's niece, Elizabeth, has come to live with them whilst her mother recovers from some health difficulties. On this day, Belinda is feeling stressed herself. Probably not the best time to address an untidy bedroom with Lottie! However, her patience has snapped as she once again has had to go in and retrieve the laundry and dirty crockery that has accumulated despite repeated requests to Lottie to bring these down.

Belinda: Lottie, I need to talk with you about your bedroom.

Lottie: I know; I will sort it out I promise.

Belinda: That isn't good enough. You have repeatedly promised me but still not done it. If I hadn't gone in today to get your laundry and crockery you would have had no clean clothes and we would have had no cups when we wanted a cup of tea.

Lottie: You went into my bedroom! You know I don't want you to mess with my things.

Belinda: Well what am I meant to do? I have asked you several times.

Lottie: Just don't mess with my stuff, right!

Belinda: I would happily respect that if you can bring me down your laundry and the crockery, but you don't.

Lottie: You are always having a go at me. I try, but it's never good enough for you. 'Miss Prissy' always gets it right. It's not fair.

Belinda: Her name is Elizabeth, and you know what a hard time she is having right now. I thought you of all people would understand.

Lottie: I hate you! You don't care about me at all. I hate you. (Lottie runs up to her room)

Belinda is left feeling cross and frustrated. She is aware that she didn't handle this very well. She makes herself a cup of tea and gives herself some time. As she has been practising in her mindfulness classes, she notices all the emotions she is feeling right now. She tries to accept and not judge herself, but a part of her is still feeling guilty and she is aware that she is being hard on herself. She decides she will call her friend later that evening. She is also a foster parent, and it will be good to talk things through with her. Taking a deep breath, she gets up and makes Lottie a cup of drinking chocolate and puts some biscuits on a plate. She calls up to Lottie.

Lottie: What do you want?

Belinda: I want to apologize. I didn't handle things very well and I have left you feeling bad. Come and sit with me and have your drink.

Lottie (shrugs, but sits down and reaches for her drink)

Belinda: Lottie, I am sorry. I know you find it hard. I am guessing you are feeling bad yourself about this. I think you would like to be tidier but this is hard for you.

Lottie (head is down, and hair covers her face, but she nods in agreement)

Belinda: I am guessing you are feeling mad at me right now?

Lottie (shrugs)

Belinda (smiling) I will take that as a yes then.

Lottie (shrugs again, but this time gives a little look at Belinda before her head goes down again)

Belinda: Sometimes I forget how hard you find it to organize things like laundry. I am wondering if I am expecting a bit too much?

Lottie (head still down and mumbling) No, I should be able to do it.

Belinda: You are feeling cross with yourself then?

Lottie (nods head)

Belinda: What do you think when I have a go at you about your bedroom?

Lottie (shrugs)

Belinda: I am wondering, maybe you think I am being mean to you?

Lottie (shakes head to say no)

Belinda: You don't? So, did you think oh no, I forgot again!

Lottie (looks up and agrees)

Belinda: How does that make you feel when you realize you had forgotten and now I was cross with you?

Lottie: I was angry!

Belinda (with empathy in her voice): So, when I told you that I wanted to talk about your bedroom you remembered that you hadn't brought the things down. And then you were cross because you had meant to and now I was having a go at you. No wonder you got mad. You want to get things right, but it seems like you never do. And then I got the stuff from your room myself, which perhaps made it worse that you hadn't done it. No wonder you got angry with me. It must have felt like I didn't trust you at all!

Lottie: You can't trust me, because I don't sort it!

Belinda: Oh Lottie, I didn't know you felt that way. You are such a good kid, but this is hard for you. Organization is so difficult.

Lottie: I'm not a good kid, I never get it right!

Belinda: Is that how it feels, like you never remember, and then I'm cross with you because I have forgotten that this is hard for you? And you have probably had the teachers on your back today as well?

Lottie (nods): I forgot my gym kit!

Belinda (feels frustration rising again, and stops herself pointing out that she had put it on the side for her so she wouldn't forget it!): So, it has been a hard day, with all of us on at you?

Lottie: No different to usual.

Belinda: That makes me feel sad. This is just usual for you. You forget things and then we all have a go at you. You know you have forgotten again, and you feel so cross with yourself, and then you really don't feel good. No wonder you get mad at us. I would get mad too if I kept being criticized for things that I find hard to do. I'm also thinking about how tidy Elizabeth is, that must be hard too?

Lottie (head goes down again and she shrugs)

Belinda: I hadn't realized quite how hard it has been for you since Elizabeth came. I am trying to support you both, but I wonder what that feels like for you?

Lottie (shrugs)

Belinda: That hard, eh! Okay, I am guessing it makes you feel bad that there are some things you don't do as well as her?

Lottie: I don't do anything as well as her!

Belinda: Nothing at all? Oh goodness, you are feeling bad about this. So, you see Elizabeth being tidy, and me spending time with her, and perhaps some other stuff and all of this makes you worried that you aren't the same, and you aren't as good as her? You don't notice the things Elizabeth gets wrong, but you certainly notice when she does things right?

Lottie: What does she get wrong?

Belinda (smiles): Well, she certainly got in a pickle the other night, do you remember? She was teasing the cat and I asked her to stop. She went right on doing it. I felt pretty cross with her right then.

Lottie: Oh, I had forgotten that.

Belinda: I think you are so worried that you aren't getting things right that sometimes it is hard to remember what you do well. Then you get really down on yourself.

Lottie: I don't want to leave here. I like living with you.

Belinda: Oh, Lottie. We like having you too. Do you really think you might have to leave? This is really big, isn't it? Is Elizabeth being here making you more worried? Like I might choose between you?

Lottie (nods)

Belinda: I hadn't realized how you felt. What horrible worries. I guess after all this time I thought you would be feeling secure here. I realize now I'm wrong. You have moved too many times before to really feel secure, and when I get cross with you it must feel like your bags are already packed.

Lottie (looks at Belinda and nods)

Belinda: I am sorry that you feel that way. I want you to know that you will always be part of our family, but I can see now how hard that is for you.

Lottie (looks sad and tearful)

Belinda knows that Lottie does not like to be hugged so she just gently touches her hand. They sit like this for a while whilst Belinda lets her know that she will help her. It won't always feel this hard. She then decides to gently think with her about the issue of her organization difficulties.

Belinda: I need to find a way of helping you to organize your bedroom that doesn't leave you feeling so bad. I will have a think about this. Let me know if you have any ideas about how I can do this. I think we need to have another chat with your teachers too. If we can find the right way to support you, it will make life easier for you. And I do need to spend time with Elizabeth right now, but I tell you what, Lottie, we will keep finding time to talk and do things together. In fact, do you want to help me with tea tonight? We could have risotto, I know you enjoy making that?

Lottie (smiles): Yes, I would like that. I just need to go up to my room. There is a cup there that you missed!

NON-PACE AND PACE DIALOGUE: ADOLESCENT LIVING IN RESIDENTIAL CARE

Justin is 16 years old and has lived in the home for the past 18 months. He came into care at the age of seven with his two older and two younger siblings. Justin has always felt to blame for this, as he was the one who disclosed physical abuse by his parents to his class teacher. Justin's older brother and sister remain in foster care and his younger sisters have been adopted. Justin has experienced ten foster placements prior to coming into residential care. His oppositional and aggressive behaviour has generally led to these breakdowns. Justin continues to have contact with his older siblings but not with his birth parents. Planning for independence is currently taking place, but staff are concerned about this as Justin is very emotionally immature. He is generally non-compliant within the home and intimidating of the two other young people also living in the home. His key worker, Rob, struggles to form a relationship with him.

This dialogue takes place in the morning. Justin returned late to the home the previous night, drunk and dishevelled. Rob doesn't want him sleeping all morning. Justin has grudgingly got up but is refusing to do the chores set for him.

Rob: Come on, Justin, get your washing in the machine and wash your breakfast things. When these are done, you can come into town with me.

Justin: Why would I want to do that?

Rob: I thought you wanted to go into the Warhammer shop to get some more paint?

Justin: I don't need you to take me. I'll go by myself later.

Rob: Well, we can get you some shopping on our way back. Remember you are cooking your own meals this week.

Justin: F*** off. I'm not going anywhere. I'm going back to bed.

Rob: You know that isn't an option. How do you expect to live in a flat by yourself if you don't start doing these things?

Justin (standing very close to Rob): At least I won't have you f****** losers on my back then.

Rob (staying calm): Just step back Justin.

Justin (continuing to stand close and prodding Rob with his finger): I don't care what you want. You're a fat loser. I bet your kids know you're a loser too. Go off shift and leave me the f*** alone.

Justin storms out. Rob is unsure what to do next. He chats to his co-workers. One of his colleagues wonders what happened the previous night. He was very threatening to the night staff, and took a long time to settle. Rob realizes that he hasn't even checked this out with Justin. He decides to let him sleep for a couple of hours and then try again.

Module Two, Session One: Activity Sheet 17

Later, Justin appears downstairs. He goes into the kitchen and makes a sandwich. As he sits down to eat it Rob sits down too.

Justin: What now? Can't you just get off my back?

Rob: Yes, I am on your back a lot, aren't I? I'm sorry. I was wondering whether you wanted anything for a headache? It was quite a skinful you had last night.

Justin: Just get the f*** away from me.

Rob: Was it a tough night?

Justin: Stop acting like you care. Aren't you off soon? (Justin turns his back on Rob.)

Rob: Justin, I get it. It doesn't feel like I care. All I do is get on at you about washing and shopping. You were back late last night. I want to check out you are all right.

Justin: I'm fine, okay? I was drinking with my mates, that's all.

Rob: So, you had a good night?

Justin: They're a load of jerks. Now leave me alone, for f***'s sake.

Rob: Not a good night then. Sounds tough?

Justin: Like you care!

Rob: I care that you are all right.

Justin: Oh yer, you're paid to care, aren't you? Trying to earn your money, are you? Well you won't have to bother for much longer.

Rob: Wow Justin, this is really bugging you. Like I only care because I'm paid. That's tough. Who cares about you just because they do? I guess it feels like no one?

Justin: No one has my whole f****** life, why should they start now? I'll be glad when you are all out of my life.

Rob: Yes, I get that. If it seems your carers have all let you down, then I get you would want to do without them. We don't want to let you down. We want to get it right for you. It's pretty scaring thinking about moving out. There I was going on about washing and shopping. No wonder you got mad with me.

Justin: I can take care of myself. I will be fine. God, I wish I could just go and get you all out of my life now!

Rob (playfully): And I just won't leave you alone. (More seriously) I know you are strong; you've had to be all your life. You don't need to do this alone though. We're here; we'll help you. It's a big step and no one is rushing you.

Justin: I don't need help, well not much anyway. Why are you bothering?

Rob: Justin, you have had it tough, I know that. And I know you think it's your fault. You have been through things no boy should go through; and you've managed it alone. You are strong; heck, you've had to be. Ten foster placements. That's too many for anyone.

Justin: Heck! Who the hell says heck? Are you a dinosaur or what?

Rob (laughing): Yer, out of date, that's me, but I know a thing or two about the world. I am going to be here whether you like it or not.

Justin: Okay, if I'm not going to get rid of you I might as well have that ride into town. No point going to the Warhammer shop though, I lost my money last night.

Rob: A really tough night then? Let me get the keys, you can tell me what happened on the way.

MODULE TWO, SESSION ONE

HANDOUTS

MIND-MINDED PARENTING, SUPPORTED BY PACE

MENTALIZATION – THE ABILITY TO BE MIND-MINDED

The parents treat their children as individuals with their own minds. The parents use their own theory of mind, the understanding that their child has thoughts, feelings, beliefs and desires which might be different to their own. With this understanding the parents can help the child discover his own mind, to organize his experience and eventually to help him put into words what he is experiencing. This in turn increases the capacity for regulation that has begun to develop within the relationship with an attuned, sensitive parent (see Fonagy *et al.* 2002).

> Mind-mindedness is an act of discovery. The parent is interested in his child's internal world, is genuinely striving to understand it. As he observes his child, talks to her, interacts with her, he is making guesses, tentative hypotheses about what the child might be experiencing. The tentativeness of this curiosity leaves him open to feedback, ready to abandon or adjust his guesses in light of the child's response to them. In this way the parent truly comes to understand the mind of his child, and can give this understanding back as a gift that will allow the child to come to know herself. *(Golding and Hughes 2012, pp.137–138)*

Begin with mentalizing own internal experience

If parents can notice their own thoughts, feelings, beliefs, worries and fears they will be more able to stay open and engaged to their child and to notice and accept the child's internal experience. They will be less defensive within their parenting.

Using PACE to discover your inner experience

- *Playfulness* is the lighter side of discovering your own inner experience. This exploration does not need to be deep and serious, it can also be light and playful. Playfulness conveys a sense of confidence and hope for the future. Experience is amplified when it is shared playfully.

- *Acceptance* creates psychological safety. The focus is on acceptance of internal experience. In accepting our own inner experience, we are not judging ourselves: this is how we feel, think, hope – it is neither right or wrong, it just is. We might evaluate our behavior but not our inner experience.

- *Curiosity:* when we curiously explore we come to know ourselves more deeply. When we direct non-judgmental curiosity towards our experience we will become more accepting and empathic towards ourselves.

- *Empathy* is the outcome of our curiosity and acceptance.
    - Acceptance + Empathy = Compassion.
    - As we know ourselves better we also experience more compassion towards ourselves.

PACE

P IS FOR PLAYFULNESS

PLAYFULNESS

Joy in relationship

To develop the relationship

Dramatizes that child is special and loveable

Fun and play is protective

Optimistic stance that things can be different

Share and amplify experience playfully

THE CHILD

Becomes more open to positive emotional experiences

Moves out of shame-based states and experiences being happy and joyful

Discovers his strengths and uniqueness

Learns reciprocal enjoyment and trust in others

Feels connected to parent as they enjoy being together

Experiences having a positive impact on the other

A IS FOR ACCEPTANCE

ACCEPTANCE

Accepting without evaluating the child's inner experience

Parent can be aware of but can't change what the child experiences

Embrace mistrust; sitting with the uncomfortable builds security for the child

THE CHILD

Experiences parent's interest in him

Shame reduces with acceptance

C IS FOR CURIOSITY

THE PARENT

Parenting that build relationships is also parenting that is curious and reflective

Attitude of not knowing

Discover who the child really is

Avoids rapid judgements and non-reflective action

Opens up the relationship rather than shutting it down

E IS FOR EMPATHY

THE CHILD

Experiences parent's different understanding and deeper acceptance through empathy

Empathy builds secure attachment

Feels more secure when inner experience is understood, accepted and empathized with

PARENTING WITH PACE

Playfulness

Acceptance

Curiousity

Empathy

Acceptance

Understanding reasons why a child behaves or experiences something in a particular way

Convey understanding via acceptance

Curiousity

Figuring out what is going on.

Understand the meaning behind the behaviour

    Wonder about the child

    Wondering with the child

Make best guesses about inner experience of child

Playfulness

A light-hearted, relaxed and playful attitude

Helps child feel connected within the relationship

Help the child to experience fun and love

Empathy

Enter imaginatively into the experience of the child

Convey acceptance of inner experience to the child

PACE IS AT THE CORE OF THERAPEUTIC PARENTING

- Parenting attitude that facilitates a connection with the child which is not possible with a narrower focus on managing the behaviour.

- This connection builds the trust and security in relationship that has previously been missing from the child's experience.

- With this connection, the child will cope better with the normal boundaries and discipline that parents need to provide for their children.

PACE IS A WAY OF BEING, NOT A STRATEGY

- If a parent is generally curious and understanding about the child's inner world, acceptance and empathy will come through in the way she is with that child.

- PACE is a way of being to help children feel more secure, rather than a strategy to change the child.

- PACE is a habitual way of engaging with the child, not a technique to turn on and off as needed.

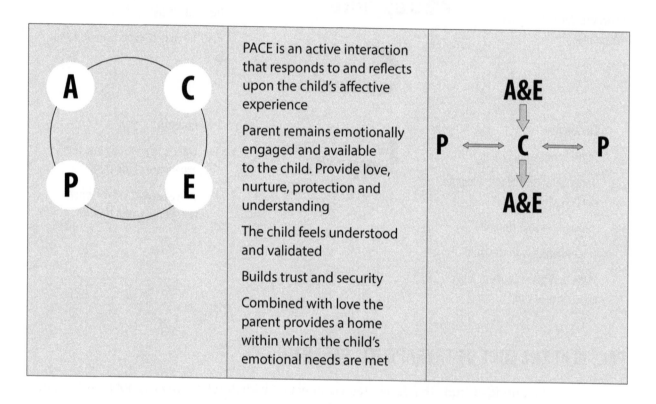

INTRODUCING PACE TO CHILDREN

Children will respond to PACE in different ways.

- They might respond positively and the parents experience a stronger connection with them.

- They might resist the feeling of closeness that PACE brings. Too strange. Doesn't fit their sense of who they are. The child feels known in a way that is unsettling.

The parents will need to approach some children more slowly; lighter PACE can gradually deepen over time; help the child get used to being known and to feel safe in this experience.

DEVELOPMENTAL SHIFTS IN RESPONDING TO PACE

Notice where the children are developmentally with making sense of internal experience:

- as an infant; needing a parent to tell them what they are experiencing

- as a toddler; helping them to know what they are experiencing

- as an older child; wonder together; help the child to discover himself.

As the parents developmentally match with the children they will be able to connect with them in a way that the children are ready for. Over time the children will learn to reflect on their experience and will be comfortable with this experiencing. At times of stress this fledgling ability to connect will reduce again; the parent can return to sitting with acceptance for the child without any pressure for the child to talk about what he is experiencing.

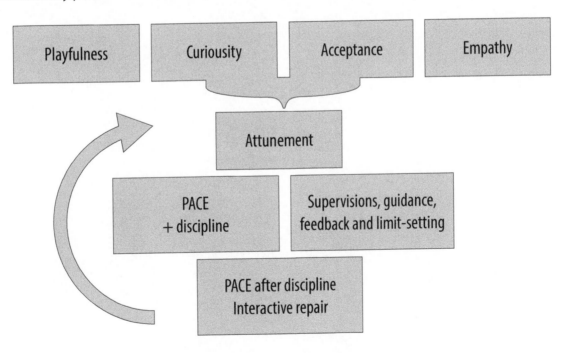

PACE WITH DISCIPLINE

- Connect with PACE before discipline; the child feels more understood and is more likely to respond to the discipline.

- Hold PACE as an attitude alongside the discipline so that it becomes a way of supporting the child's behaviour.

- Continue with PACE after discipline. This allows the child to experience guilt rather than shame and to want to make amends. Consequences become collaborative rather than imposed by the parents. Any relationship rupture is repaired.

- Ongoing PACE before, during and after discipline allows the child to continue to feel understood, accepted and unconditionally loved.

REFLECTIONS ON MIND-MINDED STATEMENTS

Mum has just gone out and Mark is standing by the front door crying.

> Dad: Come on, Mark, let's get your dinosaurs out.
>
> Mark continues crying.
>
> Dad: Tears won't bring her back, now do you want to play?

Here Dad is uncomfortable with Mark's expression of emotion. He expresses disapproval of Mark's internal experience and tries to distract him.

A mind-minded response acknowledges and accepts Mark's distress. As this is understood Mark is likely to feel soothed and to be able to play. For example, Dad might say, 'Mark, we are going to miss Mummy aren't we? Are you worried that she won't be back for a long time? I know it is hard when Mummy isn't here.'

Mum is trying to hurry Kristen up so they can get to school on time.

> Mum: Come on, Kristen, you haven't even got your socks on yet. Hurry up; we don't want to be late again.
>
> Kristen: Can you put them on, Mummy? I can't do it.
>
> Mum: Of course you can, you did it yesterday. You are a big girl now, you know.

Mum is likely to be feeling stressed about getting Kristen to school. This means she is not recognizing Kristen's internal experience and need for her support. From this scenario, we don't know why Kristen needs more support this morning, but perhaps something is making her feel more stressed. By telling her that she is a big girl, this internal distress is being dismissed. Instead Mum might say, 'Goodness me, won't those socks get on this morning? Let's see if you can do one whilst I do the other one. Are you feeling okay about going to school today? Do you have some worries that are making it harder to get your socks on?'

Raj has been out playing with some local children. He arrives home dirty and dishevelled.

> Mum: Goodness, whatever have you been doing? I'm never going to get that shirt clean again.
>
> Raj: It was Jack. He was calling me names again. I hit him and then he pushed me over!
>
> Mum: Oh Raj, why can't you just play nicely with them? You are always fighting.

In this scenario, Mum is showing no curiosity about what Raj has been experiencing. This means she is not able to understand his experience, nor how this is impacting on him emotionally. Raj is just hearing that his mum disapproves of his behaviour, and is not interested in his internal experience. Mum might show empathy and curiosity by asking him about what has happened, focusing on his experience. For example, 'That sounds horrible; being called names is not nice. No wonder you were feeling angry with Jack. It sounds like he was being very unkind.' This might lead to some further understanding about what went on. We might wonder, for example, whether there were some racist comments towards Raj. Acceptance for Raj's experience will help Raj to feel supported. He might then be able to think about how he responded to the situation.

Carol is due to go camping with her friend, but she is having second thoughts.

> Carol: I'm not sure about going. I hate camping!

> Dad: Well you liked it last month when we went! Anyway, you don't want to let them down; it is very nice of them to ask you to go.

In this scenario Dad is focused on making sure Carol doesn't let her friend and family down and this has led to a failure in curiosity, acceptance and empathy. Carol needs to know that her dad is interested in her strong emotional experience expressed by the statement 'I hate camping.' He could explore what is worrying her, and why camping with friends is making her more anxious than camping with her family. Only then will Carol be able to think about what to do, and to think about the impact on her friend if she doesn't go. For example, 'You are having doubts, aren't you? Well I guess it is harder camping without us there. You might be wondering if they will do things the same as us. Anything specific you are worried about?'

REFLECTIONS ON SPOT THE MOTIVE ACTIVITY

Twelve-year-old Karen is with her older brother whilst Mum attends to some chores. When she returns to them they are both arguing. When Mum tries to intervene, Karen turns on her and starts shouting.

Mum (with intensity and vigour): You are having a hard time today. I can see you are really angry.

Karen: I hate you, you always take his side. Always, Always!

Mum (trying to be playful, but feeling a bit frustrated): And here I am helping you right now.

Karen: I hate Paul and I hate you. (Tries to hit Mum).

Mum: I am not going to let you hurt me, Karen. I will sit with you, but I am going to keep us both safe. Now, why not tell me what the problem with your brother is?

In this example, Mum starts well. She matches Karen's affect and uses empathy to try to connect to her. She is feeling frustrated, however, and hurt by the accusation, when if anything it is her son who loses out because of all the time she needs to give to Karen. She tries to be playful but she hasn't been able to hold on to her curiosity. Mum needs some compassion for herself here. This is hard, and it is ongoing. Mum does well in that she stays calm and patient, but she moves too quickly to trying to sort out the problem between the siblings without being curious about why Karen experiences Mum as taking her brother's side. She is trying to focus Karen on her brother when Karen is feeling insecure about her mothers' interest in her. Helping Karen know that she gets that she feels no good, and that she expects Mum to prefer her brother, might help Karen to feel a bit more secure.

Nine-year-old Pascal has been kicking his football in the garden. He stomps back into the house.

Pascal: I hate that stupid ball; it's not fair!

Mum: Has it gone over the fence again?

Pascal collapses to the floor in what looks like a toddler tantrum. This takes Mum by surprise. She reassures Pascal that they can sort it out. He continues to tantrum. Mum realizes that talking with him is not going to help now. She also knows that if she tries to hold him he is likely to attack her. She therefore sits quietly near to him. She talks quietly to herself as she sits there: 'This is so hard for Pascal. All he wanted to do is kick his football. Then it went and flew over the fence. I wonder if Pascal is thinking that he is a bit rubbish at kicking that ball. It is so hard for Pascal when things go wrong. He always worries that he must be rubbish. So hard for Pascal. So hard for him to believe that I love him even when that stupid ball does go over the fence.'

Pascal crawls into Mum's lap. She sits quietly hugging him. 'I am here Pascal, I am here.'

Mum begins this interaction by trying to find out what has happened and then with reassurance. In doing this she doesn't immediately realize that Pascal is in quite a young state at this point and is feeling very emotionally vulnerable. He probably won't be receptive to Mum's wondering with him about what he is experiencing. As she picks up on this she quickly moves into using PACE to let Pascal know that she gets what is going on for him but without any expectation that he will join in. Pascal is then able to seek comfort from her.

Geoffrey is looking after his six-year-old granddaughter, Jamile. They have been playing all morning, but now he wants to sit and read the paper for a while. Jamile is not pleased. She tries to tempt him back into playing and when this doesn't work she starts aggravating him, pulling at his paper, and touching ornaments she is not allowed to touch. Geoffrey wearily puts down his paper and pulls her to him.

> Geoffrey: Well, young lady, it looks to me like you don't want me to read my paper.
>
> Jamile: Will you play with me now. You never play with me!
>
> Geoffrey: It feels like I never play with you, eh! That must be a bit tough having a granddad who doesn't play with you.
>
> Jamile: You do play with me sometimes, but I want to play now.
>
> Geoffrey: Ah, I see. You remember me playing with you this morning, but you want to play this afternoon too. I wonder what it's like when I read my paper and don't play with you?
>
> Jamile: It's boring!
>
> Geoffrey: Boring is it, even with those jigsaws to do?
>
> Jamile: Yes, you don't like me when you won't play with me.
>
> Geoffrey: Oh, I'm sorry about that. There are lots of times when I don't have time to play with you. If it feels like I don't like you at those times that sounds kind of hard. Maybe you worry that I won't ever play with you again, if I don't like you. Perhaps that's why you don't want me to read my paper.

Jamile snuggles in to Geoffrey for a few moments. She then gets her jigsaw and starts to do it at his feet.

> Geoffrey: Well, what a clever idea. Now I can read my paper, and keep an eye on what you are doing. You will know I like you because I am right here!

In this example Geoffrey manages his own frustration very well. This will be tough: to be told he never plays with her when he has played with her all morning is extremely hard. He is able, however, to stay open to Jamile's experience and to make sense of it with her with a nice use of PACE. Jamile is then able to play with her jigsaws, and Geoffrey finally gets time to read his paper. He also has a deeper understanding of Jamile's insecurity and can let her know she is still in his mind even though he isn't immediately attending to her.

Fifteen-year-old Jamie is becoming distant from his foster carers. They are trying to re-engage him back into the family, but he does not appear to be interested in any of their suggestions. Foster mum is keen to use PACE to see if this can reach him and she is looking for opportunities to have a go. She wonders with him about how he is feeling and tries to show him empathy when things have gone wrong. This just appears to be pushing him further away, however, as he angrily tells her to stop trying to get into his head.

Trying to reach an adolescent can be very tricky. In this example the foster mother is very focused on this goal and this is getting in the way of her acceptance. Jamie's wish at this moment is to keep himself more apart. This is what he needs acceptance for, even though at times he is expected to do things with the family – i.e. his internal experience of this is accepted even though he is still expected to join in at times. It is likely that Jamie is experiencing PACE as a way to change him, to make him want to be more involved in family life. Instead of genuine curiosity about why he wants to be more apart, he is experiencing a curiosity about this aimed at drawing him into family life. It may also be that Jamie doesn't really know what he is feeling right now. As is typical at adolescence, he may be feeling drawn to distancing himself from the family; but he can't explain this. Acceptance that he may not fully know what he is feeling is also important. Otherwise the young person can feel he is letting his parents down when he can't talk about his feelings, contributing to complex feelings of not being good enough.

REFLECTIONS ON HOW THE PARENTS MIGHT RESPOND WITH PACE

Robert is nine years old, and very controlling. He struggles when his parents try to make sense of his experience, tending to get hyperactive and silly. Sometimes, however, when they have helped him to calm down, he can be more mature and tell them what is going on for him. If they accept and empathize with him, so he feels understood, he can think about how he has behaved, recognizing and having empathy for others he may have hurt. He wants to make amends.

Robert struggles to relax and be open to his parents' influence. His controlling, hyperactive and silly behaviours all aim to keep his parents away from his inner experience. He becomes emotionally immature at these times. However, he is open to them helping him to regulate his emotional arousal and when he is calmer, he is more mature and able to be open to PACE. He then demonstrates his developing ability to share in figuring out what he is experiencing and what impact he is having on others. High levels of regulation, and a good length of time in using a PACE attitude towards understanding and accepting Robert's experience, are important. Robert will struggle if others try to focus on his behaviour and getting him to make amends too quickly.

Noah is much more immature than his 14 years. He is struggling with school, and has few friends. At home, he tends to stay close to his parents, ensuring that they are attending to him by talking to them all the time. He can get emotionally aroused very quickly and will have major outbursts of temper which can be prolonged. He can also get over-excited very quickly, and potentially nice events can get spoilt as a consequence. Noah struggles to talk about how he is feeling. When they try, he tends to shout at his parents or become very silly.

Noah is much more immature than his 14 years old. At times, he acts more like a toddler who just cannot manage a build-up of strong emotion. Noah needs the close presence of his parents to help him manage emotionally, but he is not yet ready to sit with them and reflect on what he is experiencing. He is likely to be more open to his parents making sense of this for him. He might cope with them using ACE to wonder aloud about how he is feeling, as long as he isn't put under pressure to respond. He is also likely to manage times of playfulness, using this to help him to feel more secure in his relationships with his parents.

Eloise is 11 years old. She has always struggled with her mother and will reject her attempts to connect, aiming physical and verbal abuse at her. She quickly experiences shame, and so any attempt to correct her generally ends in a major outburst, or her running away. When Mum expresses empathy for how hard Eloise is finding things, Eloise will shout at her to go away and leave her alone. At times Eloise can be quite perceptive, noticing, for example, that her brother was upset about not being allowed out to meet his friends because he was worried that they wouldn't invite him another time.

Eloise is struggling because she does not feel that she deserves love and attention, but also experiences a strong desire to have this. She is developmentally able to reflect on her experience, but her sense of shame makes this too frightening to do. It is easier for her to reflect on other people's experience than her own. Her anger to her mum is an expression of her own sense of not being good enough. Eloise needs her mum to understand this. Without this, empathy feels like her mum not getting how bad she feels about herself. PACE therefore needs to be high on PAC: playful moments, when possible, to build the relationship, and a high level of curiosity about how she is feeling with strong acceptance for this. For example, 'I think it is hard for you to believe I love you right now. Maybe it is hard to believe anyone can love you right now'. With this in place, Eloise might manage some light empathy, perhaps even some empathy expressed indirectly, through small notes, or overhearing Mum talking to the family dog.

Five-year-old Rachel is living with her aunt following the death of her mother. When she cries, she allows her aunt to comfort her and she has been able to tell her that she has a big worry that maybe her mum died because she was naughty. When her aunt expressed how sad it was to have a big worry, Rachel snuggled into her.

Rachel's development is in line with her chronological age. She is having a very typical reaction to a very sad event in her life and trusts that other adults, especially her aunt, can help her with this. She is fully open to the PACE attitude and is likely to use this to both explore her experience and curiosity about why her mother died, and to be helped with the strong emotions she has about this.

ACTIVITY SHEETS

PACE AND AROUSAL STATE – CHILD

Ten-year-old Summer has arrived home from school and wants to watch television. Her mum reminds her that she can't today as they must go over to her gran's house to run some errands for her. For each scene below, think about Summer's arousal level and where she is on the volcano. How might the mother use PACE and regulation to support Summer?

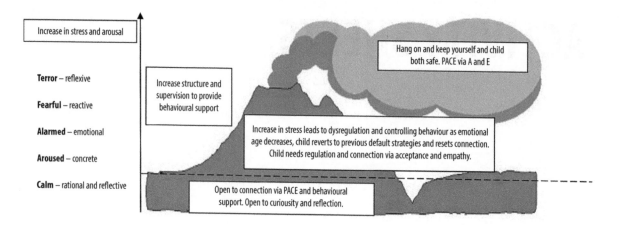

Increase in stress and arousal

Terror – reflexive

Fearful – reactive

Alarmed – emotional

Aroused – concrete

Calm – rational and reflective

Increase structure and supervision to provide behavioural support

Hang on and keep yourself and child both safe. PACE via A and E

Increase in stress leads to dysregulation and controlling behaviour as emotional age decreases, child reverts to previous default strategies and resets connection. Child needs regulation and connection via acceptance and empathy.

Open to connection via PACE and behavioural support. Open to curiousity and reflection.

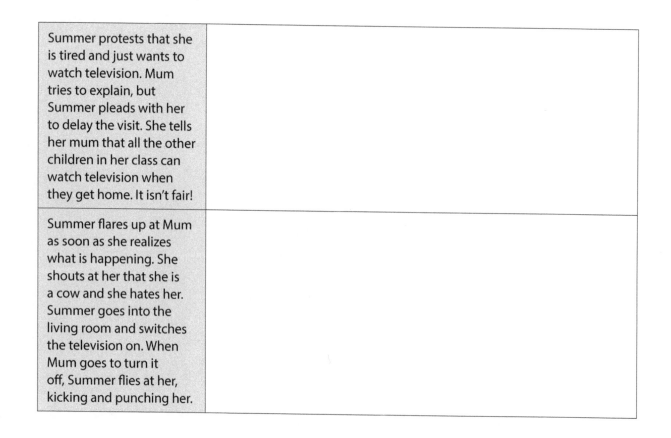

Summer protests that she is tired and just wants to watch television. Mum tries to explain, but Summer pleads with her to delay the visit. She tells her mum that all the other children in her class can watch television when they get home. It isn't fair!	
Summer flares up at Mum as soon as she realizes what is happening. She shouts at her that she is a cow and she hates her. Summer goes into the living room and switches the television on. When Mum goes to turn it off, Summer flies at her, kicking and punching her.	

Summer protests that she doesn't want to go to her gran's. She especially wanted to watch a television programme that all her friends are watching. When Mum reminds her that she had told her that morning that this would happen, Summer grudgingly accepts that she had agreed to go, but she had forgotten about the programme.	
Summer is angry with Mum when reminded about the plans. She pleads with her to change the visit, but Mum insists that they must go. Summer tells her she isn't going and why does she always do things for Gran and not for her?	
Summer doesn't even let Mum finish telling her what is going to happen. She shouts at her that she hates her gran, and why do they have to do errands for her anyway? She throws her school bag across the room and runs to her bedroom.	

PACE AND AROUSAL STATE – ADOLESCENT

Fourteen-year-old Sonja wants to go into town with her friends. She is told this is not possible as no one is available to take her or pick her up later. She had been warned about this at the start of the day. If she could arrange something later in the week, maybe this will be possible, but not today.

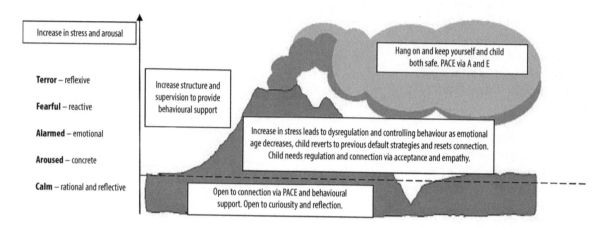

Sonja protests that she must go today, as her friends have invited her. Her carer tries to explain that it is not possible and reminds her that she had told her this earlier in the day. Sonja pleads with her to find a way. She tells her that the other girls won't ask her again if she doesn't go today. It isn't fair!	
Sonja flares up as soon as she realizes that her carer is saying no. She shouts at her that she is a cow and she hates her. Sonja goes into the living room and switches the television channel over even though another young person is watching it. When she is told to turn it over again, Sonja flies at her carer, kicking and punching her.	

★

Module Two, Session Two: Activity Sheet 19

Sonja protests that she really needs to go and meet her friends today. She is especially pleased that they asked her. When her carer reminds her that she had told her that morning that she wouldn't be able to give her a lift, Sonja grudgingly agrees that this is the case. She had forgotten when making the arrangements with her friends.	
Sonja is angry with her carer when told she can't go. She pleads with her to change her mind, but her carer insists that it isn't possible and that she had been warned that this was the case. Sonja tells her she is going anyway. No one ever does anything for her. She will just do it herself.	
Sonja doesn't even let her carer finish telling her that she can't have a lift. She shouts at her that she hates her and that she is trying to ruin her life. She throws her school bag across the room and runs to her bedroom.	

BEHAVIOUR SCENARIOS

For each child or young person, consider how the parents might provide regulation and how they can connect by understanding the young person's internal experience, using PACE to convey this understanding. Then think about the actions they might take to deal with the behaviour that has been displayed, i.e. what 'correction' they might use. Correction might consist of a consequence for the child or young person or something that the parents will change in the way that they are supporting them. Regulation and connection represent the emotional support whilst correction represents the behavioural action.

- Four-year-old Nazia has been fussing the cat. She is following him around, trying to stroke him and trying to pick him up. Dad has been telling her to leave him alone. The cat retreats under the sofa. Dad tries to distract Nazia with a game, but as he is getting it out Nazia has tried to pull the cat out. The cat, feeling cornered, scratches her. Nazia runs to Dad, crying.

- Ten-year-old Daniel has asked to go out and play with the local boys. He is allowed out for half an hour, but at the end of the half an hour he has not come home. Mum goes out to look for him and finds him throwing stones at the neighbour's car.

- Thirteen-year-old Katy has been struggling with school. She is skipping lessons and has been falling out with friends. The teachers were talking with her parents at a recent parents' evening about the importance of her changing her attitude. The very next day, Katy is caught in town with a couple of girls when she should have been in school.

- Kevin has just turned 17 and is desperate to start driving lessons. However, he is emotionally young and can still be very impulsive. His parents are concerned that he is just not ready yet for the discipline of learning to drive. Kevin is furious with his parents when they tell him this. He leaves the house and does not return until the next morning.

	Regulation	Connection	Correction
Nazia			
Daniel			
Katy			
Kevin			

LOST IN THE FOREST

In the summer of 2016, an incident got widely reported in the media of the Japanese parents who left their seven-year-old boy, Yamato, on the edge of a bear-infested forest. Once they realized that he was lost Yamato's parents requested a search, claiming that he had been lost during a family hike to pick wild vegetables.

Later, once the search was under way, Yamato's parents admitted that they had lied about what had happened. They explained what actually happened. They had, as a lesson to Yamato, left him at the side of the mountain road because he had been throwing stones at cars and people. They drove away, returning almost immediately, but by that time Yamato had wandered into the forest and could not be found. They had left him with no food or water.

More than 180 rescuers, including police officers, searched for Yamato in the mountain forest on Hokkaido. This is the northernmost of Japan's main islands. The search was hampered by heavy rain. Overnight temperatures dropped to seven degrees centigrade. Yamato was missing for six nights before being found alive. He was discovered by chance five kilometres away from where he had been left, curled up on a mattress in a one-storey wooden hut on a military exercise area. He was well, with only cuts and low body temperature to show for his ordeal. The hut was not heated and Tamato had not eaten but he had got water from a tap outside of the hut. Tamato was taken by helicopter to hospital and kept overnight as a precaution.

When father and son were reunited, the father apologized to him for causing him such an awful memory. He also apologized to his son's school, search parties and those who had supported the family, acknowledging that he had gone too far, whilst trying to do something which he had thought was for his son's own good. He described their family as loving, and said he was going to love and watch over him even more as he was growing up after this near tragedy.

(This summary is based on news reports by Guardian News and Media Ltd.)

Consider this event and reflect on:

- What were the parents' intentions?

- Would you consider this parenting to be punitive?

- What suggests that the parents were feeling defensive?

- When did the parents become open and engaged again?

- How might the parents have stayed open and engaged to their son, whilst still helping him to understand that his behaviour was not acceptable?

A DIFFICULT DAY AT SCHOOL

It is a hot day in the summer term. The children are all a bit fractious as end of term approaches. Seven-year-old Andrew has always found school difficult, and this is increased as the children become more unsettled around him. As his stress increases he is finding it harder and harder to stay regulated. He nearly blew before lunch time, but the teaching assistant managed to step in and provide him with some calm time out of the classroom. Unfortunately, this hasn't lasted. An argument over who has the football leads to Andrew hitting two of the other boys. It is decided that it would be better for Andrew to go home than for him to continue to struggle and his mum is called.

Mum puts down the phone with a sigh. The afternoon is not going to be the afternoon she had planned. She quickly phones the friend she had planned a coffee with. She reflects on how she is feeling. She is a bit frustrated that she needs to fetch Andrew. Fleetingly she wonders if they could have managed him at school without the need for him to come home. She is okay though, her empathy for how hard Andrew is finding school remains high. She thinks how to help him. She knows that Andrew is finding school difficult at the moment, and she anticipates that his emotional regulation will be very fragile after such a difficult morning. Instead of jumping in her car to collect him, she decides to take the time to walk to school. She hopes the walk home will provide some regulatory support to help Andrew to settle.

When she arrives at school Mum greets Andrew with a quick hug, acknowledging that it has been a difficult morning. She does not talk about it any further but instead they walk home chatting about what they see. They notice the birds singing and Andrew is very pleased when he recognizes the blackbird. As they get towards home, Mum notices that Andrew is becoming unsettled again. She guesses that he is anticipating a talk about school. Quietly she tells him that they will have a chat later, but for now she just wants him to have a snack and something to drink. She guesses rightly that he has not eaten much of his lunch. After a round of toast and jam and a milkshake drunk through a straw, Andrew is calm again.

'So, school was hard today?' Mum gently comments. Andrew's head immediately goes down, but he does not run away. 'It's tough being at school when you're feeling hot and tired isn't it?'

Andrew looks up: 'Yes and it was so noisy. I hated it.'

Mum nods sympathetically. 'Yes, it is much harder for you when they are noisy. I wonder why they were noisier today?'

'Mrs Jones said that we were all feeling hot and tired. She told us that it is harder not to argue when you are hot but we should try hard.'

'Do you think that is why you were finding it hard? Were the children all arguing?'

Andrew thinks about this: 'Not all of them, but Justine and Carol got very cross when they were gluing. I think their model broke.'

'Well, Andrew, no wonder you were feeling wobbly today. That was a lot to cope with, wasn't it?'

Module Two, Session Two: Activity Sheet 22

Andrew hangs his head again and then whispers, 'I hit Jack and Billy.'

'I know, sweetheart. That was when Mrs Jones called me. She isn't cross with you but she thought it would be better for you to be at home this afternoon.'

'I didn't mean to hit them, but they wouldn't let me have a turn with the ball. I had waited ages.'

'It sounds like you were trying to be patient, but then you felt very cross with them, didn't you?'

'Yes, and I tried to get the ball from them…' Andrew hesitates and then whispers, 'And then I hit them.'

Suddenly Andrew brightens. 'Mummy, can I make them cards? You know, to say sorry. Can I make a card for Jack and Billy?'

Mum smiles. 'Well, that sounds like a great plan. I will get the card and pens out and you can make them whilst I clear up a bit. We must be sure to remember to take them with us when we go to school tomorrow.'

Andrew looks pensive, and then looks at Mum with a sense of urgency: 'No Mum, no, not tomorrow. We must take the cards to school today. I don't want to wait until tomorrow.'

Mum looks puzzled. 'Well we could, but what's the hurry? It would be easier to take them with us tomorrow.'

'No Mum, that won't do,' proclaims Andrew. 'We must go back to school today. You see I don't want Jack and Billy to be upset all night!'

Mum smiles and ruffles Andrew's hair. 'Do you know, Andrew, that sounds like a great plan!'

QUESTIONS

- Think about this narrative in relation to the 'parenting in the moment' handout.

- How would you know when Andrew needs regulation and when he is ready for reflection?

- When is Andrew experiencing shame and when guilt?

- In what way does Mum use the elements of PACE?

- How does 'correction' happen in this narrative?

- What impact do you think this episode will have had on the relationship between Andrew and his mother?

HANDOUTS

PARENTING PRINCIPLES FOR SECURITY

PRINCIPLE ONE: PACE, A CONSISTENT FEATURE. DISCIPLINE BROUGHT IN AS NEEDED

- *PACE before discipline* helps child to feel emotionally connected, unconditionally loved.

- *PACE with discipline* helps to maintain this connection when the child is at her most vulnerable, experiencing shame, and fear.

- *PACE following the discipline* provides the child with a continuing sense of being unconditionally loved, repairing any ruptures in the relationship.

PRINCIPLE TWO: TWO HANDS FOR PARENTING

Hand one provides warmth and nurture, and allows children appropriate autonomy matched to their developmental age.

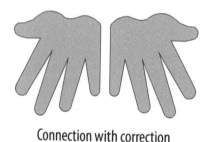

Hand two provides structure, discipline and boundaries.

Connection with correction

No correction without understanding

Connection	Correction (behavioural support)
Mind-minded parenting	Time in
PACE	Bringing child close
Open and engaged	Help child to understand cause, effect and consequences
Relationship, regulate, reflect	Descriptive praise
Understanding reasons for behaviour	
Meet hidden and expressed needs	Low-key rewards
Help child to regulate feelings of shame on the shield	Distraction, diversion
	Positive activities
Connection first	Guidance, suggestions
Attunement and relationship repair	Structure and supervision for developmental age
Stories	
Safety	Explaining, reasoning
Hand one	**Hand two**

PRINCIPLE THREE: PARENTING SANDWICH

Discipline, in the form of boundaries and consequences, is important, but it needs to be sandwiched between lots of attunement and relationship repair.

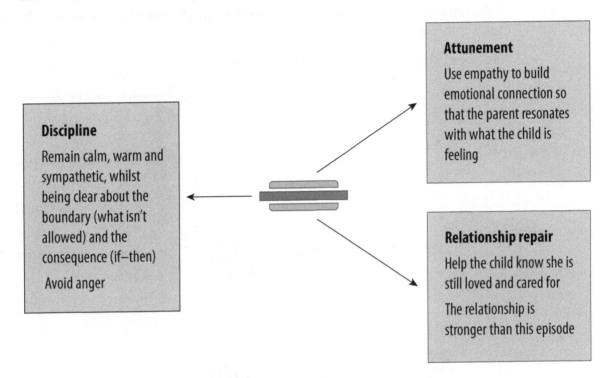

Discipline

Remain calm, warm and sympathetic, whilst being clear about the boundary (what isn't allowed) and the consequence (if–then)

Avoid anger

Attunement

Use empathy to build emotional connection so that the parent resonates with what the child is feeling

Relationship repair

Help the child know she is still loved and cared for

The relationship is stronger than this episode

PRINCIPLE FOUR: ADULT TAKES RESPONSIBILITY FOR THE RELATIONSHIP WITH THE CHILD

- Don't punish with the relationship.

- Take breaks when needed if it is practically possible.

- Take responsibility for relationship repair.

PRINCIPLE FIVE: UNDERSTANDING WITHOUT LECTURES, PREMATURE PROBLEM SOLVING AND RUSHED REASSURANCE

- Don't lecture, and delay problem solving.

- Don't rush to reassure.

- Reassure to give hope rather than to make yourself feel better.

PRINCIPLE SIX: PROVIDE APPROPRIATE LEVEL OF STRUCTURE AND SUPERVISION

- Notice child's emotional maturity and adjust expectations in line with this.

- If the consequences are piling up it is a sign that the child needs increased structure and supervision alongside empathy.

- Provide scaffolding to help child achieve more.

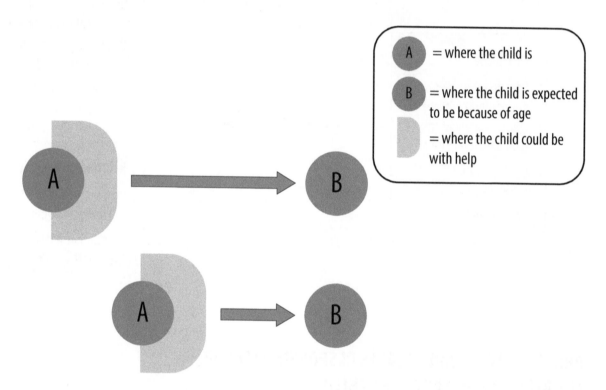

A = where the child is

B = where the child is expected to be because of age

= where the child could be with help

PRINCIPLE SEVEN: HELP THE CHILD TO MANAGE SHIFTS BETWEEN PLAYFULNESS AND PARENTAL AUTHORITY

Mistrusting children struggle to accede to parental authority. When a parent needs to use his authority for keeping the child safe, providing a boundary and structuring the environment, the child will revert to controlling behaviours. Shifting from playful times with parents ('companionship mode') to a 'parental authority mode' is difficult (Baylin and Hughes 2016). These relational transitions can lead to very rapid shifts in the child towards anger and meltdown. The parent needs to find a way to stay open and empathic to the child's struggles with letting parents have a benevolent authority over them.

PARENTING IN THE MOMENT
'CONNECTION WITH 'CORRECTION'
AN ATTITUDE OF PACE WITH BEHAVIOUR SUPPORT

This cycle demonstrates a sequence that it is helpful to take when parenting a child. By keeping this in mind it is easier to stay open and engaged with the child, rather than becoming defensive within parenting. This in turn helps to make an emotional connection with the child whilst also providing some behavioural support. When a parent connects before correcting, the child will experience unconditional love and acceptance alongside the safety that empathic boundaries and discipline can provide.

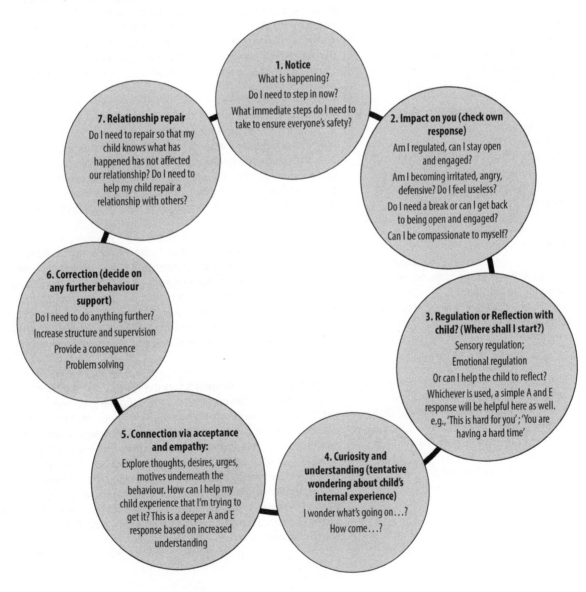

REFLECTIONS ON PACE AND AROUSAL STATE: CHILD

Summer protests that she doesn't want to go to her gran's. She especially wanted to watch a television programme that all her friends are watching. When Mum reminds her that she had told her that morning that this would happen, Summer grudgingly accepts that she had agreed to go, but she had forgotten about the programme.	*Calm. Summer is upset about the need to change her own plans but her arousal is low. She can be rational and therefore is open to reflection. She is likely to be able to explore with Mum why it feels so important to watch television and when this is understood to be able to think about Gran and her needs. She is open to PACE, and is likely to be able to go to Gran's.*
Summer protests that she is tired and just wants to watch television. Mum tries to explain but Summer pleads with her to delay the visit. She tells her Mum that all the other children in her class can watch television when they get home. It isn't fair!	*Aroused. Summer's emotional arousal is increasing and this has made her more rigid towards her mum's reasoning. She may be able to engage with Mum using PACE, but without too much expectation that she will be able to reflect, at least initially. She may respond to a bit of playfulness with acceptance and empathy. As her arousal comes down, she might be able to reflect. If her feelings are understood she may be able to go to Gran's.*
Summer is angry with Mum when reminded about the plans. She pleads with her to change the visit but Mum insists that they must go. Summer tells her she isn't going and why does she always do things for Gran and not for her?	*Alarmed. Summer is getting more emotional and this is reflected in some defiance. Dysregulation is increased, leading Summer to feel that Mum is not interested in her. Summer is unlikely to engage in reflection until she receives acceptance and empathy from Mum, who is open and engaged to what she is feeling. This means not being pulled in to responding defensively, by trying to persuade her that she does do things for her. This is likely to take some time; the trip to Gran's might be a bit late.*
Summer doesn't even let Mum finish telling her what is going to happen. She shouts at her that she hates her gran, and why do they have to do errands for her anyway? She throws her school bag across the room and runs to her bedroom.	*Fearful. Summer is now very reactive. She is angry and this is being reflected in her behaviour. If Mum can provide simple but genuine acceptance and empathy for long enough, Summer may be able to calm a little. Mum will need to be curious on Summer's behalf, making some guesses about why she is feeling so strongly about this. If Mum can take the time she may yet make the trip to Gran's, but if she tries to rush Summer so that her arousal doesn't come fully down this won't happen.*
Summer flares up at Mum as soon as she realizes what is happening. She shouts her at that she is a cow and she hates her. Summer goes into the living room and switches the television on. When Mum goes to turn it off, Summer flies at her, kicking and punching her.	*Terror. Summer becomes angry very quickly and is verbally aggressive and oppositional. This quickly turns into a fight response as Mum tries to take control. Mum can only ride the storm now, ensuring that they are both safe. PACE via A and E might provide some regulation for Summer, but with no expectation that Summer will respond quickly. Provide a sense of safety through voice and actions. As the storm passes and Summer's arousal comes down then she will need comfort and regulation. Mum needs to feel acceptance and empathy and not become defensive. The trip to Gran's will need to be delayed; later there will be a time to help Summer to make amends for this, but only once she can experience Mum's PACE towards her.*

REFLECTIONS ON PACE AND AROUSAL STATE: ADOLESCENT

Sonja protests that she really needs to go and meet her friends today. She is especially pleased that they asked her. When her carer reminds her that she had told her that morning that she wouldn't be able to give her a lift, Sonja grudgingly agrees that this is the case. She had forgotten when making the arrangements with her friends.	*Calm. Sonja is upset about the need to change her plans but her arousal is low. She can be rational and therefore is open to reflection. She is likely to be able to explore with her carer why it feels so important to meet her friends and when this is understood to be able to think about how she can change her arrangements to later in the week. She is open to PACE, and is likely to be able to let her carer sort this out with her.*
Sonja protests that she must go today, as her friends have invited her. Her carer tries to explain that it is not possible and reminds her that she had told her this earlier in the day. Sonja pleads with her to find a way. She tells her that the other girls won't ask her again if she doesn't go today. It isn't fair!	*Aroused. Sonja's emotional arousal is increasing and this has made her more rigid towards her carer's reasoning. She may be able to engage with her carer using PACE, but without too much expectation that she will be able to reflect, at least initially. She may respond to a bit of playfulness with acceptance and empathy. As her arousal comes down she might be able to reflect. If her feelings are understood she may be able to let her carer sort this out with her.*
Sonja is angry with her carer when told she can't go. She pleads with her to change her mind but her carer insists that it isn't possible and that she had been warned that this was the case. Sonja tells her she is going anyway. No one ever does anything for her. She will just do it herself.	*Alarmed. Sonja is getting more emotional and this is reflected in some defiance. Dysregulation is increased, leading Sonja to feel that her carer is not interested in her. Sonja is unlikely to engage in reflection until she receives acceptance and empathy from her carer, who is open and engaged to what she is feeling. This means not being pulled in to responding defensively by trying to persuade her that she does do things for her. This is likely to take some time before Sonja will let her carer sort this out with her.*
Sonja doesn't even let her carer finish telling her that she can't have a lift. She shouts at her that she hates her and that she is trying to ruin her life. She throws her school bag across the room and runs to her bedroom.	*Fearful. Sonja is now very reactive. She is angry and this is being reflected in her behaviour. If her carer can provide simple but genuine acceptance and empathy for long enough, Sonja may be able to calm a little. Her carer will need to be curious on Sonja's behalf, making some guesses about why she is feeling so strongly about this. If her carer can take the time to support Sonja she may be able to agree to her sorting this out, but if she tries to rush her so that her arousal doesn't come fully down this won't happen and this is likely to build up during the evening.*
Sonja flares up as soon as she realizes that her carer is saying no. She shouts at her that she is a cow and she hates her. Sonja goes into the living room and switches the television channel over even though another young person is watching it. When she is told to turn it over again Sonja flies at her carer, kicking and punching her.	*Terror. Sonja becomes angry very quickly and is verbally aggressive and oppositional. This quickly turns into a fight response as the carer tries to take control. The carer can only ride the storm now, ensuring that they are both safe. PACE via A and E might provide some regulation for Sonja, but with no expectation that Sonja will respond quickly. Provide a sense of safety through voice and actions. As the storm passes and Sonja's arousal comes down then she will need comfort and regulation. The carer needs to feel acceptance and empathy and not become defensive. Later there will be a time to help Sonja to make amends for her behaviour, but only once she can experience her carer's PACE towards her.*

REFLECTIONS ON THE BEHAVIOUR SCENARIOS

	Regulation	Connection	Correction
Nazia	Nazia will need to be soothed and regulated before she can think about the cat.	Dad will then need to connect with her internal experience. For example, he might notice how much she wants to love the cat, and her disappointment that the cat did not like the way she 'loved' him.	Now Dad can help Nazia to think about the cat, and how it might hurt him when she picks him up and pulls him. They might make a story book together about how to be gentle with the cat. Nazia might be encouraged to help with feeding the cat. Dad might also think about how he can supervise Nazia a bit more closely around the cat.
Daniel	Mum will need to help Daniel to come indoors away from the other children. She might notice that he is quite wound up and therefore might choose a calming activity for them to do together.	Mum then needs to connect with Daniel's internal experience. She might wonder about Daniel's experience of the other children, and perhaps his need to fit in. She might acknowledge that it is difficult to come away when the children are expecting him to join in.	Now Mum can think with Daniel about any actions he needs to take to put things right. She might offer to help him write a letter of apology to their neighbour, for example. Mum will also need to think about whether Daniel can manage this unstructured time with the local children. Does he need extra help with peer relationships? Might she need to provide an opportunity for him to have a friend home where she can keep a closer eye on him and be able to help if he is struggling?

	Regulation	Connection	Correction
Katy	Mum and Dad need to seek a time when Katy is calm and regulated so that they can have a quiet chat with her.	Mum and Dad need to start with Katy's experience first. Is she struggling with school generally or is it friendships that are causing her most difficulty? What was her experience of being out of school with the girls? For example, was she excited or worried? Whatever the feelings, they will acknowledge that these feelings are understandable, as is her desire to get on with her peers.	Now Mum and Dad can think with Katy about how school can be more tolerable for her. Does she need some extra support, for example? They can plan together about how they will let the school staff know about this. They can also think about ways to help her with friendships. Perhaps a local youth or theatre club might be a safe setting for her to manage peer relationships.

They can also think together about what consequence Katy might have for being out of school. Katy is likely to be quite hard on herself in her choice of consequences and Mum and Dad can offer a more lenient option! |
| **Kevin** | Dad lets Kevin get some sleep. He makes him a meal for when he wakes up. Kevin is still cross with him but agrees that they can take the dog out together. | Dad uses this walk as an opportunity to talk with him. First he starts with Kevin's experience of being told no to driving lessons, acknowledging his strong desire to drive and the frustration of not being able to start. Dad expresses his understanding that Kevin is likely to stay cross with him for quite a time. | If Kevin is staying regulated Dad might now explain why he is concerned about Kevin learning to drive just now, but also maintain his belief that Kevin will be a successful driver in the future. He might suggest an off-road driving experience, offering to top up his birthday money to afford this. Finally, Dad might observe how much time they spent looking for and worrying about Kevin overnight. They might think together about some jobs that Kevin can do for them to help pay them back for the time they spent looking for him. |

ACTIVITY SHEETS

HOW DOES MY EXPERIENCE OF PAST RELATIONSHIPS IMPACT ON ME AS A PARENT?

Reflect on the parenting you experienced as a child. Think about the words you would use to describe your parents. What words would you use to describe yourself as a parent or as the parent you hope to be?	
How would you describe the relationship that you had with your parents as a child? How has this changed over time? Are there ways you try, or want to try, to be like or not like your parents?	
Think about other relationships you experienced in the past. Reflect on difficulties and pleasures in these relationships. Are any of these difficulties or pleasures reflected, or likely to be reflected, in your relationship with your child?	
What are your relationship triggers? *i.e. things that make you feel defensive as you become angry, withdrawn, upset, anxious or fearful.*	
How has this impacted on you as an individual? *Notice strengths and resiliencies as well as vulnerabilities.*	Are there ways that this has, or you anticipate it might, impact on your parenting? *Reflect on how it might have increased or reduced flexibility.*

Module Three, Session One: Activity Sheet 23

How did you seek comfort when you were distressed as a child? How do you seek comfort when distressed as an adult? How do you help, or expect to help, your child to seek comfort?	
How did you feel soothed when you were ill as a child? How do you get soothed when ill as an adult? How do you soothe, or expect to soothe, your child?	
Think about when you were happy or excited as a child. How did your parents respond to you? How do you respond, or expect to respond, to your child when happy or excited?	
Did you experience any major separations or losses as a child? How were you supported to cope with these? How have you supported, or expect to support, your child to manage separation and loss?	
How has this impacted on you as an individual? *Notice strengths and resiliencies as well as vulnerabilities.*	Are there ways that this has impacted on your parenting? *Reflect on how it might have increased or reduced flexibility.*

WHAT IS YOUR ATTACHMENT STATE OF MIND?

Mark on the line where you think you fit in relation to the descriptions:

I don't like to think about the past. What's done is done. I feel it is best just to get on with things.

I can reflect on my past without getting overly preoccupied. I can see how negative and positive experiences have made me the person I am.

When I think about past relationships I get easily upset or angry. It is hard to focus on what is happening now at these times.

What impact does this have on the way that you parent?

MODULE THREE, SESSION ONE

HANDOUTS

EXPLORING ATTACHMENT HISTORY

Attachment state of mind	Reflection on childhood experience	Impact on parenting ability
Autonomous *Balanced and valuing* You experienced a secure attachment history or have resolved difficult attachment experience through reflection and understanding leading to earned security.	You are likely to talk about childhood realistically. You will be able to give a coherent account of difficult experience or loss. You will be aware of the influence of your past on your present.	You are likely to find it relatively easy to be a sensitive and responsive parent. You are likely to remain regulated (open and engaged) when your child displays distress and need for comfort. You are likely to be able to provide comfort for your child's distress, providing a secure base for your child.
Dismissing *Minimizing* You experienced an avoidant attachment history which has led you to a tendency to distrust emotional expression and to value self-reliance.	When talking about your childhood you are likely to focus on positives rather than negatives, but may struggle to remember actual experiences. You are likely to feel that negative experiences have not made any difference to you. You are likely to value self-reliance and devalue dependence.	You are likely to find it difficult to recognize your child's attachment needs. You are likely to feel uncomfortable when your child is distressed. You may minimize emotional distress in your child, encouraging him to get over it. You are likely to value independence in your child.
Preoccupied *Maximizing* You experienced an ambivalent-resistant attachment history which has led to a tendency to use emotional expression to keep others engaged with you.	When talking about your childhood you are likely to be preoccupied with this experience. It will be harder for you to feel distanced from these past events. You may find yourself feeling easily angry and emotional within current relationships. You may often expect to be let down and you work hard to try to prevent this.	You may find your child's needs to be overwhelming. You are likely to try hard to be a good parent who is valued by your child, but doubts will make it hard to focus on your child's needs.
Unresolved *For past loss or trauma* You had frightening experience with parents or they could be highly unavailable to you, which you experienced as traumatic. This might have included difficult losses or separations.	You are likely to still experience a lot of grief related to past relationship experience. You may find it hard to talk about traumatic events, leading to incoherence when talking about these.	You are likely to find that your child's distress can trigger fear and be emotionally overwhelming. This may make it hard for you to protect or reassure your child. You may experience fear of your child, or loss of control with your child.

MODULE 3, SESSION 2

ACTIVITY SHEETS

HOW WELL DO I CARE FOR MYSELF?

	Not at all	Sometimes	Reasonable amount of the time	Often	All the time
I give myself time and space to recover from an illness.					
I visit the doctor when I need advice or help.					
I am comfortable letting others help me when I am under the weather.					
I take time for myself when I notice myself getting stressed.					
I can turn to others when I have a problem or worry.					
I can sit and relax without worrying about things I should be doing.					
I have hobbies and interests and feel it is important to have times for these.					
I make sure I take regular exercise.					
I make sure I eat healthily.					
I don't feel guilty if I have an occasional treat.					
I make sure that I get enough sleep.					
I can say no to others when I need to.					
I have time during the week which is just for me.					
I make time in a month to spend time with friends.					
I have people in my life who I can talk about anything to.					

AM I AT RISK OF DEVELOPING BLOCKED CARE?

What past experience have I had that might increase my risk of blocked care? *e.g. past relationships that were difficult; previous parenting experience; historical attachment experience*	
What current experience do I have that might increase my risk of blocked care? *e.g. Parenting demands; other demands; challenging child*	
What are the challenges that my child currently or could potentially present to me that might increase my risk of blocked care? *e.g. think about the child's earlier experience and reflect on the challenges we have explored earlier in the programme with trust, intersubjectivity, shame and attachment difficulties*	

How might you notice that you are in danger of moving into blocked care? *e.g. think about ways you respond to stress; signs that you are becoming more defensive in your responses to others; what your child might present that is difficult for you*

MY SELF-CARE PLAN

What am I going to do to increase my self-care and increase my resilience to blocked care?	
How will I increase my self-care?	
How will I develop my use of PACE?	
How will I use other relationships to increase my resilience?	
What else might I do to increase my resilience and reduce my risk to blocked care? *e.g. mindfulness practice, therapy*	

HANDOUTS

SELF-CARE

Self-care is a critical part of parenting children with relationship difficulties. It:

- ensures that you get a good level of emotional support
- builds emotional reserves
- reduces feelings of being emotionally overwhelmed
- protects from blocked care
- helps to recover from blocked care.

'HEALTHY MIND PLATTER' FOR SELF-CARE

Dan Siegel and colleague suggest that parents attend to:

Physical health. Aerobic exercise increases heart rate and improves physical health.

Focus. Periods of focusing on one thing at a time.

Down time. Allowing time in the day when nothing needs to be attended to.

Connecting. Time to connect with others and receive social support.

Sleep. Getting enough good-quality sleep.

Play. Time to be spontaneous and have fun.

Time in. Reflecting on inner world (see mindfulness).

(Adapted from Rock and Siegel 2011)

MINDFULNESS

The ability to deliberately focus attention on feelings, thoughts and experiences in the present moment and in a non-judgmental and accepting way (Kabat-Zinn 2004).

- Mindful parents notice their here-and-now experience without evaluation.
- PACE facilitates a mindful approach to parenting.

BLOCKED CARE*

Caregiving in the adult synchronizes with attachment in the child. Each activates the other. This leads to five regions in the brain working well:

- *Approach:* The hormone oxytocin facilitates caring for child. Parents can stay open and engaged rather than defensive. Approach activated and avoidance deactivated. When caring for a child is difficult, less oxytocin is released; the parent is more likely to avoid than approach.

- *Reward:* Social engagement leads to release of hormone dopamine. Reciprocal process as each enjoys being with the other, sustaining caregiving process. Relationship is pleasurable. Lack of reciprocity leads to reduction in dopamine. Less pleasure and disengagement is more likely.

- *Child reading*: Deep interest in the child, parent wants to make sense of the child's experience. Parents use mind-minded abilities and empathy to understand and communicate with the child. When the attuned relationship fails, empathy and mind-mindedness decline. The parents become defensive and not open and engaged to the child's experience. High levels of stress reduce mind-mindedness, impacting upon this ability to make sense of the child's experience; parenting becomes focused narrowly on changing behaviour, whilst empathy and compassion are reduced.

- *Meaning making*: Links with history of attachment and relationships. Make meaning of current relationship through the lens of past relationships. Under stress tend to make negative meanings, as memories of past relationship stresses are activated. Under stress parents are more likely to hold negative narratives about their child or themselves, which increases their defensiveness.

- *Executive system:* This integrative centre of the brain makes all this work. Executive functioning allows purposeful, goal-directed and problem-solving behaviours, less dependent upon the child's influence upon the parent. Executive functioning will reduce under stress. If the parents have developed reasonable executive function they will be able to care for the child, but without the other caregiving systems working well the joy in this parenting is lost. The parents do the job, but experience no pleasure in this.

---

*   Adapted from Hughes and Baylin 2012.

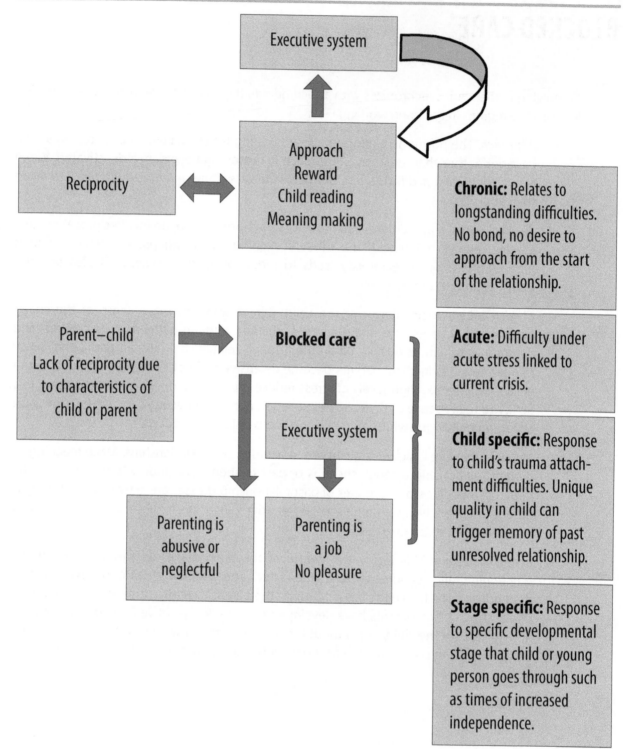

PROTECTION AND RECOVERY FROM BLOCKED CARE

RELATIONSHIPS

Reliable and supportive relationships can allow you to experience PACE from another. This increases social support, building resilience and increasing emotional reserves.

MIND-MINDED AND PACE-FUL TO SELF

- Notice and understand own experience.

- Increase empathy and self-compassion.

- Reduce feelings of failure and hopelessness.

- Able to stay in touch with child's internal experience.

USE ATTACHMENT HISTORY EXPLORATION

Notice any tendencies to:

- try to avoid feeling things, preferring to rationalize and intellectualize

- be easily overwhelmed by emotional experience without being able to reflect on this experience.

Use supportive relationships to help you find the balance between these two.
In this way, you will:

- become open to your emotional experience

- be able to reflect on this experience without being overwhelmed.

INCREASE CAPACITY TO REFLECT AND REGULATE

Practise remaining open to emotional experience, noticing what you are experiencing and regulating this experience with support from others.

Reflecting on this experience will increase your capacity to remain open and engaged to yourself, allowing you to move more easily from defensive to open and engaged when responding to your child. Regular mindfulness practice has also been shown to be useful for restoring balance in the brain, strengthening healthy reflection and regulation.

THERAPY

It can be hard to seek therapeutic help for yourself when your children have high needs. Therapy when you are struggling will also be therapeutic for your children.

THE HOUSE MODEL OF PARENTING

Thinking, feeling and behavioural choices

Supporting feelings and containing behaviours

Choices and consequences   *Praise and rewards*

MANAGING BEHAVIOUR

Stepping aside from confrontation
Empathy before discipline, remain calm, avoid battles

Structure and supervision
Provide predictability, help child to feel safe

Parenting with PACE
Regulate emotion, make sense of experience

Playfulness   Acceptance   *Curiosity   Empathy*

Family   Friends   **Helping children enjoy relationships**   *School*

BUILDING RELATIONSHIPS

Rest, relaxation, reflection   **Looking after yourself**   *Support to manage stress*

Rituals   **Belonging**   *Claiming*

Family atmosphere

Provide emotional support, empathy and interactive repair   **Attunement**   *Reflection Understand yourself*

Acceptance   **Empathy**   *Curiosity*

SECURE BASE

Glossary

Abandonment

Children who do not receive the physical or emotional care that they need experience this as abandonment by their parents. This leads to continuing fears that this abandonment will be repeated in the future from significant people in their life.

Arousal state

Our arousal state describes how physiologically alert we are. As arousal increases, a person moves from calm and reflective to increasingly reactive.

Attachment theory

Psychiatrist John Bowlby developed attachment theory to describe the bond that develops between a child and parent. This bond is a response to the degree to which a parent helps a child to feel safe and secure.

Attachment is dependent upon an *attachment behavioural system*. Children have an innate predisposition to display attachment behaviours when they are feeling insecure or distressed in some way. The attachment behavioural system is activated leading to the child seeking proximity to the attachment figure, protesting separation from that person and therefore seeking to use the caregiver as a secure base. This behavioural system works together with the *exploratory behavioural system*. This is also an innate predisposition, this time to seek novelty and new experience. It focuses attention onto exploration and learning. These two behavioural systems are complementary: as one is activated the other deactivates dependent upon current circumstances.

The way that parents respond to the cues or signals that children give about their need to attach or explore represents the degree to which they are sensitive or insensitive to these signals. From this experience children develop attachment patterns.

- *Secure:* The attachment that children develop when a parent is experienced as sensitive and responsive to their emotional needs. The child learns trust in others and appropriate self-reliance.

- *Ambivalent-resistant:* Also called anxious attachment, this is the attachment pattern or style of relating that develops when attachment needs are triggered but the child has experienced the parent as inconsistent and unpredictable. The child maximizes the expression of attachment need in order to maintain the availability of the parent.

- *Avoidant:* This is the attachment pattern or style of relating that develops when attachment needs are triggered but the child has experienced the parent as rejecting. The child minimizes the expression of attachment need in order to maintain the availability of the parent.

- *Disorganized-controlling:* This is the attachment pattern or style of relating that develops when attachment needs are triggered but the child has experienced the parent as frightened or frightening. The child has trouble organizing his behaviour at times of stress. As they grow older, children with these patterns of relating under stress learn to control relationships to force predictability. Controlling relationships develop instead of reciprocal relationships.

Within the insecure patterns children develop ways of hiding and expressing needs in line with their expectations of their parents.

This attachment experience leads to the development of an *internal working model.* This is a cognitive model of the relationship (i.e. a memory or template) that the child has experienced. This model influences how the child will respond to future relationships.

Children develop multiple models of attachment influenced by the range of relationships that they have experienced. The model guides the behaviour that they will display within the different relationships that they go on to encounter.

Through adolescence and into adulthood, these attachment patterns based on multiple models transform into an attachment state of mind, based on the way the multiple models combine to give the adult a single more complex model to guide behaviour. Four states of mind are described which can be linked to the childhood patterns:

- *Autonomous attachment state of mind* emerges from secure patterns. The individual with this model is likely to have experienced a secure attachment relationship or to have resolved difficult experience with attachment figures. This experience will help the individual to be a sensitive and responsive parent.

- *Dismissing attachment state of mind* emerges from avoidant patterns. This individual is likely to have learnt to distrust emotional expression and to value self-reliance. As a parent, this experience will make it harder for the individual to recognize the child's attachment needs, will increase discomfort with the child's distress and will lead to a valuing of independence in the child.

- *Preoccupied attachment state of mind* emerges from ambivalent patterns. This individual is likely to have learnt to coercively use expression of emotion to keep others engaged. As a parent, this individual is likely to find the child's needs to be overwhelming, and will quickly feel emotional and angry towards the child.

- *Unresolved attachment state of mind* emerges from disorganized-controlling patterns. Past loss and frightening experiences remain a source of trauma. As a parent, the child's distress can trigger memories of this early trauma, meaning that the parent is unavailable to the child when needed most.

Attunement

An emotional connection between two people in which one person mirrors or matches the rhythm, vitality and affect (externally displayed mood) of the other.

Authoritative parenting

Parenting that provides a child with a high degree of warmth and nurture alongside clear and appropriate boundaries. The child is enabled to develop autonomy (independence) in line with the developmental stage he is at.

Autonomy

This represents the degree of personal independence an individual possesses.

Behaviour management

Behaviour management (sometimes called behaviour modification) provides a set of strategies for parents to use with the focus on changing the behaviour of the child. The aim is to reduce challenging behaviour and to increase prosocial behaviour: the behaviours we want to see children using. This is achieved through the use of consequences, sanctions, praise and rewards. In this programme I use the term *behaviour support* to describe an approach that has a focus on relationship, building connection and helping regulation; the support for the behaviour is then provided in the context of this relationship. This is captured in the expression *connection with correction* (see also **social learning theory**).

Blocked care

In a healthy parent–child relationship, caregiving in the adult synchronizes with care-seeking in the child. This is supported by five regions in the brain which, when working well, will help the adult to be a caregiver. These systems are:

- *Approach.* The parent seeks connection with the child.

- *Pleasure.* Reciprocal process as each enjoys being with the other.

- *Child reading.* The parent wants to make sense of the child.

- *Meaning making.* The parent seeks to understand the child. This links with past experience of attachment and relationships. Parents make meaning through the lens of past relationships.

- *Executive system.* This integrative centre of the brain makes all of this work but is less dependent upon the child's influence.

A state of blocked care can result when the child is unable to engage in a reciprocal relationship with the parent. The brain regions 1–4 deactivate, leaving only the executive system working.

Blocked trust

Blocked trust is a failure in social relatedness. It develops as a response to frightening and painful relationship experiences with caregivers. The innate need for comfort and companionship is suppressed, leading to chronic defensiveness and a lack of social engagement. The child strives to be self-sufficient, keeping the caregiver at a distance through controlling rather than reciprocal relationships. This adaptation means that the child is not getting the social buffering needed to manage stress and alarm in the world.

In blocked trust, five systems in the brain have adapted to living in a harsh social world.

- The *stress system* is chronically activated, easily triggered and hard to switch off.

- The *social switching system* does not move easily between social engagement and self-defence, as appraisal of threat and danger during interactions is set very high.

- The *social engagement system* is suppressed.

- The *self-defence system* is activated.

- The experience of *social pain* is blocked.

Co-construction

Within DDP this describes the joint discovery of a story or narrative about the person's experience. Through the relationship the story emerges, helping the individual make sense of current or past experience.

Consequences

Any piece of behaviour is followed by consequences. These consequences will to some extent determine what we do in the future. Consequences therefore can be used to help someone to behave differently. In this programme I have called this use of consequences *coercive consequences*, as they are used in an effort to change the behaviour of the other. When the child is supported in a relationship he comes to understand his behaviour and the impact it has had on another. This can lead to feelings of remorse and a desire to make amends. The child seeks a consequence which can help him to repair. The parent can support him with this and thus the consequence becomes part of a collaborative process of planning for and making this repair. Thus, in this programme I have called these *collaborative consequences*.

Controlling behaviours

Controlling behaviours represent a need to feel in charge within the relationship. This is generally because the person fears a relationship which is reciprocal. She feels vulnerable being open to the influence of the other, so she seeks to coercively influence instead.

DDP

Dyadic Developmental Psychotherapy was originally developed by Dan Hughes as a therapeutic intervention for families who were fostering or had adopted children with significant developmental trauma and insecurity of attachment. The therapist facilitates the child's relationship with his parents through the development and maintenance of an affective-reflective (a-r) dialogue which explores all aspects of the child's life: safe and traumatic, present and past. The therapist and parent's intersubjective experience of the child provide the child with new meanings which can become integrated into his autobiographical narrative, which in turn becomes more coherent. In this way the child experiences healing of past trauma and achieves safety within current relationships. The conversations and interactions (verbal and non-verbal) within the therapy room are all based upon PACE and have a quality of story-telling. Dyadic Developmental Psychotherapy therefore is an approach within which the child and parents work together with the therapist. The child gains relationship experience which helps him to grow and heal emotionally as family members develop healthy patterns of relating and communicating.

DDP has a broader application as Dyadic Developmental Practice (see Figure Glossary 1). This provides a set of principles that can support networks, inform and enrich parenting, and support the child outside of the home, for example in residential settings and at school.

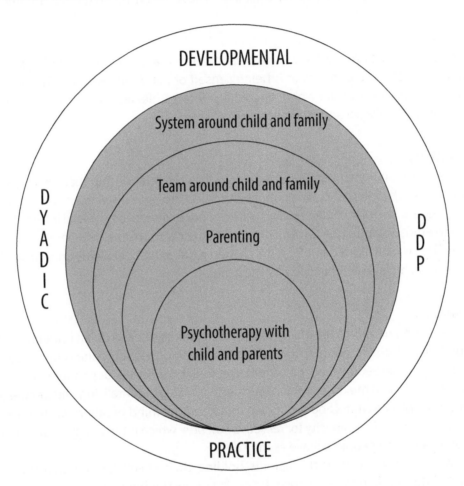

Figure Glossary 1: Model of Dyadic Developmental Practice and its relationship to Dyadic Developmental Psychotherapy

DDP is theoretically based on the models of attachment theory and intersubjectivity, and is consistent with the needs of children and young people who have experienced developmental trauma.

Defensive

When we experience physical or psychological threat, we instinctively move to defend ourselves, through a range of fight/flight behaviours. If these options are not available to us we will move into shut-down responses (dissociation) as a means of survival. These defensive reactions are governed by the nervous system which can be sensitized to react more quickly for individuals whose earliest experience has been frightening.

Discipline

Discipline means giving another skills and knowledge through teaching. In childhood parents use discipline to teach children about their expectations of them and to give them guidelines and principles they can use to live their lives. These are based on the parents' morals and values.

Dissociation

This describes the process by which a person defends against overwhelming stress by cutting off from conscious awareness what is being sensed or felt. At its extreme, the person cuts off from contact with others or the world, becoming numb, unfeeling or unaware. Dissociation reduces the ability to make sense of self or others.

Intersubjectivity

In child development, intersubjectivity describes the relationship that develops between infant and parent. The infant has an innate ability to co-ordinate his actions with that of his parent so that they are both synchronized. This is necessary experience for social interactions. Children are able to emotionally connect with others, with their responses contingent on the response of the other. This is a bit like a game of tennis, when a ball is hit backwards and forwards between two players. Each player is influenced by the other.

Mentalization

Mentalization describes the ability to predict responses based on an understanding of the inner experience of others. For example, an understanding that someone is upset by an event might lead to an expectation that the other person will cry. This is dependent on the ability to take the perspective of the other person (*perspective-taking*). Mentalizing and perspective-taking rest upon the ability to think about our own mind and the mind of others, i.e. to have *theory of mind*. This in turn leads to a capacity for *reflective function*, which is the ability to understand why things happen and why people behave as they do.

Mentalization involves the parents holding their child's mind within their own mind and helping the children to experience the parent's mind within theirs.

One aspect of mentalization is the ability to be *mind-minded*, i.e. to be able to understand and take into account the mental state of another person, what the person might be thinking, feeling, wishing, believing, desiring, etc. When a parent can understand the internal experience of the child it is easier for her to emotionally connect with him.

Mindfulness

Mindfulness is the process of bringing attention to experiences occurring in the present moment. Attention can be directed to internal experience, for example our internal world of thinking and feeling. Alternatively, it can be directed to external experience, for example, to what we are seeing, hearing, smelling, tasting or sensing. When we are mindful, we are living fully in the present. It is therefore difficult to be mindful when feeling depressed, as this tends to take our attention to the past, or when anxious, as this tends to focus attention on to the future. Regular practice of mindfulness has been found to improve mental health.

Narrative

A narrative is a cohesive story of real or imaginary events. The narrative is at the heart of story-telling. Discovering the story is an important part of DDP, as we make sense of the experience of the other.

PACE

PACE is the therapeutic attitude that is used within the DDP model to facilitate emotional connection. The attitude of PACE offers an unconditional relationship expressed through playfulness, acceptance, curiosity and empathy.

Regulation

This represents an individual's ability to control and modulate his level of emotional arousal. This ability to regulate is influenced by the experience of *emotional co-regulation*. This is the experience children need when parents help them to manage their emotional arousal. *Emotional dysregulation* represents a lack of regulatory ability. This occurs when an individual fails to control and modulate his level of emotional arousal. The emotional experience overwhelms the individual.

Relationship repair

This is a psychological term used to describe the process whereby one person in a relationship repairs a rupture that has occurred within the relationship. A parent can re-establish a positive emotional connection between herself and a child (attunement) following a time when the relationship was ruptured, either because of the behaviour of the child or of the parent.

Self-esteem

This describes how people perceive themselves and their abilities. It represents their sense of their own worth. High self-esteem suggests that an individual perceives himself positively whilst low self-esteem represents a low opinion of self and worth to others.

Shame

A complex emotional state within which a person experiences negative feelings about herself; a feeling of inferiority, not feeling good enough.

Social engagement

Social engagement is the capacity to engage in social relationships, being open to responding to, as well as influencing, others in the relationship. Biologically, we are innately prepared to engage with others, but when we experience fear and trauma such engagement reduces. Within the DDP model the phrase *open and engaged* is used to describe a relationship where partners within the relationship are open to social engagement with each other. This is the opposite state to *social defensiveness*, when social engagement is reduced.

Socialization

Socialization is a developmental process of helping children to acquire the skills that they will need to engage in social relationships. This includes learning cultural norms and values so that the children are equipped to live within their own communities. This socialization process goes on through childhood and into adulthood, influencing behaviour, beliefs and the way that people make relationships.

Social learning theory

In behavioural psychology (social learning theory) the term 'reinforcement' refers to the consequence to behaviour. This consequence can be a *negative reinforcer*. This is experienced as unpleasant. The person behaves in a certain way in order to avoid the negative consequence. For example, a parent may buy a child some sweets to stop him crying. The sweet-buying behaviour in the parent has been negatively reinforced. Alternatively, it can be a *positive reinforcer*. This refers to a consequence to a behaviour that is experienced as pleasant and thus rewarding. The person behaves in a certain way in order to gain the pleasant consequence, for example, the child cries because the crying has been rewarded by sweets. The child's crying behaviour has been positively reinforced. Reinforcement, which is strengthening of behaviour, can be contrasted with *punishment*, which is weakening of behaviour. In behavioural psychology, punishment refers to a consequence to a behaviour that is experienced as unpleasant. The person stops behaving in order to avoid the unpleasant consequence. For example, if a child was smacked when crying for sweets, the child's crying behaviour would be punished, leading to the child stopping crying. As punishment also leads to shame and feelings of low self-worth and doesn't teach the child what behaviour is acceptable, it is generally considered to be a poor parenting technique. Parents are advised to reward good behaviour rather than punish bad behaviour.

Social learning theory has less focus on relationship and emotional connection and therefore is not attachment focused.

Therapeutic parenting

Therapeutic parenting is a general term to describe any parenting approach that aims to heal the child as well as to parent the child. There are lots of different parenting ideas described as therapeutic parenting. In this programme, a DDP-informed therapeutic parenting approach is described.

Trauma

In this context we are reflecting on psychological trauma rather than a physical trauma, such as a break to a bone, although both can overlap. Trauma is an experience of an event or events that involves actual or threatened death or serious injury to self or witnessing such an event to another person. Learning about unexpected or violent death, serious harm or threat of death or injury to family or friends can also represent a trauma. For the event to be traumatizing, the response by the individual is of intense fear, helplessness or horror. In other words, it is the experience of the event that determines whether it is a trauma for the individual. An event is traumatic if it is extremely upsetting and at least temporarily overwhelms an individual's internal resources. Such traumas can include extreme emotional abuse, major losses or separations, degradation and humiliation.

Complex trauma occurs when an individual is exposed to multiple traumatic events with an impact on immediate and long-term outcomes (e.g. war, ethnic cleansing).

When complex trauma occurs through childhood with early onset, is chronic and prolonged, occurs from within the family, and impacts on development, it is described by some researchers as *developmental trauma*. This is a useful description of the experience of children who develop attachment difficulties, blocked trust and fear of relationship. The children can become trauma organized in a pattern of highly controlling behaviours. When parents are trauma informed they can help the children to discover other ways of being.

Unconditional love

Unconditional love represents a love which will be given 'no matter what'. When love is only given if certain circumstances exist it is described as conditional: 'I will love you only if…', instead of 'no matter what'.

Verbal and non-verbal communication

Verbal represents the use of words to communicate, whereas non-verbal is the way we communicate without words. Communication is generally a mixture of verbal and non-verbal behaviours.

Zone of proximal development (ZPD)

Russian psychologist, Lev Vygotsky suggested the zone of proximal development to describe how children can achieve more when the adults or older peers provide them with support to do this. He describes the ZPD as 'the distance between the actual developmental level as determined by independent problem solving and the level of potential development as determined through problem solving under adult guidance, or in collaboration with more capable peers' (Vygotsky 1978, p.86). In this programme, I am using this idea as a helpful way for thinking about the structure and supervision that children need to support their emotional development as well as their cognitive development. Expectations that are beyond the child's ability are outside ZPD, whilst low expectations mean that the child is not in the zone and doesn't make progress. If the parent provides support within the zone the child is likely to make emotional progress.

Everyday Parenting with Security and Love
Using PACE to Provide Foundations for Attachment

Kim S. Golding

Foreword by Dan Hughes

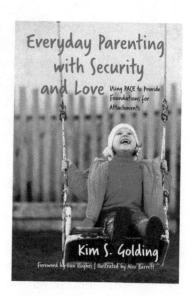

Paperback: £16.99 / $27.95
ISBN: 978 1 78592 115 5
eISBN: 978 1 78450 384 0
240 pages

Children that have experienced trauma, loss or separation early in life need special care and attention; they need to be parented with love and security in a way that allows them to heal and rebuild emotional bonds. This comprehensive book provides parents and carers with crucial advice and guidance on how to strengthen attachment and trust.

Based on Dan Hughes' proven 'PACE' model of therapeutic parenting, this book explains how to implement PACE techniques to overcome the challenges faced by children who struggle to connect emotionally. Barriers to stable relationships such as a lack of trust, fear of emotional intimacy, and high levels of shame are all explained. It explores techniques to overcome these barriers by teaching how to support the child's behaviour at the same time as building empathy and trust.

The practical parenting guidance offered throughout is essential for carers or parents of troubled children, and will help build safe, secure emotional relationships.

Kim S. Golding is a consultant clinical psychologist. She is author of several books including bestsellers Creating Loving Attachments and Nurturing Attachments.